Prentice Hall **Realidades 3**

Leveled Vocabulary and Grammar Workbook
Core Practice

PEARSON

Boston, Massachusetts   Chandler, Arizona   Glenview, Illinois   Upper Saddle River, New Jersey

PEARSON

ISBN-13: 978-0-13-322573-0
ISBN-10:   0-13-322573-9

12   16

Table of Contents

Realidades 3

Para empezar

Tu vida diaria

Nombre _____

Fecha _____

Hora _____

Core Practice **P-1**

Entre amigos

Todos los días haces cosas diferentes. Responde las preguntas de tu amigo usando las ilustraciones.

Modelo
— ¿Qué traes?
— *Traigo unos libros.*

1. —¿Qué tienes que escribir?

   _____

2. —¿Cuándo desayunas?

   _____

3. —¿Qué oyes?

   _____

4. —¿Adónde vas?

   _____

5. —¿Qué pones en la mochila?

   _____

6. —¿A qué hora sales de casa?

   _____

7. —¿Qué desayunas?

   _____

8. —¿Qué eres?

   _____

realidades.com
• Web Code: jed-0001

Realidades 3

Para empezar

Tu vida diaria

Nombre _____

Fecha _____

Hora _____

Core Practice **P-2**

¿Qué quieres (o no quieres) hacer?

A veces la gente quiere hacer cosas, y a veces no quiere hacerlas. Di lo que estas personas quieren o no quieren hacer, utilizando los elementos que aparecen entre paréntesis.

Modelo	¿Lavo el coche? (querer / mañana)

Quiero lavar el coche mañana.

1. ¿Juegas al fútbol? (querer / por la tarde)

   _____

2. ¿Voy al supermercado contigo? (poder / a las 5:00)

   _____

3. ¿Sirven la cena? (empezar / a las 8:00)

   _____

4. ¿Hilda da de comer al perro? (preferir / por la noche)

   _____

5. ¿Pierde Juan el partido? (no querer / la semana próxima)

   _____

6. ¿Jugamos hoy? (comenzar / esta tarde)

   _____

7. ¿Cortan Uds. el césped? (no poder / ahora)

   _____

8. ¿Hace Ud. el desayuno? (preferir / temprano por la mañana)

   _____

realidades.com

• Web Code: jed-0002

Realidades 3

Para empezar

Tu vida diaria

Nombre _____

Fecha _____

Hora _____

Core Practice **P-3**

¿A qué hora?

Todos los días hacemos actividades a la misma hora. Escribe frases para expresar lo que hacen estas personas a cada hora.

Pablo

Modelo *Se lava la cara a las siete de la mañana.*

1. Rolando

_____

2. yo

_____

3. tú

_____

4. yo

_____

5. Andrés

_____

6. Ud.

_____

7. nosotros

_____

Realidades ③

Para empezar

Días especiales

Nombre _____

Fecha _____

Hora _____

Core Practice **P-4**

¿Qué te gusta?

¿Qué les gusta hacer a estas personas? Primero contesta la pregunta, y luego escribe una frase usando una de las expresiones del recuadro.

encantar las fiestas	encantar hablar con ellos	gustar el béisbol
encantar la guitarra	encantar las películas policíacas	interesar la ropa
interesar los bailes	encantar las telenovelas	

Modelo   ¿Qué te gusta hacer? (ver la televisión)
Me gusta ver la televisión porque me encantan las telenovelas.

1. ¿Qué les gusta hacer a Uds.? (ir al cine)

    _____

2. ¿Qué le interesa hacer a Octavio? (practicar deportes)

    _____

3. ¿Qué les encanta hacer a tus amigos? (ir a bailar)

    _____

4. ¿Qué te gusta hacer? (reunirse con mis amigos)

    _____

5. ¿Qué le gusta hacer a Ud.? (tocar un instrumento musical)

    _____

6. ¿Qué nos gusta hacer (ir de compras)

    _____

7. ¿Qué me gusta hacer? (celebrar mi cumpleaños)

realidades.com
• Web Code: jed-0004

Realidades 3

Para empezar

Días especiales

Nombre _____

Fecha _____

Hora _____

Core Practice **P-5**

Tiempo libre

A. Isabel habla de cómo son las vacaciones con su familia. Completa el párrafo con los posesivos que faltan.

Mis padres y hermanos son muy divertidos. Me encanta ir de vacaciones con

(1.) _____ familia. Viajo con **(2.)** _____ padres y **(3.)** _____ dos

hermanos. Tenemos un perro. Este año podemos llevar a **(4.)** _____ perro también

porque vamos en coche. Vamos a un hotel que está en la playa. **(5.)** _____ mamá

está muy contenta porque no tiene que hacer los quehaceres de la casa cuando estamos

de vacaciones. Mi hermano Paquito está contento porque no tiene que hacer

(6.) _____ tarea. Y mi hermana Rosita está contenta porque no tiene que ayudar

a mamá con los quehaceres. Papá está contento también porque no tiene que pensar en

(7.) _____ trabajo. Todos **(8.)** _____ días son especiales cuando estamos de

vacaciones. Y ahora, dime tú, ¿cómo son las vacaciones con **(9.)** _____ familia?

B. Tu maestra tiene muchas preguntas sobre tus amigos y tu familia. Completa las respuestas usando el adjetivo posesivo apropiado.

| Modelo | ¿Tu amiga está aquí? No, _____*mi*_____ amiga no está aquí.

1. ¿La ropa de Matilde es elegante? Sí, _____ ropa es elegante.

2. ¿Están de vacaciones tus padres? No, _____ padres no están de vacaciones.

3. ¿El equipo de José y Alberto es bueno? Sí, _____ equipo es bueno.

4. ¿Vas a la fiesta sorpresa de Gerardo? No, no voy a _____ fiesta sorpresa.

5. ¿Las fiestas de Uds. son especiales? No, _____ fiestas no son especiales.

6. ¿Mis libros están en la maleta? No, _____ libros no están en la maleta.

7. ¿Están emocionadas las hermanas de Felipe? Sí, _____ hermanas están emocionadas.

8. ¿Quieres ir a tu club? Sí, quiero ir a _____ club.

Realidades 3

Para empezar

Nombre _____

Fecha _____

Hora _____

Core Practice **P-6**

Grammar

1. Write the first-person form for the present indicative of the following verbs:

   conocer _____   ver _____

   dar _____   caer _____

2. Conjugate the following verbs in the present indicative:

   perder

   poder

   pedir

3. What are the two parts of a Spanish reflexive verb? Give three examples.

   _____

   _____

4. List the reflexive pronouns.

5. What do the verbs *encantar, importar,* and *interesar* have in common with the verb *gustar?*

   _____

6. When do we use the singular form of the above verbs and when do we use the plural?

   _____

7. What prepositional phrase can we use instead of the possessive pronouns *su / sus* for clarity or emphasis?

   _____

realidades.com
● Web Code: jed-0006

Realidades ③

Capítulo 1

Nombre _____

Fecha _____

Hora _____

Core Practice **1–1**

A ver si recuerdas . . .

Vacaciones inolvidables

Usa la información que te damos para contar lo que estas personas hicieron durante las vacaciones. Escribe los verbos en pretérito.

Modelo	Emilia / ir al mar

Emilia fue al mar.

1. nosotros / montar a caballo

_____

2. tú / ir al campo

_____

3. los hermanos Ortega / dar una caminata

_____

4. yo / montar en bicicleta

_____

5. Uds. / viajar a las montañas

_____

6. Roberto / ir de pesca

_____

7. Ud. / sacar fotos

_____

8. Paquita / ver monos en un zoológico

_____

Realidades 3

Capítulo 1

Nombre _____

Hora _____

Fecha _____

Core Practice **1-2**

A ver si recuerdas . . .

Actividades al aire libre

Mira los dibujos y escribe lo que hicieron estos jóvenes la semana pasada. Usa el pretérito de los verbos.

Modelo _____ Juan Luis _montó en monopatín_ _____.

1. _____ Margarita _____.

2. _____ Nicolás y Pedro _____.

3. _____ Estela _____.

4. _____ Lourdes y Consuelo _____.

5. _____ Mario _____.

6. _____ Ramón _____.

• Web Code: jed-0101

Realidades 3

Capítulo 1

Nombre _____

Fecha _____

Hora _____

Core Practice **1-3**

¡Qué aventura!

Usa la información que te damos y los dibujos para contar lo que hicieron estos amigos en la sierra.

Modelo

Los chicos lo ___*pasaron bien*___ cuando fueron de cámping.

1. Ellos llevaron su _____ a la sierra.

2. Al _____, ellos usaron _____ para ver.

3. Marcos durmió en _____.

4. Mis amigos y yo dimos _____ por un _____ con pocos árboles.

5. Mis amigos y yo _____. en la cabaña cuando empezó a _____.

6. Trajimos _____ para no _____.

Realidades 3

Capítulo 1

Nombre _____

Fecha _____

Hora _____

Core Practice **1-4**

Van de cámping

A. Contesta las preguntas con frases completas usando palabras de la lección.

Modelo ¿Dónde te refugias cuando vas de cámping?

Me refugio en una tienda de acampar.

1. ¿Qué usas cuando te molestan los mosquitos?

_____

2. ¿Qué usaron ellas para ver de lejos?

_____

3. Él se despierta muy temprano. ¿Cuándo se despierta?

_____

4. ¿Por qué te caes cuando te tropiezas con una roca?

_____

B. Usa las palabras del recuadro para completar la historia de Carmen y sus amigas.

la oeccanher	nua zev laíl	cihaa	aceraper
sía	ejdó ed	nu trao	

Mis amigas y yo fuimos a acampar en la sierra. Luisa conocía un lugar ideal. Caminamos

una hora para llegar. **(1.)** _____, sacamos la tienda de acampar. De repente,

empezó a caer granizo. Corrimos **(2.)** _____ la tienda y nos refugiamos.

Cuando **(3.)** _____ llover, salimos otra vez y fuimos a ver el lago. Pasamos

(4.) _____ allí. **(5.)** _____ hicimos una fogata y

(6.) _____ pudimos preparar la cena. ¡Qué bien lo pasamos!

realidades.com

• Web Code: jed-0102

Realidades 3

Capítulo 1

Nombre _____

Fecha _____

Hora _____

Core Practice **1-5**

Desastres horribles

A. Completa esta conversación con el pretérito del verbo apropiado.

Modelo Nadie _____*creyó*_____ (*creer / destruir*) lo que dije.

—Yo **(1.)** _____ (*leer / creer*) algo horrible en el periódico. No sé si lo

(2.) _____ (*caer / leer*) tú también. Hubo una tormenta terrible en

Nicaragua.

—Mi hermano y yo **(3.)** _____ (*oír / leer*) la noticia en la radio. Parece

que la tormenta **(4.)** _____ (*destruir / caerse*) muchas casas.

—También **(5.)** _____ (*caerse / leer*) muchos árboles.

—Muchas personas **(6.)** _____ (*creer / destruir*) que iban a morir.

B. Completa esta noticia con el pretérito del verbo apropiado.

Mis amigos no **(1.)** _____ (*creer / caer*) lo que pasó ayer. Hubo un terremoto en

el centro de la ciudad. A las once y veintidós yo **(2.)** _____ (*oír / creer*)

un ruido terrible. La tierra **(3.)** _____ (*dejar / empezar*) a temblar.

(4.) _____ (*caerse / leer*) muchas casas.

El terremoto **(5.)** _____ (*caerse / destruir*) muchos edificios. Hoy, todos

(6.) _____ (*leer / oír*) las noticias sobre el terremoto en la radio,

y **(7.)** _____ (*leer / creer*) lo que pasó en los periódicos.

Realidades **3**

Capítulo 1

Nombre _____

Fecha _____

Hora _____

Core Practice **1-6**

Un día en la sierra

Tú y tus amigos pasaron un día en la sierra. Completa esta historia con el pretérito de los verbos que aparecen entre paréntesis.

Mis amigos y yo fuimos a la sierra. Mis padres nos **(1.)** _____ (decir) que

el paisaje era muy hermoso. Mi hermanita **(2.)** _____ (venir)

con nosotros. Marcos **(3.)** _____ (decir) que no podía venir.

Él **(4.)** _____ (tener) que ir con sus primos al centro.

Después de llegar a la sierra, mis amigos y yo **(5.)** _____ (poder) hacer

una fogata. Entonces nosotros **(6.)** _____ (decir): "¡Vamos a comer!". Después

de comer, nosotros **(7.)** _____ (andar) mucho por los senderos del bosque.

Todos mis amigos **(8.)** _____ (traer) sus brújulas, y por eso nosotros no

(9.) _____ (tener) problemas. Yo **(10.)** _____ (poner) el

repelente de insectos en mi mochila.

Después, mi hermanita y yo **(11.)** _____ (ir) al lago. Yo

(12.) _____ (poder) pescar un poco. Otros **(13.)** _____ (andar)

alrededor del lago. Estábamos muy cansados y **(14.)** _____ (tener) que

descansar antes de volver a casa. Después de nuestro día en la sierra nosotros

(15.) _____ (estar) muy contentos.

realidades.com

• Web Code: jed-0104

Realidades 3

Capítulo 1

Nombre _____

Fecha _____

Hora _____

Core Practice **1-7**

¿Todos se divierten?

A. ¿Qué le pasó a Andrea anoche? Completa su cuento usando el pretérito del verbo apropiado del recuadro.

divertirse	dormir	morir	preferir	sentir	sugerir

Anoche Andrea tuvo mucho sueño y se **(1.)** _____ temprano. De repente **(2.)**

_____ que la cama temblaba. ¡Era un terremoto! Andrea recordó lo que un

amigo le **(3.)** _____ una vez: estar debajo de la puerta. Por suerte, nadie **(4.)**

_____ ni hubo heridos. Pobre Andrea no **(5.)** _____

para nada.

B. Claudia y Patricia acamparon en la sierra durante las vacaciones de primavera. Para saber cómo lo pasaron, completa el párrafo con el pretérito de los verbos apropiados del recuadro.

andar	divertirse	dormirse	estar
leer	oír	traer	vestirse

Claudia **(1.)** _____ en el periódico sobre la Sierra Altamira. Decidió ir a la

sierra con su amiga Patricia. Ellas **(2.)** _____ con ropa adecuada. Claudia

(3.) _____ su tienda de acampar y Patricia llevó dos sacos de dormir.

Salieron al amanecer y **(4.)** _____ por un largo camino hasta llegar a la sierra.

Escalaron una rocas y luego acamparon. Por la noche, **(5.)** _____ temprano.

De repente, Patricia se despertó porque **(6.)** _____ un ruido. Por eso **(7.)**

_____ nerviosas toda la noche y no pudieron dormir. Al día siguiente, las

chicas dieron un paseo por la sierra. Luego regresaron a casa. Claudia y Patricia lo pasaron

bien y se divirtieron mucho aunque durmieron poco.

Realidades ③

Capítulo 1

Nombre _____

Fecha _____

Hora _____

Core Practice **1-8**

Una carrera atlética

¿Qué pasó en la competencia? Mira los dibujos y completa las oraciones.

Modelo

Martín y Marcos ——— *se inscriben* ——— para participar en la carrera.

1. Marianela obtuvo ——————————.

2. Cuando Marianela ganó la competencia, su hermanito le dijo ——————————.

3. Yo pasé mucho tiempo ——————————— antes de participar en la carrera.

4. Asistimos a la ceremonia de ——————————.

5. Alberto es el campeón. Recibió ——————————.

6. Matilde es campeona. Tiene su ——————————.

7. Los padres de Matilde están muy ——————————— de su hija.

realidades.com

• Web Code: jed-0106

Una carta

Eugenia le escribe una carta a su primo Carlos para contarle algo maravilloso. Lee su carta y contesta las preguntas que siguen.

> Querido Carlos:
>
> ¿Cómo estás? ¿Y tus padres? Aquí todos estamos bien. Te escribo para contarte algo increíble. ¿Te acuerdas que te dije que yo iba a participar en la carrera de San Marcos el domingo? Me inscribí hace dos meses y pasé mucho tiempo entrenándome. Y ¿sabes, Carlos? ¡Alcancé mi meta! Fue una carrera muy dura, pero la gané. ¡Cuánto me emocioné! Después de la carrera hubo una entrega de premios. Mis padres estaban muy orgullosos cuando me vieron con el trofeo que obtuve.
>
> La semana pasada me inscribí para las carreras de verano que tienen lugar en julio. Esas carreras son muy difíciles porque en ellas participan jóvenes de todo el país. Me doy cuenta de que tengo que hacer un esfuerzo muy grande y ya he empezado el entrenamiento. ¡Si gano esas carreras obtendré una medalla!
>
> Bueno, Carlos, muchos saludos a tus padres y un beso de tu prima.
>
> Eugenia

Preguntas

1. ¿En qué competencia atlética participó Eugenia?

_____

2. ¿Qué le dieron a Eugenia en la ceremonia?

_____

3. ¿Cómo se sintieron los padres de Eugenia?

_____

4. ¿En que otra competencia va a participar Eugenia?

_____

5. ¿Qué debe hacer para ganar esa competencia?

Realidades ❸

Capítulo 1

Nombre _____

Fecha _____

Hora _____

Core Practice **1-10**

El trofeo de Victoria

Completa la historia de Victoria y su trofeo, usando el pretérito o el imperfecto del verbo apropiado. La primera frase ya está hecha.

A Victoria Martínez siempre le **(1.)** _____*gustaban*_____ (*gustar / comer*) las

competencias deportivas. Todos los días **(2.)** _____ (*pensar / correr*) en ganar

un trofeo. Por eso ella **(3.)** _____ (*leer / entrenarse*) todas las semanas,

(4.) _____ (*correr / destruir*) ocho kilómetros cada día y

(5.) _____ (*hacer / venir*) mucho ejercicio. Todos los días

(6.) _____ (*oír / leer*) el periódico para ver cuándo **(7.)** _____

(*ser / saber*) las carreras de Santo Tomás. Un día leyó que las carreras

(8.) _____ (*ir / destruir*) a tener lugar en agosto y entonces Victoria se

inscribió. Ella **(9.)** _____ (*creer / tener*) tres meses para prepararse.

Por fin llegó el día de la carrera. Victoria **(10.)** _____ (*caer / saber*) que

(11.) _____ (*beber / competir*) con los mejores atletas del país. Sin embargo, no

se desanimó. Cuando empezó la carrera, Victoria **(12.)** _____ (*sentirse / ir*) en

cuarto lugar, pero después hizo un esfuerzo y ganó. ¡Le dieron su trofeo! Todos sus amigos

(13.) _____ (*estar / competir*) emocionados y gritaban "¡Felicitaciones!".

realidades.com ✔
• Web Code: jed-0107

Realidades 3

Capítulo 1

Nombre _____

Fecha _____

Hora _____

Core Practice **1-11**

Mi tío el atleta

A. Consuelo te habla sobre su tío Antonio. Ella te cuenta lo que le pasó a su equipo de fútbol. Completa el párrafo con el pretérito o el imperfecto del verbo apropiado del recuadro.

ir	ser	ganar	beber
gustar	obtener	jugar	

Déjame contarte algo acerca de mi tío. Mi tío Antonio **(1.)** _____ muy

deportista y siempre le **(2.)** _____ mucho los deportes. De niño siempre

(3.) _____ a los partidos de fútbol con su papá. Antonio también

(4.) _____ al fútbol por dos años. Su equipo no era muy bueno y casi nunca

(5.) _____. Pero una vez ellos **(6.)** _____ el trofeo del primer

lugar.

B. Ahora Amanda, la hermana de Consuelo, sigue contando la historia de su tío Antonio. Completa el párrafo con el pretérito o el imperfecto del verbo apropiado del recuadro.

hacer	dar	haber	entrenar
emocionarse	contar	nadar	

Antonio me **(1.)** _____ cómo pasó eso. Me dijo que los jugadores de su

equipo se **(2.)** _____ todos los días. El día del partido, el equipo

(3.) _____ un esfuerzo y logró ganar. Después **(4.)** _____ una

entrega de premios y le **(5.)** _____ al equipo de Antonio el trofeo. Todos los

jugadores **(6.)** _____ mucho.

Realidades 3

Capítulo 1

Nombre _____

Fecha _____

Hora _____

Core Practice **1-12**

La competencia

Un amigo te hace preguntas acerca de una competencia. Primero completa la pregunta, usando el pretérito o el imperfecto del verbo según el caso. Luego escribe la respuesta.

Modelo

¿En qué mes _____*fue*_____ (ser) la competencia?

La competencia fue en julio.

1. ¿Dónde _____ (tener) lugar esa competencia?

_____

2. Generalmente, ¿qué competencia _____ (haber)?

_____

3. ¿Qué hora _____ (ser) cuando empezó la competencia?

_____

4. ¿_____ (hacer) calor o frío cuando empezó la competencia?

_____

5. Generalmente, ¿cuántos atletas _____ (participar) en la competencia?

_____

6. ¿Qué _____ (haber) ayer después de la competencia?

_____

7. ¿Qué _____ (obtener) el ganador de la competencia todos los años?

_____

Realidades 3

Capítulo 1

Nombre _____

Hora _____

Fecha _____

Core Practice **1-13**

Organizer

I. Vocabulary

Actividades al aire libre

_____
_____
_____
_____

Para describir la naturaleza

_____
_____
_____
_____

Para hablar de cámping

_____
_____
_____
_____

Para hablar del tiempo

_____
_____
_____
_____

Para hablar de competencias deportivas

_____
_____
_____

Para expresar emociones e impresiones

_____
_____
_____

Para indicar cuándo sucede algo

_____
_____
_____

Para prepararse para un evento deportivo

_____
_____
_____

Organizer

II. Grammar

1. In verbs ending in *-uir*, the letter _____ changes to the letter _____ in the

   Ud. / él / ella forms of the preterite.

2. The preterite forms of *poner* are: The preterite forms of *decir* are:

   _____   _____   _____   _____

   _____   _____   _____   _____

   _____   _____   _____   _____

3. The preterite forms of *pedir* are: The preterite forms of *dormir* are:

   _____   _____   _____   _____

   _____   _____   _____   _____

   _____   _____   _____   _____

4. The imperfect endings of *-ar* verbs are:

   yo _____   nosotros(as) _____

   tú _____   vosotros(as) _____

   el/ella _____   Uds. _____

   The imperfect endings for regular *-er/-ir* verbs are:

   yo _____   nosotros(as) _____

   tú _____   vosotros(as) _____

   el/ella _____   Uds. _____

5. List three uses of the imperfect tense.

   a. _____

   b. _____

   c. _____

A ver si recuerdas . . .

Hablemos de arte

Luis y Ernesto quieren hacer comparaciones sobre arte. Ayúdalos escribiendo frases completas con la información que te damos.

| Modelo | esta obra de arte / + sencillo / esa obra de arte |

Esta obra de arte es más sencilla que esa obra de arte.

esta obra de arte / - sencillo / esa obra de arte

Esta obra de arte es menos sencilla que esa obra de arte.

esta obra de arte / = sencillo / esa obra de arte

Esta obra de arte es tan sencilla como esa obra de arte.

1. el museo de arte de Bilbao / + moderno / el museo de arte de Madrid

_____

2. estos pintores / – interesante / esos pintores

_____

3. tus obras de arte / = feo / mis obras de arte

_____

4. las estatuas de la plaza / – realista / las estatuas del parque

_____

5. el estilo de Carrillo / = complicado / el estilo de Obregón

_____

6. esta artista / + serio / esa artista

_____

7. esos cuadros / – bonito / estos cuadros

_____

8. los paisajes de este museo / + bueno / los paisajes de otros museos

_____

A ver si recuerdas . . .

Mis amigos artistas

Carla te está hablando de sus amigos artistas. Usa los dibujos para escribir frases superlativas.

cómico

Modelo

👍 *Fernando es el actor más cómico de todos.*

👎 *Fernando es el actor menos cómico de todos.*

1. 👎 talentoso _____

2. 👍 inolvidable _____

3. 👎 interesante _____

4. 👍 malo _____

5. 👍 perezoso _____

6. 👍 bueno _____

22 *A ver si recuerdas . . .*

Realidades ③

Capítulo 2

Nombre _____

Fecha _____

Hora _____

Core Practice **2-3**

Pintura y escultura

Estás de visita en un taller de arte. Mira los dibujos y completa las frases para decribir lo que ves.

1. Simón y Cristina pintan _____ en la pared.

2. Lorenza tiene varios colores en su _____.

3. Rogelio hace una _____ abstracta.

4. Los estudiantes pintan dentro del _____ de arte.

5. Juan José pinta _____.

6. Raquel y Elena trabajan _____.

7. Olivia tiene un _____.

Realidades 3

Capítulo 2

Nombre _____

Fecha _____

Hora _____

Core Practice **2-4**

La pintora y el crítico

A. Martín Dávila, crítico de arte, visita el taller de Mercedes Valenzuela. Completa las palabras para saber qué dice él acerca de esta pintora.

El taller de Mercedes Valenzuela **(1.)** m __ __ __ t __ __ por qué esta artista

es tan respetada. Sus cuadros **(2.)** __ __ p __ __ __ __ n muchos sentimientos

diferentes. Sus **(3.)** __ __ m __ s favoritos son la naturaleza y la familia, y

(4.) r __ __ __ __ __ __ __ t __ __ su amor por la vida. Se puede ver que el

pintor Armando Reverón **(5.)** i __ __ __ __ __ e mucho en su estilo. Las pinturas de

Valenzuela se vuelven más **(6.)** __ b __ __ __ __ c __ __ __ cada día. Esta pintora

ya es muy **(7.)** f __ m __ __ __ y yo creo que es una de las mejores artistas de este

(8.) s __ __ l __.

B. Ahora Mercedes Valenzuela nos habla de su arte. Completa las frases, sustituyendo *(substituting)* las palabras en paréntesis por palabras del vocabulario.

Mi estilo **(1.)** _____ *(se hace)* más complicado todos los días. Los críticos

dicen que mis **(2.)** _____ *(dibujos y pinturas)* son muy interesantes. Voy a mi

(3.) _____ *(estudio de arte)* todos los días. Yo prefiero estar

(4.) _____ *(en una silla)* cuando trabajo. A veces pinto

(5.) _____ *(cuadros de mí misma)*. Me gusta expresar

(6.) _____ *(alegría y tristeza)* en mis pinturas. Ahora estoy pintando un

paisaje. Al **(7.)** _____ *(la parte de atrás)* del cuadro se ven unas montañas.

Hay unos árboles en el **(8.)** _____ *(la parte de adelante)*.

Realidades ③

Capítulo 2

Nombre _____ Hora _____

Fecha _____ Core Practice **2-5**

No sabes lo que pasó

María le explica a su amiga Carmen por qué llegó tarde a la clase de arte. Completa su conversación con el pretérito o el imperfecto de los verbos que aparecen entre paréntesis, según el contexto.

CARMEN: ¿Qué pasó? Yo **(1.)** _____ *(ver)* que tú

(2.) _____ *(llegar)* tarde a la clase de arte.

MARÍA: Yo **(3.)** _____ *(salir)* de mi casa a tiempo, pero el autobús **(4.)**

_____ *(llegar)* tarde. Cuando yo

(5.) _____ *(entrar)* en la sala de clases, los estudiantes ya

(6.) _____ *(estar)* sentados.

CARMEN: Creo que **(7.)** _____ *(ser)* las nueve y diez cuando llegaste.

MARÍA: Creo que el profesor **(8.)** _____ *(estar)* enojado conmigo. No sé si

viste cómo me **(9.)** _____ *(mirar)* cuando me vio entrar tarde.

CARMEN: Yo vi que él **(10.)** _____ *(dejar)* de pintar.

(11.) _____ *(poner)* su pincel y su paleta en la mesa.

MARÍA: El profesor no **(12.)** _____ *(decir)* nada, pero sus ojos

(13.) _____ *(expresar)* sus sentimientos.

CARMEN: Sí, él **(14.)** _____ *(empezar)* el taller a las nueve, como de costumbre.

MARÍA: ¡Ay! No quiero que el profesor esté enojado conmigo. Su taller de arte es mi clase

favorita. Tengo que hablar con él para explicarle por qué yo

(15.) _____ *(llegar)* tarde.

CARMEN: Me parece buena idea.

realidades.com ⓥ
• Web Code: jed-0203

Realidades 3

Capítulo 2

Nombre _____

Hora _____

Fecha _____

Core Practice **2-6**

Una escena misteriosa

¿Qué ha pasado en el taller de arte? Usa *estar* + participio para contestar las preguntas y describir la escena.

Modelo
¿Alguien abrió la puerta del taller?

No, la puerta del taller ya estaba abierta. _____

1. ¿Alguien cerró las ventanas?

_____

2. ¿Los artistas hicieron el trabajo?

_____

3. ¿Ellas pintaron los cuadros?

_____

4. ¿Los estudiantes pusieron las paletas en la mesa?

_____

5. ¿Ellos decoraron el taller?

_____

6. ¿Alguien apagó las luces?

_____

7. ¿El profesor se acaba de dormir?

_____

8. ¿Los estudiantes escondieron las esculturas?

_____

• Web Code: jed-0205

Realidades ③

Capítulo 2

Nombre _____

Fecha _____

Hora _____

Core Practice **2-7**

Una visita al museo

A. Herminia está haciendo una lista de cosas que hizo cuando fue al Museo de Arte Nacional. Completa las frases usando el pretérito, el imperfecto o el imperfecto de *estar* y el participio pasado de los verbos, según el caso.

1. *(Ser)* _____ las once de la mañana cuando llegué al museo.

2. El guía del museo ya *(sentar)* _____ en su oficina.

3. El guía me dijo que *(llamarse)* _____ Manuel.

4. Manuel me *(hablar)* _____ sobre los cuadros mientras nosotros dos

   (caminar) _____.

5. Al final del día, yo *(cansar)* _____.

B. Sergio cuenta la visita que hicieron él y su hermana al museo de arte el viernes. Completa su historia usando el pretérito, el imperfecto, o el imperfecto de *estar* y el participio pasado de los verbos, según el caso.

El viernes pasado mi hermana y yo no **(1.)**_____ *(tener)* nada que

hacer. No **(2.)**_____ *(hacer)* muy buen tiempo, y por eso nosotros **(3.)**

_____ *(decidir)* ir al museo de arte. Nuestro profesor de arte nos dijo que **(4.)**

_____ *(haber)* muchas obras de arte interesantes allí. **(5.)**_____

(Ser) las nueve y diez cuando llegamos y el museo ya **(6.)**_____ *(abrir)*.

Nosotros **(7.)**_____ *(entrar)* y

(8.)_____ *(empezar)* a mirar la colección del museo. Mi hermana y yo **(9.)**

_____ *(ver)* a unas personas que **(10.)**_____ *(parar)* delante de

una escultura abstracta.

Después de pasar dos horas en las salas del museo, le **(11.)**_____

(decir) a mi hermana que **(12.)**_____ *(tener)* hambre. Ella también **(13.)**

_____ *(querer)* comer y **(14.)**_____ *(ir)* al restaurante del

museo. Después **(15.)**_____ *(visitar)* la librería del museo. Fue un día muy

agradable.

• Web Code: jed-0202, jed-0205

Realidades 3

Capítulo 2

Nombre _____

Fecha _____

Hora _____

Core Practice **2-8**

Estudiantes talentosos

Todas estas personas realizan actividades artísticas. Mira los dibujos y completa las frases.

1. Pedro y Tomás _____.

2. Nos encantó el _____ de salsa.

3. Ramón _____.

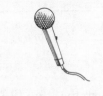

4. Teresa es una _____ de cuentos para niños.

5. Diego usa _____ cuando canta.

6. Leonora y Carlos aprenden _____ del tango.

7. Necesito comprar dos _____ para el espectáculo.

realidades.com

• Web Code: jed-0206

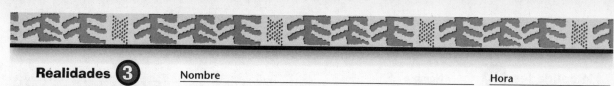

Realidades 3

Capítulo 2

Nombre _____

Fecha _____

Hora _____

Core Practice **2-9**

¿Adónde vamos a ir?

Elena y Jorge quieren salir esta noche, pero no pueden decidir adónde. Lee la conversación y completa el diálogo, sustituyendo (substituting) las palabras en paréntesis por palabras de vocabulario. No olvides usar los artículos determinados (el / la / los / las) o indeterminados (un / una / unos / unas), según el caso.

ELENA: Me gustaría ver **(1.)** _____ (baile estilo ballet) esta noche. ¿Qué te parece?

JORGE: Yo prefiero ver al **(2.)** _____ (grupo) de salsa "Bandoleros".

ELENA: ¿Qué sabes de ellos?

JORGE: Un crítico **(3.)** _____ (muy conocido) los recomendó en

(4.) _____ (artículo) del periódico.

ELENA: ¿Y qué escribió?

JORGE: Dijo que las canciones de "Bandoleros" tienen excelente

(5.) _____ (palabras de la canción) y

(6.) _____ (música).

ELENA: ¿El grupo "Bandoleros" **(7.)** _____ (ser similar) al grupo "Los chicos"?

JORGE: Sí. Los dos tocan salsa, pero tienen **(8.)** _____ (compases) diferentes. ¿Qué sabes del ballet?

ELENA: Los bailarines son famosos y muy buenos. El año pasado

(9.) _____ (actuaron) "El lago de los cisnes".

JORGE: ¿Y este año?

ELENA: Este año van a **(10.)** _____ (hacer) "El cascanueces".

JORGE: El ballet va a estar toda la semana y el grupo de salsa esta noche solamente. Vamos a ver a "Bandoleros" hoy y mañana podemos ir a ver el ballet que es

(11.) _____ (obra) más serio.

ELENA: De acuerdo. Yo voy a comprar **(12.)** _____ (boletos) para "Bandoleros" ahora mismo.

JORGE: ¡Y compra las de "El cascanueces" al mismo tiempo!

Realidades 3

Capítulo 2

Nombre _____

Fecha _____

Hora _____

Core Practice **2-10**

El teatro de los estudiantes

Los estudiantes presentan una obra de teatro, y hoy es la primera noche. Para saber cómo estuvieron las cosas, completa estas frases con el imperfecto de *ser* o *estar*, según el contexto.

1. _____ las siete y media.

2. El teatro _____ abierto.

3. Los actores ya _____ allí.

4. Todos los actores _____ estudiantes.

5. Ellos _____ muy nerviosos.

6. El escenario _____ muy bonito.

7. Mucha gente _____ sentada en el teatro.

8. La obra _____ argentina.

9. _____ una obra muy original.

10. La interpretación _____ muy interesante.

11. Los papeles _____ difíciles.

12. El público _____ muy entusiasmado.

• Web Code: jed-0207

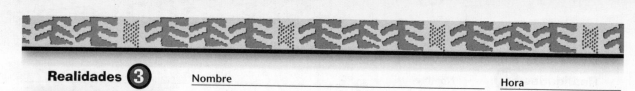

Realidades 3

Capítulo 2

Nombre _____

Hora _____

Fecha _____

Core Practice **2-11**

Preguntas y respuestas

Un amigo te pregunta algunas cosas acerca del conjunto "Los abuelos". Completa las preguntas con el pretérito o el imperfecto de los verbos indicados. Luego responde las preguntas utilizando el mismo verbo en pretérito o imperfecto, según el contexto.

Modelo conocer

—¿Tú _____*conocías*_____ al cantante de "Los abuelos"?

—No. *Lo conocí ayer después del concierto.* _____

1. **saber**

   —¿Tú _____ que el conjunto tocaba merengue?

   —No. _____

2. **querer**

   —¿Tu hermana _____ ver ese espectáculo?

   —Sí. _____

3. **poder**

   —¿Ellos _____ comprar las entradas ayer?

   —Sí. _____

4. **no querer**

   —¿Ustedes dijeron que _____ comprar el disco de "Los abuelos"?

   —No. _____

5. **conocer**

   —¿Tú _____ a Marta en el concierto?

   —No. Ya _____

6. **poder**

   —¿Marta _____ aprenderse la letra de las canciones antes del concierto?

   —No. _____

Realidades ❸

Capítulo 2

Nombre _____

Fecha _____

Hora _____

Core Practice **2-12**

Hablando de una artista

Laura y Paco hablan de la señora Piñedo, una artista que conocen. Completa su conversación con el pretérito o imperfecto de los verbos entre paréntesis.

LAURA: Ayer **(1.)** _____ (conocer/saber) a la señora Piñedo.

PACO: Entonces ¿tú no la **(2.)** _____ (ser/conocer)?

LAURA: No. Nunca **(3.)** _____ (poder/estar) ir a verla en su taller.

PACO: ¿Tú ya **(4.)** _____ (saber/querer) cómo llegar?

LAURA: Sí. **(5.)** _____ (ser/estar) fácil llegar al taller.

PACO: ¿Cómo **(6.)** _____ (ser/estar) la señora Piñedo?

LAURA: Muy bien. Y el taller **(7.)** _____ (ser/estar) muy grande. Las paredes

(8.) _____ (ser/estar) pintadas.

PACO: ¿Viste sus cuadros?

LAURA: Sí. **(9.)** _____ (poder/conocer) ver muchos cuadros de la señora Piñedo.

PACO: Al principio, la señora Piñedo **(10.)** _____ (ser/estar) una artista

realista, y después su arte se volvió abstracto. Ella ya no

(11.) _____ (conocer/querer) pintar más cuadros realistas.

LAURA: Bueno, los cuadros que yo vi **(12.)** _____ (ser/estar) muy abstractos. Yo

no **(13.)** _____ (poder/conocer) los cuadros realistas de ella.

PACO: Antes ella hacía esculturas también. ¿ **(14.)** _____ (poder/saber) verlas?

LAURA: **(15.)** _____ (Querer/Conocer) verlas, pero no

(16.) _____ (saber/poder). Creo que las esculturas

(17.) _____ (ser/estar) en otro taller.

PACO: Yo estudio pintura con la señora Piñedo. Antes de estudiar con ella, yo no

(18.) _____ (ser/estar) tan buen pintor. Ahora pinto mejor.

LAURA: Siempre **(19.)** _____ (querer/saber) estudiar con la señora Piñedo.

Podemos estudiar juntos.

PACO: ¡Excelente idea!

32 *Manos a la obra 2* ▬ *Gramática y vocabulario en uso*

realidades.com ▼

• Web Code: jed-0210

Realidades 3

Capítulo 2

Nombre _____

Fecha _____

Hora _____

Core Practice **2-13**

Organizer

I. Vocabulary

Formas y géneros de arte

_____

_____

_____

_____

_____

Para describir una obra de arte

_____

_____

_____

_____

_____

En el escenario

_____

_____

_____

_____

_____

Para hablar sobre la música y la danza

_____

_____

_____

_____

_____

Para hablar sobre la actuación

_____

_____

_____

_____

_____

Profesiones artísticas y materiales de arte

_____

_____

_____

_____

_____

Realidades 3

Capítulo 2

Nombre _____

Fecha _____

Hora _____

Core Practice **2-14**

Organizer

II. Grammar

1. List two uses of the preterite and two uses of the imperfect.

_____

_____

_____

_____

2. How is *estar* + past participle used?

_____

_____

3. Write the past participle of the following verbs:

abrir _____ hacer _____

decir _____ escribir _____

volver _____ romper _____

4. List two uses of *ser* and two uses of *estar*.

_____

_____

_____

_____

5. What meanings do these verbs have in the different tenses?

	IMPERFECT	PRETERITE
saber		
conocer		
querer		
no querer		
poder		

realidades.com

• Web Code: jed-0211

A ver si recuerdas . . .

Los enfermos

Cuenta lo que les pasó hoy a estas personas que no se sienten bien. Contesta las preguntas usando los dibujos. Usa el pretérito y un pronombre de complemento indirecto.

Modelo

A María le dolía el tobillo. ¿Qué hizo la médica?

La médica le examinó el tobillo.

1. Marisol estaba enferma. ¿Qué hizo la enfermera?

_____

2. Pablo necesitaba una medicina. ¿Qué hizo el médico?

_____

3. A Uds. les dolía la garganta. ¿Qué recomendó la médica?

_____

4. Los niños se sentían mal. ¿Qué preparó su mamá?

_____

5. Andrés quería sentirse bien. ¿Qué le dijo el médico?

_____

6. Manuel se rompió el brazo. ¿Qué hicieron los enfermeros?

_____

7. Roberto y tú siempre estaban cansados. ¿Qué recomendó el médico? _____

A ver si recuerdas . . .

¡Qué rica comida!

¿Qué les gusta y qué no les gusta a estas personas? Completa cada pregunta y escribe las dos formas posibles de la respuesta, usando el gerundio y un pronombre de complemento directo.

Modelo

— ¿Juan come ____el pastel____?

— *No, no está comiéndolo.* (o) *No, no lo está comiendo.*

1.

—¿Isabel prueba _____?

—_____. (o) _____.

2.

—¿Pepe y Anita compran _____?

—_____. (o) _____.

3.

—¿La señora Salas sirve _____?

—_____. (o) _____.

4.

—¿Matilde come _____?

—_____. (o) _____.

5.

—¿Ernesto prepara _____?

—_____. (o) _____.

6.

—¿Antonia y Rebeca comen _____?

—_____. (o) _____.

7.

—¿El señor Tamayo prueba _____?

—_____. (o) _____.

realidades.com
• Web Code: jed-0301

Realidades 3

Nombre _____   Hora _____

Capítulo 3

Fecha _____   Core Practice **3-3**

La clínica del doctor Ramírez

Guillermo no se siente bien y va al médico. Completa la conversación con las palabras que faltan.

MÉDICO: ¿Qué tienes, Guillermo? ¿Qué te duele?

GUILLERMO: No estoy seguro. Me siento mal. Creo que tengo fiebre.

MÉDICO: Voy a tomarte la temperatura.

GUILLERMO: ¿Tengo fiebre, doctor?

MÉDICO: Sí. Tienes una fiebre de 39 **(1.)** _____.

GUILLERMO: No sé, doctor. No oigo bien. Me duelen **(2.)** _____.

MÉDICO: ¿Y la garganta y el pecho también? Oigo que tienes una

                    (3.) _____ muy fuerte.

GUILLERMO: También me molesta la nariz. Yo **(4.)** _____ mucho. ¿Puede

                    ser una alergia? ¿Estoy resfriado?

MÉDICO: Creo que tienes **(5.)** _____. Te voy a recetar un

                    (6.) _____. Tómalo con la comida. No lo tomes con el

                    estómago vacío. Y si te duele la cabeza, toma unas **(7.)** _____.

GUILLERMO: ¿Puedo comer, doctor?

MÉDICO: Claro, Guillermo, pero evita la **(8.)** _____, como las papas

                    fritas y las hamburguesas. Debes seguir una **(9.)** _____

                    equilibrada, como siempre.

Realidades 3

Capítulo 3

Nombre _____

Fecha _____

Hora _____

Core Practice **3-4**

Consejos para los atletas

El entrenador les explica a los atletas lo que deben hacer para mantenerse en forma. Completa el párrafo.

Bueno, mis queridos atletas, les voy a dar algunos consejos para que se mantengan

(1.) ___ a ___ ___ d ___ ___ ___ ___ ___. Tener buenos **(2.)** ___ á ___ ___ t ___ ___

___ ___ ___ m ___ ___ t ___ ___ ___ ___ ___ es muy importante. Deben

comer muchas frutas y verduras. Por ejemplo, las espinacas contienen un alto

(3.) ___ ___ v ___ l de **(4.)** ___ ___ ___ r r ___. La leche tiene **(5.)** ___ ___ l c ___ ___,

que ayuda a poner los huesos fuertes. Pero tengan cuidado con los

(6.) ___ ___ ___ b ___ h ___ ___ r ___ ___ ___. Éstos dan **(7.)** ___ ___ ___ r g ___ ___,

pero no se deben comer demasiados. Los huevos tienen muchas

(8.) ___ r ___ t ___ ___ ___ ___ ___, pero tampoco hay que comer demasiados.

Recuerden no saltarse comidas, pero también deben evitar comer mucho en las

(9.) ___ ___ r ___ ___ n ___ ___ ___. Coman cuando tengan hambre,

pero cuando se sientan **(10.)** ___ ___ e n ___ ___, dejen de comer. Es muy importante

también **(11.)** t ___ ___ ___ r mucha agua siempre y, sobre todo, cuando

hace mucho calor.

realidades.com

• Web Code: jed-0302

Realidades 3

Capítulo 3

Nombre _____

Fecha _____

Hora _____

Core Practice **3-5**

Ideas para tus amigos

Tus amigos quieren vivir mejor y tú les das consejos sobre su alimentación y lo que deben hacer todos los días. Escríbeles consejos con mandatos afirmativos con *tú*, usando los verbos del recuadro.

levantarse	hacer	evitar	cepillarse
tomar	comer	beber	correr

Modelo   *Come mucha fruta.* _____

1. _____

2. _____

3. _____

4. _____

5. _____

6. _____

7. _____

Realidades 3

Nombre _____

Hora _____

Capítulo 3

Fecha _____

Core Practice **3-6**

Buenos consejos

Tu amigo Fernando te pregunta lo que no debe hacer para estar bien de salud y tener éxito en la escuela. Primero escoge el verbo correcto para cada uno de sus comentarios. Luego contesta sus preguntas usando mandatos negativos con *tú*. La primera respuesta ya está escrita.

FERNANDO: Creo que no tengo buenos hábitos alimenticios. Por ejemplo,

(*como* / *estornudo* / *hago*) muchos dulces.

TÚ: **(1.)** *Pues entonces, no comas muchos dulces.*

FERNANDO: Además, generalmente tengo sed durante el día. Siempre me

(*olvido* / *como* / *duermo*) de beber agua.

TÚ: **(2.)** _____

FERNANDO: Nunca traigo mi almuerzo. Siempre (*baño* / *corto* / *compro*) comida basura.

TÚ: **(3.)** _____

FERNANDO: También me (*bebo* / *salto* / *descanso*) comidas durante el día. Por ejemplo, no

tomo el desayuno.

TÚ: **(4.)** _____

FERNANDO: Sí, pero no es fácil. Es que me (*hago* / *pruebo* / *pongo*) nervioso en la escuela.

TÚ: **(5.)** _____

FERNANDO: Quisiera ser más fuerte. Pero siempre (*examino* / *evito* / *duermo*) hacer ejercicio.

TÚ: **(6.)** _____

FERNANDO: No es fácil. (*Soy* / *Corro* / *Paseo*) muy perezoso.

TÚ: **(7.)** _____

FERNANDO: Cuando llego a la casa, no estudio. (*Cierro* / *Navego* / *Miro*) la televisión.

TÚ: **(8.)** _____

FERNANDO: Además, me gusta (*jugar* / *evitar* / *pensar*) videojuegos.

TÚ: **(9.)** _____

FERNANDO: Trataré de seguir tus consejos. Gracias.

• Web Code: jed-0304

Realidades 3

Capítulo 3

Nombre _____

Fecha _____

Hora _____

Core Practice **3-7**

El Dr. Peña dice . . .

El Dr. Peña está en el hospital. Cuando visita a sus pacientes, les dice lo que deben y no deben hacer. Algunos(as) pacientes reciben instrucciones especiales. Escribe lo que les dice el Dr. Peña, usando mandatos con *Ud.* y *Uds.*

Modelo   (todas) escuchar bien / al médico
Escúchenlo bien.
_____

1. (todos) tomarse / la temperatura

   _____

2. (Sra. Laínez) no tomar / hierro

   _____

3. (todos) hacer / esta dieta

   _____

4. (Sra. Gómez) comer / verduras

   _____

5. (todas) dormirse / temprano

   _____

6. (Sr. Pérez y Srta. Pardo) seguir / mis consejos

   _____

7. (todas) no saltar / el desayuno

   _____

8. (todos) hacer / ejercicio

   _____

9. (Sra. Ruiz) evitar / tomar el sol

   _____

10. (Sra. Paz) no poner / las vitaminas en la basura

    _____

Realidades 3

Capítulo 3

Nombre _____

Fecha _____

Hora _____

Core Practice **3-8**

Gente en forma

Mira los dibujos y escribe una frase para describir cada uno.

Modelo Manuel

Manuel flexiona la rodilla. _____

1. Sonia

_____

2. Ramiro

_____

3. Luz y Clarita

_____

4. Marcos

_____

5. Marta y Nola

_____

6.  Berta

_____

7.  Nicolás

_____

realidades.com

• Web Code: jed-0306

Realidades 3

Capítulo 3

Nombre _____

Fecha _____

Hora _____

Core Practice **3-9**

Aconsejando a una amiga

Laura y Mirna están hablando de los problemas que tiene Laura. Lee la conversación y completa las frases con palabras o expresiones que signifiquen lo mismo que las expresiones entre paréntesis.

MIRNA: Laura, te ves muy cansada.

LAURA: Sí, es que anoche no dormí bien. Y ahora **(1.)** _____

(*tengo muchas ganas de dormir*).

MIRNA: Vamos, no te **(2.)** _____ (*decir lo que te molesta*).

LAURA: ¡Es en serio! Y siempre estoy en la luna. Trato de leer pero no puedo

(3.) _____ (*pensar en lo que quiero*).

MIRNA: ¿Y qué otros problemas tienes?

LAURA: A ver . . . también estoy muy **(4.)** _____ (*nerviosa*). En general, me

siento **(5.)** _____ (*muy mal*).

MIRNA: Bueno, tal vez yo pueda **(6.)** _____ (*decir qué hacer*).

LAURA: Sí, tal vez. Tú eres una persona que siempre está

(7.) _____ (*contenta*). No sé cómo lo haces.

MIRNA: Bueno, dime . . . ¿por qué crees que te sientes así?

LAURA: Creo que en el trabajo me **(8.)** _____ (*piden*) mucho. Hay

demasiado que hacer.

MIRNA: ¿Por qué no intentas **(9.)** _____ (*estar tranquila*) un poco?

LAURA: Es que no sé cómo hacerlo. La verdad, ya no **(10.)** _____ (*puedo*) más.

MIRNA: Pues te recomiendo que hagas yoga. Cuando yo hice yoga, aprendí a

(11.) _____ (*tomar aire*) mejor. Eso me ayuda a sentirme

bien siempre.

LAURA: ¿Sabes qué? No es mala idea. Esta noche me inscribo en una clase de yoga.

Realidades 3

Capítulo 3

Nombre _____

Fecha _____

Hora _____

Core Practice **3-10**

Instructora de ejercicio

María es instructora en un club deportivo. Ahora le enseña a un grupo nuevo lo que tiene que hacer en el programa de ejercicios. Mira los dibujos y completa sus instrucciones. Hay un verbo del recuadro que se usa varias veces.

hacer	buscar	estirar	flexionar	descansar

Modelo Sugiero que Uds. _hagan ejercicios aeróbicos_ para empezar.

1. Primero, _____ un buen lugar para hacer ejercicio.

2. Quiero que Juan _____ la pierna.

3. Después, recomiendo que todos nosotros _____.

4. Es bueno que todo el mundo _____ también.

5. Marta, te aconsejo que _____ los músculos.

6. Aconsejo que los más fuertes _____.

7. Después de hacer ejercicio, exijo que Uds. _____

• Web Code: jed-0307

Realidades 3

Capítulo 3

Nombre _____

Fecha _____

Hora _____

Core Practice **3-11**

Ser consejero(a)

¿Puedes ayudar a los estudiantes que tienen problemas? Escoge entre las soluciones propuestas y da tu consejo, usando el subjuntivo.

evitar la comida basura	estar menos estresado(a)
ir al cine con amigos(as)	ser más paciente con los (las) amigos(as)
hacer ejercicio	saber escoger bien los alimentos
hacer clases de ejercicios aeróbicos	comenzar con ejercicios para entrar en calor
dar un paseo	

Modelo Martín quiere perder peso. ¿Qué recomiendas?
Recomiendo que evite la comida basura.

1. Rosaura se enoja con todo el mundo. ¿Qué es necesario que haga?

   _____

2. Carla y Paula quieren ser más fuertes. ¿Qué sugieres?

   _____

3. No quiero tener calambres cuando corro. ¿Qué es importante que haga?

   _____

4. Nosotros no tenemos energía. ¿Qué es necesario que hagamos?

   _____

5. Estoy siempre muy nerviosa. ¿Qué recomiendas?

   _____

6. Pedro está muy aburrido. ¿Qué aconsejas?

   _____

7. Los estudiantes necesitan estar en forma. ¿Qué es necesario?

   _____

8. Los chicos quieren relajarse. ¿Qué es bueno?

Realidades **3**

Nombre _____

Hora _____

Capítulo 3

Fecha _____

Core Practice **3-12**

Los padres y los hijos

Los padres y los hijos no siempre están de acuerdo. A veces los hijos hacen algo, y sus padres quieren que hagan otra cosa. Primero completa la frase del hijo con el verbo adecuado del recuadro. Luego en base a los elementos dados, escribe lo que quieren sus padres, usando el subjuntivo.

| tomar | correr | jugar | levantarse | beber | hacer |

Modelo

JUAN: Yo _____*corro*_____ en el gimnasio.

MADRE DE JUAN: *Quiero que Juan corra en el parque.*

MELISSA: Yo _____ ejercicios aeróbicos.

1. PADRE DE MELISSA: _____

ROBERTO: Yo _____ jugo de naranja.

2. PADRE DE ROBERTO: _____

CRISTINA: Yo _____ vitaminas.

3. PADRE DE CRISTINA: _____

MARISOL: Yo _____ al fútbol.

4. MADRE DE MARISOL: _____

GABRIEL: Yo _____ tarde en la mañana.

5. PADRE DE GABRIEL: _____

realidades.com

• Web Code: jed-0309

Realidades 3

Capítulo 3

Nombre _____

Fecha _____

Hora _____

Core Practice **3-13**

Organizer

I. Vocabulary

Tipos de ejercicio

_____

_____

_____

_____

Estados de ánimo

_____

_____

_____

_____

Elementos de la comida

_____

_____

_____

_____

Aspectos de la nutrición

_____

_____

_____

_____

Síntomas y medicinas

_____

_____

_____

_____

Actividades relacionadas con la salud

_____

_____

_____

_____

Realidades 3

Capítulo 3

Nombre _____

Fecha _____

Hora _____

Core Practice **3-14**

II. Grammar

1. What is the form of the affirmative *tú* commands with regular verbs?

   _____

2. How do you form negative *tú* commands with regular verbs?

   _____

3. What are the irregular affirmative *tú* command forms of these verbs?

   decir _____   hacer _____

   poner _____   ser _____

   tener _____   salir _____

   ir _____   mantener _____

4. How do you form *Ud.* and *Uds.* commands?

   _____

5. Summarize the position of object pronouns with command forms.

   _____

   _____

6. Provide the subjunctive forms of these verbs.

   tomar   **poder**

   _____ _____   _____ _____

   _____ _____   _____ _____

   _____ _____   _____ _____

   pedir   **ir**

   _____ _____   _____ _____

   _____ _____   _____ _____

   _____ _____   _____ _____

realidades.com
• Web Code: jed-0311

A ver si recuerdas . . .

¿Cómo se relaciona la gente con los demás?

Irene habla de las relaciones que tienen sus amigos y su familia. Escribe lo que dice con frases completas, usando los verbos reflexivos sugeridos.

> **Modelo** Leti y yo / llevarse / muy bien
> *Leti y yo nos llevamos muy bien.*

1. Patricia y Plácido / verse / durante los fines de semana

   _____

2. mis amigos y yo / hablarse / todos los días por la noche

   _____

3. Carlitos y mi primo / pelearse / cuando juegan al fútbol

   _____

4. tú y yo / escribirse / por correo electrónico

   _____

5. mis padres y nosotros / entenderse / muy bien

   _____

6. Mari Carmen y yo / llamarse / por la tarde

   _____

7. Felipe y Luisa / conocerse / desde hace tres años

   _____

8. mi mamá y mi hermanito / abrazarse / a menudo

   _____

9. Juan, Elena y Gregorio / reunirse /durante los días festivos

   _____

10. Marta y su esposo / quedarse / en casa

    _____

Realidades ③

Capítulo 4

Nombre _____

Hora _____

Fecha _____

Core Practice **4-2**

A ver si recuerdas . . .

Los niños y los jóvenes

¿Qué les pasa a estas personas? Mira los dibujos y completa las frases para saber lo que sucede.

Modelo   Manolo _____*se enojó*_____ con Rafael.

1.   Angélica _____ cuando María le

_____.

2.   Raquel _____ mucho cuando vio el programa
de televisión.

3.   Martín _____ nervioso cuando su amigo

_____ tarde.

4.   Perla y Victoria _____ en el centro.

5.   Margarita y Francisca _____ porque estaban
aburridas.

6.   Anita y Enrique _____ por los juguetes.

7.   Nicolás se puso _____ porque Lorenzo era muy

_____ y no quería hacer nada.

8.   Bertín _____ loco cuando su equipo perdió
el partido.

realidades.com

• Web Code: jed-0401

Realidades ③

Capítulo 4

Nombre _____

Fecha _____

Hora _____

Core Practice **4-3**

¿Cómo son los amigos?

A Pedro y Jimena les encanta hablar de los amigos. Lee el diálogo y complétalo con las palabras adecuadas. Luego responde las preguntas.

PEDRO: Jimena, ¿conoces a Sarita Fernández?

JIMENA: Claro. Es una chica muy sincera y **(1.)** _____. Siempre dice la verdad.

PEDRO: Ella trata de no lastimar los sentimientos de sus amigos. Es muy simpática.

Para mí es la persona más **(2.)** _____ que conozco.

JIMENA: Si, además es muy **(3.)** _____. Siempre que nos vemos me da un

gran abrazo.

PEDRO: Es cierto. Sin embargo, siempre se anda mirando en el espejo.

JIMENA: Sí, es bastante **(4.)** _____.

PEDRO: Ella es la novia de Lorenzo, ¿no?

JIMENA: Sí. Pero a mí no me gusta él.

PEDRO: ¿Por qué? Él siempre me escucha y me aconseja. Entiende mis problemas y es muy

(5.) _____. Me ayuda y me **(6.)** _____ en los momentos difíciles.

JIMENA: Pues a mí me parece que sólo piensa en sí mismo. Es **(7.)** _____.

PEDRO: No te creo. Lo único malo que tiene Lorenzo es que le gusta saber lo que hacen

y dicen los demás. Es un poco **(8.)** _____.

JIMENA: ¿Un poco? ¡Yo diría que mucho! Y luego le cuenta todo a su hermana.

PEDRO: Ella sí que es **(9.)** _____. Le encanta hablar de los demás.

JIMENA: Menos mal que nosotros no somos así.

PEDRO: Sí. Menos mal.

10. ¿Cuáles son dos cualidades buenas de Sarita Fernández?

_____

11. ¿Cuáles son dos cualidades malas de Lorenzo?

_____

Realidades ③

Capítulo 4

Nombre _____

Fecha _____

Hora _____

Core Practice **4-4**

Amigos íntimos

Fernando habla sobre cómo debe ser un buen amigo. Completa lo que dice con las palabras que faltan. Pon las letras de las palabras en orden.

caetap	lagero	oayop	clddsuaiae
iadmast	raudarg	ratnoc	númco

1. Para mí, es muy importante tener buenos amigos. La _____ es muy

   importante.

2. Es necesario que un amigo sepa _____ un secreto.

3. Si tu amigo les cuenta tus secretos a otros, tú no puedes _____ con él.

4. Es bueno si los amigos tienen interés en las mismas cosas. Los buenos amigos

   siempre tienen mucho en _____.

5. Un buen amigo no trata de cambiarte. Te _____ tal como eres.

6. Yo también soy un buen amigo. Cuando mis amigos tienen momentos felices, yo

   me _____ por ellos.

7. Y también los _____ en los momentos tristes.

8. Un buen amigo debe ser honesto, comprensivo y considerado. Son las

   _____ más importantes, en mi opinión.

realidades.com

• Web Code: jed-0402

Realidades 3

Capítulo 4

Nombre _____

Fecha _____

Hora _____

Core Practice **4-5**

¿Cómo deben ser los amigos?

Los estudiantes expresan sus ideas sobre los amigos y la amistad. Escribe lo que dicen, formando frases con los elementos dados.

 alegrarse   temer   sorprenderse   preocuparse   sentir

Modelo

 Los amigos (*pasar / apoyar*) mucho tiempo juntos.

Me alegro que los amigos pasen mucho tiempo juntos.

 Tú (*tener / saludarse*) muchos amigos aquí.

1. _____

 Uds. no (*temer / pasar*) mucho tiempo con Pablo.

2. _____

Carla no (*saber / alegrarse*) guardar secretos.

3. _____

 Esos jóvenes no (*confiar / tener*) mucho en común.

4. _____

 Paula no (*guardar / apoyar*) a Marcos.

5. _____

 Siempre (*poder / temer*) contar con Susana.

6. _____

 Raúl (*desconfiar / esperar*) de sus amigos.

7. _____

Realidades 3

Capítulo 4

Nombre _____

Fecha _____

Hora _____

Core Practice **4-6**

Conversaciones entre amigas

Julia y Daniel tienen problemas en su relación. Completa estas conversaciones con *por* o *para* para saber lo que pasa.

LAURA: Elena, te llamé **(1.)** _____ pedirte un consejo. Estoy muy preocupada

(2.) _____ Julia y Daniel. ¿Tienes tiempo ahora **(3.)** _____ hablar?

ELENA: **(4.)** _____ supuesto que sí, Laura. Dime lo que pasa.

LAURA: No lo vas a creer, pero ellos se pelearon **(5.)** _____ algo. Ayer yo caminaba

(6.) _____ el parque **(7.)** _____ volver a casa y los vi. Estuvieron discutiendo

(8.) _____ mucho tiempo.

ELENA: ¿No oíste lo que decían?

LAURA: No me acerqué. No quise ser entrometida.

ELENA: Julia es mi amiga. Hoy **(9.)** _____ la noche voy a llamarla **(10.)** _____

teléfono.

Elena llama a Julia.

ELENA: ¿Julia? Te habla Elena. Llamé **(11.)** _____ ver cómo estabas.

JULIA: Hola, Elena. Pues, no muy bien. Daniel y yo no nos vamos a ver más.

ELENA: ¿Cómo? Julia, ¡lo siento! ¿Qué pasó?

JULIA: En los últimos meses, Daniel cambió mucho. Antes era muy comprensivo y

cariñoso. Yo podía contar con él **(12.)** _____ todo, pero ahora es muy egoísta.

(13.) _____ ejemplo, nunca me ayuda cuando lo necesito.

ELENA: ¿**(14.)** _____ qué crees que cambió tanto?

JULIA: No tengo idea, pero sé que no puedo seguir así.

ELENA: Entonces, es mejor no verlo más.

JULIA: Sé que tienes razón, pero **(15.)** _____ mí es muy difícil.

En familia

La señora Almudena dice lo que piensa de todo lo que pasa en su familia. Primero completa la pregunta con *por* o *para.* Luego escribe la respuesta, usando los elementos sugeridos para formar frases. Usa el subjuntivo o el indicativo, según el caso.

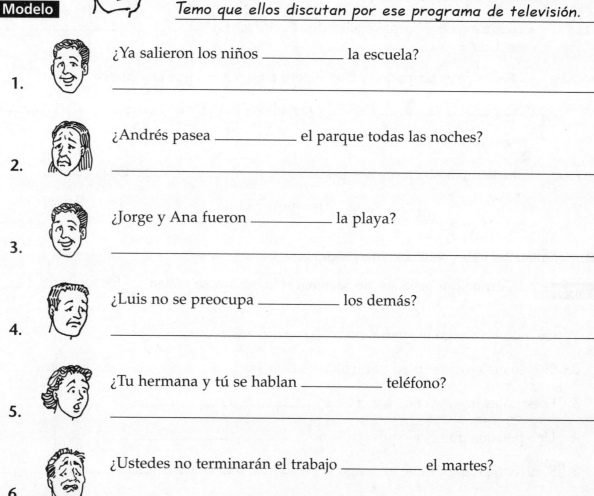

alegrarse   temer   sorprenderse   preocuparse   sentir

Modelo

¿Ellos van a discutir ___*por*___ ese programa de televisión?

Temo que ellos discutan por ese programa de televisión.

1. ¿Ya salieron los niños _____ la escuela?

   _____

2. ¿Andrés pasea _____ el parque todas las noches?

   _____

3. ¿Jorge y Ana fueron _____ la playa?

   _____

4. ¿Luis no se preocupa _____ los demás?

   _____

5. ¿Tu hermana y tú se hablan _____ teléfono?

   _____

6. ¿Ustedes no terminarán el trabajo _____ el martes?

   _____

Realidades ❸

Capítulo 4

Nombre _____

Fecha _____

Hora _____

Core Practice **4-8**

Conversación

A. Completa la conversación con los elementos apropiados del recuadro. Pon las letras de las palabras en orden.

ncoliosfct	iafeendircs de iopónni	lendnmadotei
roponde	imecitacrr	epsain ne ís simmo
et cciorenlsiate	ghaan als cpaes	abloraco

ELENA: ¿Por fin **(1.)** _____ con tu hermano?

TOMÁS: No. Yo no **(2.)** _____ a Federico por **(3.)** _____ delante de mis papás.

ELENA: Tu hermano tiene buenas cualidades. Puede ser un **(4.)** _____ entre Uds.

TOMÁS: Sí, Federico es simpático y cortés pero también es egoísta y nunca

(5.) _____ con nadie. Sólo **(6.)** _____.

Por eso ocurren **(7.)** _____ en mi familia.

ELENA: Entre hermanos siempre hay **(8.)** _____. Ojalá que

(9.) _____ pronto.

B. Completa las frases de una manera lógica.

Modelo   Cuando dos personas deciden hacer lo mismo, se ponen ____*de acuerdo*____.

1. Cuando un amigo te ignora, no _____.

2. Si algo malo ocurre pero tú no hiciste nada, no _____.

3. Si estudias más, tus notas van a _____.

4. Una persona que está equivocada no _____.

5. Si no entiendes por qué tu amigo se portó mal, pídele una _____.

6. Cuando tengo una _____ con un amigo le grito y luego me voy.

realidades.com ⓥ
• Web Code: jed-0406

Realidades ③

Capítulo 4

Nombre _____

Fecha _____

Hora _____

Core Practice **4-9**

La encuesta

Te están haciendo una encuesta sobre la amistad. Escribe respuestas a las preguntas, cambiando las palabras subrayadas por palabras del vocabulario.

Modelo   ¿Tú y tus amigos se ayudan?

Sí, mis amigos y yo colaboramos.

1. ¿Tus amigos no te hacen caso?

   No, _____

2. ¿Tú y tus amigos a veces no piensan lo mismo?

   Sí, _____

3. ¿Tu mejor amigo tiene una buena manera de actuar?

   Sí, _____

4. ¿Tu mejor amigo a veces dice que haces algo mal?

   No, _____

5. Cuando se pelean, ¿tus amigos te dicen "Lo siento"?

   Sí, _____

6. Después de pelearse, ¿tú y tus amigos hacen las paces?

   Sí, _____

7. Cuando están equivocados, ¿tus amigos lo aceptan?

   Sí, _____

8. ¿Tus amigos son egoístas?

   No, _____

Realidades ③

Capítulo 4

Nombre _____

Fecha _____

Hora _____

Core Practice **4-10**

Situaciones

Sugiere una solución para cada una de estas situaciones. Escoge el verbo o expresión más apropiado del recuadro y responde con un mandato con *nosotros*.

refugiarse allí	ponerse de acuerdo	hacer las paces	guardar su secreto
pedirle el dinero	no mentirle	no desconfiar de él	buscarlo

Modelo   Necesito hacer ejercicio. (salir a correr)

Salgamos a correr. _____

1. Alicia me dijo que no sale más con Felipe Ramírez y que no quiere que nadie lo sepa.

_____

2. Alfredo quiere que tengamos confianza en lo que dice.

_____

3. Yo creo que papá nos dará los mil pesos que necesitamos.

_____

4. No quiero que tú y yo sigamos enojados.

_____

5. Cada uno quiere hacer otra cosa. Tenemos que decidirnos.

_____

6. Creo que nuestro gato se perdió.

_____

7. Empieza a caer granizo.

_____

8. El profesor exige que le digamos la verdad.

_____

Realidades **3**

Capítulo 4

Nombre _____

Hora _____

Fecha _____

Core Practice **4-11**

¿Qué sucede con los míos?

Mira los dibujos y describe lo que ves en dos frases completas. La segunda frase debe tener un pronombre posesivo.

Modelo

Los padres de Lorenzo

mis padres

estar enojados

Los padres de Lorenzo
están enojados.
Los míos no están enojados.

1. el novio de Luisa

tu novio

ser celoso

_____

_____

_____

2. las amigas de Francisca

nuestras amigas

ser chismosas

_____

_____

_____

3. la tía de Pablo

su tía (de ustedes)

ser cariñosa

_____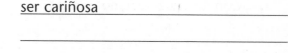

_____

_____

4. el hijo de los Valdez

el hijo de usted

tener la culpa

_____

_____

_____

5. la explicación de tu profesora

la explicación de mi profesora

ser buena

_____

_____

_____

• Web Code: jed-0409

Realidades 3

Capítulo 4

Nombre _____

Fecha _____

Hora _____

Core Practice **4-12**

¿Cuál debemos escoger?

¡Tu amigo no puede decidirse! Te hace varias preguntas sobre algunas personas para que tú le digas qué hacer. Responde las preguntas de tu amigo, rechazando la primera posibilidad y aceptando la segunda. Usa mandatos con *nosotros* y pronombres posesivos.

Modelo ¿A quién le debemos pedir perdón? ¿A tu amigo o al amigo de Carlos?

No le pidamos perdón al mío. Pidámosle perdón al suyo.

1. ¿A quién debemos escoger? ¿A nuestro capitán o al capitán del otro equipo?

   _____

2. ¿A quién debemos criticar? ¿A los profesores de Paula o a nuestros profesores?

   _____

3. ¿A quiénes les debemos hacer caso? ¿A los padres de nuestros amigos o a mis padres?

   _____

4. ¿A quién debemos apoyar? ¿A nuestra entrenadora o a la entrenadora de ellos?

   _____

5. ¿Con quiénes debemos contar? ¿Con tus amigas o con las amigas de Silvia?

   _____

6. ¿Qué problemas debemos resolver? ¿Mis problemas o los problemas de ustedes?

   _____

7. ¿Qué secretos debemos guardar? ¿Los secretos de Daniela o tus secretos?

   _____

8. ¿Cuál debemos empezar? ¿La tarea mía o la tarea de mis hermanos?

   _____

realidades.com
• Web Code: jed-0410

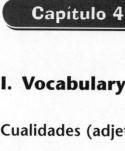

Realidades 3

Capítulo 4

Nombre _____

Hora _____

Fecha _____

Core Practice **4-13**

Organizer

I. Vocabulary

Cualidades (adjetivos)

_____

_____

_____

_____

_____

_____

Sustantivos que describen relaciones humanas

_____

_____

_____

_____

_____

_____

Verbos que expresan conflictos

_____

_____

_____

_____

_____

_____

Verbos que expresan emociones y sentimientos

_____

_____

_____

_____

_____

_____

Expresiones que describen relaciones humanas

_____

_____

_____

_____

_____

_____

Realidades 3

Capítulo 4

Nombre _____

Fecha _____

Hora _____

Core Practice **4-14**

II. Grammar

1. List six expressions of emotion that are followed by the subjunctive.

   _____   _____

   _____   _____

   _____   _____

2. What does the preposition *por* indicate?

   _____

   _____

3. What does the preposition *para* indicate?

   _____

   _____

4. List two expressions with the preposition *por*.

   _____ _____

5. How do you form *nosotros* commands?

   _____

   _____

6. List the possessive pronouns corresponding to each of the subject pronouns.

	masculine sing.	feminine sing.	masculine plural	feminine plural
yo	_____	_____	_____	_____
tú	_____	_____	_____	_____
él, ella, Ud.	_____	_____	_____	_____
nosotros(as)	_____	_____	_____	_____
vosotros(as)	_____	_____	_____	_____
ellos, ellas, Uds.	_____	_____	_____	_____

realidades.com
• Web Code: jed-0411

A ver si recuerdas . . .

¿En qué están trabajando?

Un amigo te pregunta quiénes están haciendo varios trabajos. Responde sus preguntas con frases completas.

Modelo ¿Quién enseña una clase?

La profesora está enseñando una clase.

1. ¿Quién saca fotos?

   _____

2. ¿Quién apaga el incendio?

   _____

3. ¿Quién investiga el crimen?

   _____

4. ¿Quién sirve comida en el restaurante?

   _____

5. ¿Quién te ayuda a planear un viaje?

   _____

6. ¿Quién le dice al atleta lo que tiene que hacer?

   _____

7. ¿Quién habla en el programa de radio?

   _____

8. ¿Quién te limpia los dientes?

   _____

Realidades ③

Capítulo 5

Nombre _____

Fecha _____

Hora _____

Core Practice **5-2**

A ver si recuerdas . . .

Hay mucho que hacer

A. Sara está diciéndoles a sus hermanitos que hagan los quehaceres, pero ellos ya están haciéndolos. Escribe las respuestas de sus hermanitos usando los pronombres apropiados.

> **Modelo**   José, recoge la basura del césped.
>
> _____*Ya la estoy recogiendo.*_____ (o) _____*Ya estoy recogiéndola.*_____

1. José y María, laven el coche.

   _____ (o) _____

2. María, limpia los baños.

   _____ (o) _____

3. María y José, paseen al perro.

   _____ (o) _____

4. José, pasa la aspiradora en la sala.

   _____ (o) _____

B. Luis es director de cine y está haciendo una película sobre un terremoto. Usa los pronombres apropiados para escribir los mandatos que les da a los actores.

> **Modelo**   Los detectives deben llevar a las víctimas al hospital.
>
> _____*Llévenlas al hospital.*_____

1. Los ancianos deben llamar a la policía.

   _____

2. Manuel y Antonia deben comenzar la explosión en el laboratorio.

   _____

3. Los médicos no deben abrir el consultorio.

   _____

4. Los voluntarios no deben apagar el incendio.

   _____

realidades.com ✔
• Web Code: jed-0501

Realidades ③

Capítulo 5

Nombre

Fecha

Hora

Core Practice **5-3**

En la compañía

En esta compañía trabajan muchas personas. Contesta las preguntas en base a la ilustración. Escribe frases completas.

1. ¿Qué puesto tiene Margarita en la compañía?

_____

2. ¿Qué tiene José en la mano?

_____

3. ¿Quién es el (la) gerente?

_____

4. ¿Qué trabajo tiene Pedro?

_____

5. ¿Qué trabajo hace Carlos?

_____

6. ¿Quién crees que va a tener una entrevista de trabajo?

_____

Realidades 3

Capítulo 5

Nombre _____

Fecha _____

Hora _____

Core Practice **5-4**

¿Qué puedes hacer?

Lee estos anuncios clasificados. Luego escribe qué persona debe responder a cada anuncio y cómo debe ser esa persona.

Modelo   Se necesita empleado para trabajar con atletas en club deportivo. Tiene que ser amable y considerado.

Se busca _entrenador agradable._ _____

1. Se necesita alguien que cuide niños. Debe trabajar desde las ocho hasta las once de la mañana.

   Se busca _____

2. Se solicita alguien que trabaje con niños en el campamento. Debe poder trabajar cuando se lo pidamos.

   Se busca _____

3. Club deportivo busca a alguien que cuide a la gente en la piscina. Debe trabajar desde las nueve de la mañana hasta las cinco de la tarde.

   Se busca _____

4. Compañía necesita alguien que entregue paquetes dentro de la oficina. Debe llegar al trabajo a tiempo, todos los días.

   Se busca _____

5. Se necesita alguien que conteste los teléfonos. Debe traer una carta de recomendación.

   Se busca _____

6. Se necesita alguien que prepare platos deliciosos. Debe saber mucho de alimentación.

   Se busca _____

• Web Code: jed-0502

Realidades 3

Capítulo 5

Nombre

Fecha

Hora

Core Practice **5-5**

Entrevista para un nuevo puesto

La Sra. Cádiz está entrevistando gente para unos puestos en su compañía. Escribe las respuestas usando el presente perfecto y los pronombres apropiados.

Modelo   ¿Reparó Ud. computadoras como las nuestras?

Muchas veces *las he reparado*.

1. ¿Se llevaron bien Ud. y su gerente?

   Siempre _____

2. ¿Repartió Ud. paquetes antes?

   Sí, _____

3. ¿Atendió Ud. a los clientes de su compañía?

   Muchas veces _____

4. ¿Tuvo Ud. beneficios en su trabajo?

   Siempre _____

5. ¿Solicitó Ud. empleo antes?

   Nunca _____

6. ¿Escribió Ud. anuncios clasificados?

   Muchas veces _____

7. ¿Fue Ud. mensajero antes?

   No, nunca _____

8. ¿Llenó Ud. la solicitud de empleo?

   Sí, ya _____

Realidades 3

Capítulo 5

Nombre _____

Fecha _____

Hora _____

Core Practice **5-6**

El nuevo puesto de Jorge

Ramiro y Antonio hablan de Jorge y su búsqueda de trabajo. Para saber lo que ha pasado, completa el diálogo usando el pluscuamperfecto del verbo que corresponda.

RAMIRO: No sabía que Jorge **(1.)** _____ *(conseguir / tener / atender)* trabajo.

ANTONIO: Bueno, sabías que él **(2.)** _____ *(querer / salir / ser)* cambiar de trabajo.

RAMIRO: Sí, él me **(3.)** _____ *(preguntar / decir / cumplir)* que no le

gustaba el trabajo que tenía. Pero yo no me di cuenta de que él ya

(4.) _____ *(querer / empezar / reparar)* a buscar otro puesto.

ANTONIO: Jorge **(5.)** _____ *(recibir / escribir / saber)* muchas cartas y

(6.) _____ *(repartir / leer / reparar)* muchos anuncios clasificados.

Él **(7.)** _____ *(solicitar / hacer / ir)* mucho para buscar trabajo.

RAMIRO: ¿Y no encontró nada?

ANTONIO: No, las compañías siempre le **(8.)** _____ *(dar / presentarse / estar)*

el puesto a otra persona. ¡Hay tanta gente que busca trabajo! Él y yo

(9.) _____ *(expresar / hablar / encargarse)* mucho del problema.

RAMIRO: Entonces, ¿qué hizo finalmente?

ANTONIO: Supo que alguien **(10.)** _____ *(dejar / hacer / saber)*

su trabajo en la biblioteca de la universidad y se presentó enseguida.

RAMIRO: Y se lo dieron a él. ¡Qué suerte!

• Web Code: jed-0504

Realidades 3

Capítulo 5

Nombre _____

Fecha _____

Hora _____

Core Practice **5-7**

En el mundo del trabajo

Escribe diálogos sobre lo que pasa en el trabajo. Usa el presente perfecto y el pluscuamperfecto para decir que las siguientes cosas ya se habían hecho cuando la gente llegó.

Modelo   Juan / encender las luces / la empleada

— *¿Juan ha encendido las luces?*

— *No, la empleada ya las había encendido.*

1. tú / abrir las cartas / la secretaria

   _____

   _____

2. Uds. /escribir el horario de hoy / el gerente

   _____

   _____

3. el dueño / atender a los clientes / la recepcionista

   _____

   _____

4. tú/ leer las cartas de recomendación / el jefe

   _____

   _____

5. el agente / poner el correo en la mesa / yo

   _____

   _____

6. el repartidor / traer el almuerzo / el secretario

   _____

   _____

7. ellos / terminar el informe / Juan

   _____

   _____

Realidades 3

Capítulo 5

Nombre _____

Fecha _____

Hora _____

Core Practice **5-8**

¿Adónde debo ir?

Sugiere a tu amigo(a) adónde debe ir para participar en la vida de su comunidad y para ayudar a los demás.

Modelo

—Quiero ayudar a las personas que no tienen hogar.

—*Debes ir al refugio para gente sin hogar.*

—Quiero ver los cuadros que han pintado mis vecinos.

1. _____

—Quiero ayudar a la gente como mis abuelos.

2. _____

—Quiero servirles comida a las personas pobres.

3. _____

—Quiero jugar con los niños que han tenido accidentes.

4. _____

—Quiero hacer un proyecto de arte y practicar deportes.

5. _____

realidades.com
• Web Code: jed-0506

Realidades 3

Capítulo 5

Nombre _____

Fecha _____

Hora _____

Core Practice **5-9**

Cosas que pasan en la comunidad

Unos estudiantes hablan de lo que está pasando en su comunidad. Vuelve a escribir las frases, cambiando la(s) palabra(s) subrayada(s) por otra(s) palabra(s).

Modelo Quiero ayudar a <u>las personas que no tienen casa</u>.

Quiero ayudar a la gente sin hogar.

1. Nosotros <u>no queremos</u> que cierren el centro de la comunidad.

   _____

2. Ellos <u>sí quieren</u> que lo cierren.

   _____

3. Los maestros deben <u>enseñar</u> a los niños.

   _____

4. Estos jóvenes están tratando de <u>obtener dinero</u> para la campaña.

   _____

5. Creo que el centro recreativo va a <u>ser bueno para</u> la comunidad.

   _____

6. Yo no entiendo <u>las reglas</u> de inmigración.

   _____

7. <u>No puedo de ninguna manera</u> ir al hogar de ancianos hoy.

   _____

8. Quiero <u>dar</u> comida para el comedor de beneficencia.

   _____

9. <u>Me gustaría mucho</u> ayudar a la gente pobre.

   _____

• Web Code: jed-0506

Realidades ③

Capítulo 5

Nombre _____

Fecha _____

Hora _____

Core Practice **5-10**

En la comunidad

José, Reynaldo y Gabriela están hablando de las cosas que pasan en su comunidad. Lee lo que dicen y luego responde las preguntas. La primera respuesta ya está escrita.

JOSÉ: ¿Escucharon la noticia? Se construyó un nuevo centro recreativo. ¡Eso sí es bueno!

GABRIELA: Sí, porque los jóvenes necesitamos un lugar para divertirnos.

JOSÉ: ¿Sabían que también se abrió un comedor de beneficencia?

REYNALDO: Eso es excelente. Ayudará a la gente pobre.

GABRIELA: Hay tanta gente pobre. Es una lástima.

JOSÉ: Ahora pueden usar el centro de rehabilitación también.

REYNALDO: Sí. La comunidad cambió las leyes. Eso me alegra.

GABRIELA: Mi padre ayudó a que no cerraran el hogar de ancianos.

JOSÉ: ¿El hogar de ancianos no cerró? ¡Qué bueno!

GABRIELA: Lo bueno es que los ancianos se pueden quedar allí.

1. ¿¿Qué dice José sobre el nuevo centro recreativo?

Él dice que es bueno que hayan construido un nuevo centro recreativo.

2. ¿Qué dice Reynaldo sobre el comedor de beneficencia?

_____

3. ¿Qué dice Gabriela de la gente pobre?

_____

4. ¿Qué dice Reynaldo de las leyes?

_____

5. ¿Qué dice José del hogar de ancianos?

_____

6. ¿Qué dice Gabriela de los ancianos?

_____

realidades.com ✔
• Web Code: jed-0507

Realidades 3

Capítulo 5

Nombre _____

Fecha _____

Hora _____

Core Practice **5-11**

¿Qué debo hacer?

Usa los dibujos para decirle a tu amigo(a) lo que debe hacer. Primero completa la pregunta con un adjetivo demostrativo. Luego escribe la respuesta con un pronombre demostrativo. Recuerda que el dibujo de la derecha es el que está más cerca de ti.

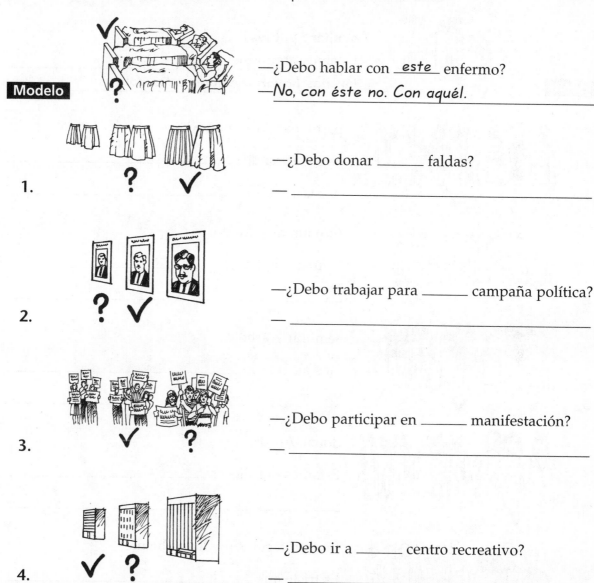

Modelo

—¿Debo hablar con ___este___ enfermo?

—*No, con éste no. Con aquél.*

1. —¿Debo donar _____ faldas?

— _____

2. —¿Debo trabajar para _____ campaña política?

— _____

3. —¿Debo participar en _____ manifestación?

— _____

4. —¿Debo ir a _____ centro recreativo?

— _____

5. —¿Debo sembrar _____ árboles?

— _____

realidades.com

• Web Code: jed-0509

Manos a la obra 2 ━ *Gramática y vocabulario en uso* **73**

Realidades 3

Capítulo 5

Nombre _____

Fecha _____

Hora _____

Core Practice **5-12**

¿Te gusta lo que han hecho los jóvenes?

¿Qué opina la gente acerca de lo que hacen los jóvenes? Completa las frases, usando el presente perfecto del subjuntivo y los adjetivos demostrativos. Recuerda que el dibujo de la izquierda es el que está mas cerca de ti.

Modelo

ayudar / pobres

Estamos orgullosos *de que estos*

jóvenes hayan ayudado a los pobres.

1. participar / campaña

Nos sorprende _____

_____

2. (no) juntar / fondos

Es una lástima _____

_____

3. sembrar / árboles

Nos alegra _____

_____

4. donar / ropa

Estamos orgullosos _____

_____

5. (no) proteger / medio ambiente

Es triste que _____

_____

6. asistir / marcha

Es bueno _____

_____

realidades.com
• Web Code: jed-0510

Realidades 3

Capítulo 5

Nombre _____

Fecha _____

Hora _____

Core Practice **5-13**

Organizer

I. Vocabulary

Cualidades y características

_____

_____

_____

_____

_____

Lugares en la comunidad

_____

_____

_____

_____

_____

Palabras para la entrevista

_____

_____

_____

_____

_____

Acciones

_____

_____

_____

_____

_____

Palabras para el trabajo

_____

_____

_____

_____

_____

La comunidad

_____

_____

_____

_____

_____

Realidades 3

Capítulo 5

Nombre _____

Fecha _____

Hora _____

Core Practice **5-14**

Organizer

II. Grammar

1. How do you form the present perfect tense?

_____

2. How do you form the pluperfect tense?

_____

3. How do you form the present perfect subjunctive?

_____

4. Conjugate the verb *cantar*
   in the pluperfect.

   Conjugate the verb *escribir* in
   the present perfect subjunctive.

   _____ _____   _____ _____

   _____ _____   _____ _____

   _____ _____   _____ _____

5. Fill in the chart with the demonstrative adjectives and pronouns. Write the masculine and feminine singular, and the masculine and feminine plural forms for each.

	Close to you	Close to the person you are talking to	Far from both of you
Adjectives			
Pronouns			

6. Give the forms of the pronouns that refer to an idea, or something that has not been identified.

_____

realidades.com
• Web Code: jed-0511

A ver si recuerdas . . .

¿Quién conoce a quién?

Tú y tus amigos conocen a personas importantes. Completa las frases para decir a quiénes conocen, y qué saben hacer esas personas.

repara coches	escribe poemas	baila muy bien
cura perritos	actúa muy bien	hace esculturas de piedra

Modelo Marta *conoce a un cantante que sabe cantar* *canciones.*

1. Pedro y Eugenia _____

_____.

2. Beatriz _____

_____.

3. Sandra y yo _____

_____.

4. Yo _____

_____.

5. Fernando _____

_____.

6. Tú _____

_____.

Realidades 3

Nombre _____

Hora _____

Capítulo 6

Fecha _____

Core Practice **6-2**

A ver si recuerdas . . .

Dice que . . .

Un amigo te pide que le expliques lo que dicen algunos anuncios del periódico. Lee los siguientes anuncios y escribe una frase explicando lo que dice cada uno.

¿Animales enfermos?

Los veterinarios de "Cuidanimales" están aquí para cuidarlos.

Modelo   *En "Cuidanimales" se cuidan animales enfermos.*

¿Necesita computadora portátil?

En "Compucasa" las vendemos.

1. _____

¿Televisor roto?

En "Electrolandia" lo arreglamos.

2. _____

¿Quiere vender su computadora usada?

La compramos en "Tecnitienda".

3. _____

¿El coche no anda?

En "Autotaller" lo reparamos.

4. _____

¿Quiere un mural?

En "Artestudio" lo pintamos.

5. _____

¿Quiere una casa?

"Fernández y Compañía" la construirá.

6. _____

realidades.com

• Web Code: jed-0601

Realidades 3

Capítulo 6

Nombre _____

Fecha _____

Hora _____

Core Practice **6-3**

¿A qué se dedican?

Mira los dibujos de las siguientes personas haciendo diferentes trabajos. Completa las frases con las palabras que faltan para describir el trabajo que hace cada una.

Modelo

¿A qué se dedica Ramiro?

Ramiro es programador. _____

1.  ¿A qué se dedica Isabel? _____

2.   ¿A qué se dedica Marcelo? _____

3.   ¿A qué se dedica Federico? _____

4.   ¿A qué se dedica Pedro? _____

5.   ¿A qué se dedica Juana? _____

6.   ¿A qué se dedica Enrique? _____

• Web Code: jed-0602

Realidades 3

Capítulo 6

Nombre

Fecha

Hora

Core Practice **6-4**

Hablemos del futuro

Tu maestra te habla de algunos jóvenes y sus intereses. Escribe lo que va a ser cada uno algún día.

Modelo Octavio hace unos platos riquísimos.

Octavio será cocinero.

1. Matilde es bilingüe y le gusta traducir libros.

   _____

2. A Mateo le gusta dibujar edificios y casas.

   _____

3. Lidia quiere tener un puesto en una oficina en donde se encargará de otros empleados.

   _____

4. Sofía y Roberto estudian derecho. No les interesa ser jueces.

   _____

5. Ana se encarga del dinero de su familia y le encantan los números.

   _____

6. Gabriel y su esposa Felisa quieren desempeñar un cargo en el banco.

   _____

7. Laura quiere dedicarse a corregir el trabajo de otros escritores.

   _____

8. Andrés dice que nunca se va a casar.

   _____

realidades.com

• Web Code: jed-0602

Realidades 3

Capítulo 6

Nombre _____

Fecha _____

Hora _____

Core Practice **6-5**

¿Qué harán en el futuro?

¿Qué profesión correspondería a estos jóvenes? Escoge la situación más lógica del recuadro y completa las descripciones.

aprender a ser peluquera	tener que mudarse a otra ciudad
querer trabajar de voluntarios	dedicarse a las finanzas
seguir una carrera de arquitecto	hacerse diseñadoras
abrir su propia empresa	

Modelo   A Micaela le gusta arreglarles el pelo a sus amigas.
Por eso, aprenderá a ser peluquera.

1. A Luisa y Carmen les fascina la moda y la ropa.

   _____

2. En mi ciudad no hay universidad que ofrezca los programas que yo quiero.

   _____

3. A ti siempre te han fascinado los edificios viejos y las casas modernas.

   _____

4. A Juan y Alfredo les encanta la economía.

   _____

5. Sonia y yo queremos ayudar a los ancianos. No nos importa si ganamos dinero o no.

   _____

6. Pablo no quiere trabajar para ningún jefe.

¿Qué será?

¿Qué hacen estas personas? Lee las descripciones sobre las actividades de estas personas. Luego usa el futuro de probabilidad para decir lo que crees que hacen.

asistir a la universidad	querer ser agricultores
trabajar de redactora	hacerse abogado(a)
estudiar para ser ingeniero	buscar el puesto de contador
ser científicos	

Modelo No creo que Juan Morales trabaje. Siempre lo veo con muchos libros.
Asistirá a la universidad.

1. Martín y Eva dicen que no quieren quedarse en la ciudad. Quieren vivir en el campo.

   _____

2. Tú siempre te encargas del dinero de todos los clubes.

   _____

3. Alicia siempre ve si algo está mal escrito en las composiciones de sus amigos.

   _____

4. A Ramiro le encantan los puentes. Siempre nos explica cómo han sido construidos.

   _____

5. A mí me gustan las leyes y los derechos de los ciudadanos.

   _____

6. Mi tío y mi tía trabajan en un laboratorio haciendo investigaciones.

   _____

realidades.com
• Web Code: jed-0604

Realidades 3

Capítulo 6

Nombre _____

Fecha _____

Hora _____

Core Practice **6-7**

¿Qué estarán haciendo?

Estos amigos se hacen preguntas y respuestas sobre varias personas, tratando de imaginar lo que hacen. Escribe los diálogos, usando el futuro de probabilidad de los verbos.

Modelo — dónde / el abuelo / estar / durmiendo / en la cama
— *¿Dónde estará el abuelo?*
— *Estará durmiendo en la cama.*

1. qué / nosotros / comer / esta noche / mamá / tener / algunas ideas

_____

_____

2. dónde / aquel médico / trabajar / atender / el hospital del barrio

_____

_____

3. por qué / Ana María / ir / la universidad / querer / ser científica

_____

_____

4. cuándo / Pablo / estudiar / de noche

_____

_____

5. adónde / tus amigos / viajar / ir / Venezuela

_____

_____

6. cuántos idiomas / Francisco / hablar / saber / por lo menos dos

_____

_____

Realidades 3

Nombre _____

Hora _____

Capítulo 6

Fecha _____

Core Practice **6-8**

¿Cómo será el futuro?

Tu amiga te dice cómo piensa ella que serán las cosas en el futuro. Cambia las palabras o frases entre paréntesis por sus sinónimos.

Modelo Las personas podrán (*hablarse*) ___*comunicarse*___ a través de la televisión.

1. La vida se va a (*durar más tiempo*) _____.

2. La gente podrá (*saber*) _____ de las noticias más rápidamente.

3. Se van a (*resolver*) _____ ciertas enfermedades.

4. Los discos compactos van a (*no existir*) _____.

5. Habrá más (*necesidad*) _____ de teléfonos celulares.

6. Se va a (*encontrar*) _____ que hay vida en otros planetas.

7. Los coches eléctricos van a (*hacer que haya menos*) _____ la contaminación.

8. Los televisores 3D van a (*tomar el lugar de*) _____ los televisores tradicionales.

9. Creo que se va a inventar una máquina que pueda (*imaginar lo que va a pasar*) _____ el futuro.

10. Desafortunadamente, creo que va a (*haber más*) _____ el número de fábricas.

11. La gente tendrá más oportunidad de comprar una (*casa o apartamento*) _____.

12. Yo también pienso que habrá más demanda en la industria de la (*hoteles y empresas turísticas*) _____.

Realidades 3

Capítulo 6

Nombre _____

Fecha _____

Hora _____

Core Practice **6-9**

Hablando del futuro . . .

Mateo y Elena están hablando del futuro. Completa las palabras o expresiones que faltan.

MATEO: ¿Verdad que es interesante pensar en los **(1.)** ___ v ___ ___ c ___ ___ tecnológicos y científicos?

ELENA: Ah sí. Por ejemplo, con la energía solar, se puede calentar las viviendas sin **(2.)** ___ ___ ___ t ___ m ___ ___ ___ ___ el medio ambiente.

MATEO: Y con la televisión **(3.)** ___ í ___ ___ ___ t ___ l ___ ___ ___ nos enteramos inmediatamente de lo que pasa en el mundo.

ELENA: La gente puede **(4.)** ___ ___ m ___ n ___ ___ ___ ___ ___ ___ desde muchos lugares gracias al teléfono celular.

MATEO: Dicen que en el futuro trabajaremos menos y que tendremos más tiempo de **(5.)** ___ ___ i ___. ¡Eso sí me gusta!

ELENA: Y vivirás más años gracias a los avances en **(6.)** ___ ___ n ___ t ___ ___ ___.

MATEO: Sí. Creo que con **(7.)** ___ l ___ s ___ de los genes se van a curar muchas **(8.)** ___ n ___ ___ ___ ___ ___ d ___ ___ ___ s.

ELENA: Sí. Tienes razón.

MATEO: A mí me encanta la realidad virtual. Se vive una experiencia **(9.)** ___ o ___ o s ___ ___ u ___ ___ ___ real.

ELENA: Es importante **(10.)** ___ ___ n ___ ___ ___ n ___ u ___ ___ t ___ que la informática es la profesión del futuro.

MATEO: Sí. Creo que cada vez habrá más trabajo en este **(11.)** ___ ___ m ___ ___.

ELENA: Definitivamente, en el futuro se van a **(12.)** ___ n ___ ___ ___ t ___ ___ muchas cosas nuevas.

Realidades 3

Capítulo 6

Nombre _____

Fecha _____

Hora _____

Core Practice **6-10**

Futuro y pasado

A. Explica en cada caso por qué será un poco tarde para hacer estas cosas. Usa el futuro perfecto.

Modelo   Voy a venir esta tarde para ver a tus primos. (dentro de dos horas / irse)
Pero dentro de dos horas se habrán ido.

1. El jueves vengo a ayudarte con el informe. (para el miércoles / entregar el informe)

_____

2. Llegaremos dentro de media hora para verlos a Uds. (dentro de media hora / salir)

_____

3. Estaré a las siete para comer con ellas. (a las siete ya / cenar)

_____

4. En el año 2100 seguiremos usando gasolina. (para aquel año / descubrirse nuevas fuentes de energía)

_____

B. ¿Cómo han logrado estas personas hacer las cosas que hacen? Escribe una explicación para cada una de estas situaciones, usando el futuro perfecto.

aprender a manejar	conseguir el dinero del banco	tomar un taxi
comprarse un robot	comprar un aparato de calefacción solar	

Modelo   María llegó muy rápidamente. *Habrá tomado un taxi.*

1. La señora Díaz dice que pasa menos tiempo ahora con los quehaceres de la casa.

_____

2. Los Gómez gastan menos ahora para calentar su casa.

_____

3. Carlos ya va a todas partes en coche.

_____

4. ¿Cómo pudo Sarita pagarse el viaje a Florida?

_____

Realidades 3

Capítulo 6

Nombre _____

Hora _____

Fecha _____

Core Practice **6-11**

Ayudando a los demás

A. Completa los siguientes diálogos usando la información dada. En tu respuesta incluye dos pronombres: uno de complemento directo y otro de complemento indirecto.

> **Modelo** — Necesito leer ese artículo. ¿Lo tienes? (prestar / esta tarde)
> — *Sí, yo te lo prestaré esta tarde.*

1. —¿Uds. tienen el programa de realidad virtual? Nosotros lo necesitamos. (enviar / mañana)

   _____

2. —El coche de Anita no funciona. ¿Puedes ayudarla? (reparar / en el taller)

   _____

3. —¿Tienes el CD de "Solares"? A Juan y a Laura les encanta. (regalar / para su cumpleaños)

   _____

4. —Raquel se compró una casa nueva y quiere que sus amigos la vean. ¿Sabes cuándo? (enseñar / el fin de semana)

   _____

B. Tus amigos no saben qué hacer, pero tú los ayudas. Escribe una respuesta para cada pregunta, usando la forma de mandatos.

> **Modelo** — Alfonso necesita esos libros. ¿Qué debo hacer? (dar)
> — *Dáselos.*

1. —El profesor quiere el informe hoy. ¿Qué debo hacer? (entregar)

   _____

2. —Mis amigos quieren saber la historia. ¿Qué sugieres? (contar)

   _____

3. —Nosotros tenemos refrescos para los invitados. ¿Qué debemos hacer? (ofrecer)

   _____

4. —Tengo las medicinas que Uds. necesitan. ¿Qué debo hacer? (traer)

   _____

Realidades ③

Capítulo 6

Nombre _____

Fecha _____

Hora _____

Core Practice **6-12**

Explica estas cosas

Explica por qué han pasado estas cosas, usando el futuro perfecto y los complementos directos e indirectos.

Modelo ¿Cómo es que tiene Paula aquel informe? (Juan / dar)

Juan se lo habrá dado.

1. ¿Quién le dio a Isabel un vestido tan bonito? (sus padres / regalar)

_____

2. Vi a José manejando el coche de Vera. (ella / vender)

_____

3. ¿Cómo nos llegó esta tarjeta postal? (nuestros primos / enviar)

_____

4. Luis dice que ya entiende los problemas de matemáticas. (el profesor / explicar)

_____

5. Clara dice que sabe tus planes. (alguien / decir)

_____

6. ¿Sabes que yo ya he visto las fotos de Teresa? (su novio / mostrar)

_____

7. Ellos van al mismo hotel que Alberto. (él / recomendar)

_____

8. ¿Cómo es que no tienes aquellos discos digitales? (mis amigos / llevarse)

_____

Realidades 3

Capítulo 6

Nombre _____

Fecha _____

Hora _____

Core Practice **6-13**

Organizer

I. Vocabulary

Profesiones y oficios

_____

_____

_____

_____

_____

Cualidades

_____

_____

_____

_____

_____

Verbos que tienen que ver con el trabajo

_____

_____

_____

_____

_____

Otros verbos y expresiones

_____

_____

_____

_____

_____

Campos y carreras del futuro

_____

_____

_____

_____

_____

Palabras asociadas con el futuro

_____

_____

_____

_____

_____

Realidades 3

Capítulo 6

Nombre _____

Fecha _____

Hora _____

Core Practice **6-14**

II. Grammar

1. What are the endings of the future tense?

   yo _____ tú _____ él/ella/Ud. _____ nosotros(as) _____

   vosotros(as) _____ ellos/ellas/Uds. _____

2. What is the *yo* form of the future of each of these verbs?

   haber _____ **poder** _____ **querer** _____ **hacer** _____

   decir _____ **poner** _____ **saber** _____ **salir** _____

3. What is the future of probability used for? _____

   _____

4. How do you form the future perfect tense? _____

   _____

5. Conjugate these verbs in the future perfect.

   curar   **descubrir**

   _____   _____   _____   _____

   _____   _____   _____   _____

   _____   _____   _____   _____

6. What is the order of the object pronouns when you have an indirect and a direct pronoun occurring together?

   _____

7. What happens to the indirect object pronoun *le* or *les* when it comes before the indirect objects *lo, la, los, las*?

   _____

8. How do you clarify whom the pronoun *se* refers to in the combinations *se lo, se la, se los*, and *se las*?

   _____

9. What do you add when the object pronouns are attached to the infinitive, a command or a present participle?

   _____

realidades.com

• Web Code: jed-0611

Realidades 3

Nombre _____

Hora _____

Capítulo 7

Fecha _____

Core Practice **7-1**

A ver si recuerdas . . .

¿Qué viste en tus vacaciones?

Un amigo y tú fueron de vacaciones y les pasaron cosas muy diferentes. Escribe una frase para decir algo opuesto a lo que le pasó a tu amigo, usando los elementos dados.

Modelo

Siempre me molestaban las moscas.

Nunca me molestaban a mí.

1. _____

No vi ninguno.

2. _____

Yo vi algunas.

3. _____

Yo no vi nada.

4. _____

Nunca cayeron.

5. _____

Alguien me explicó su historia.

6. _____

Yo sí vi alguno.

Realidades ③

Capítulo 7

Nombre _____

Fecha _____

Hora _____

Core Practice **7-2**

A ver si recuerdas . . .

¿Cuál quieres ver?

Imagina que estás en un lugar que no conoces y quieres ver las distintas cosas que hay allí. Completa las preguntas con las palabras que faltan y contéstalas usando adjetivos en forma de sustantivos.

Modelo

¿Quieres ver el _____río_____ grande? (pequeño)

No, el grande no. Quiero ver el pequeño.

1. ¿Quieres ver un _____ antiguo? (moderno)

_____

2. ¿Quieres ir a la _____ pequeña? (grande)

_____

3. ¿Quieres jugar con los _____ negros? (gris)

_____

4. ¿Quieres ver unos _____ horribles? (hermoso)

_____

5. ¿Quieres ver unas _____ negras? (rojo)

_____

6. ¿Quieres subir las _____ de la derecha? (izquierda)

_____

realidades.com

• Web Code: jed-0701

La arqueología, en otras palabras

Puedes hablar de la arqueología usando sinónimos. Completa las siguientes frases, expresando la misma idea con palabras de este capítulo.

Modelo El monumento pesaba _____*toneladas*_____ (miles de kilos).

1. Son _____ (*pueblos*) que existieron hace muchos años.

2. Vimos un _____ (*edificio donde se estudiaban los movimientos del sol y de la luna*).

3. Es un _____ (*algo que no se sabe*) por qué se construyeron estas grandes ciudades.

4. Se ven _____ (*dibujos*) geométricos en las paredes de ese castillo.

5. Esa pirámide tiene dibujos de _____ (*objetos de cuatro lados*).

6. Ése es un fenómeno _____ (*que nadie sabe explicar*).

7. Los arqueólogos _____ (*no creen*) que existan más ruinas allí.

8. Esa piedra _____ (*estaba encima de*) una estructura.

9. Nadie sabe cuál era _____ (*el uso*) de esa figura.

10. Es _____ (*casi seguro*) que esas ruinas tengan miles de años.

Realidades 3

Capítulo 7

Nombre _____

Fecha _____

Hora _____

Core Practice **7-4**

El trabajo de arqueólogo

Tus compañeros y tú están ayudando a un grupo de arqueólogos en una excavación. Primero mira los dibujos. Después lee las preguntas y contéstalas escribiendo una frase.

Modelo

¿Qué traza Pablo en la tierra?

Pablo traza un óvalo en la tierra.

¿Qué mide Leonor?

1. _____

¿Qué hacen Antonio y sus ayudantes?

2. _____

¿Qué mide Daniela?

3. _____

¿Qué mides?

4. _____

¿Qué hace Marisol?

5. _____

¿Qué estudian Teresa y Silvio?

6. _____

¿Qué es el señor Bermúdez?

7. _____

realidades.com

• Web Code: jed-0702

Realidades 3

Capítulo 7

Nombre _____

Fecha _____

Hora _____

Core Practice **7-5**

Hablando entre arqueólogos

Imagina que eres un(a) arqueólogo(a). Expresa tu opinión sobre las ideas de los otros arqueólogos con quienes trabajas. Usa la expresión dada y el subjuntivo o el indicativo, según corresponda.

Modelo   Estas piedras pesan tres toneladas. (es imposible)

Es imposible que pesen tres toneladas.

1. Empezamos a excavar hoy. (dudo)

   _____

2. ¿Son antiguos estos diseños? (es evidente)

   _____

3. Hoy encontraremos más ruinas. (no creo)

   _____

4. ¿Descubrirán los científicos el misterio? (no es probable)

   _____

5. Hay una ciudad antigua por aquí. (me parece dudoso)

   _____

6. Algún día sabremos por qué se construyeron estos edificios. (no dudamos)

   _____

7. Esto es una evidencia de que hay extraterrestres. (no es verdad)

   _____

8. Trazaremos la distancia hoy. (no es posible)

   _____

Realidades 3

Capítulo 7

Nombre _____

Hora _____

Fecha _____

Core Practice **7-6**

Intercambio de ideas

Dile a tu compañero(a) que no estás de acuerdo con él (ella). Completa la primera frase con el verbo correcto en pretérito. Luego usa la expresión entre paréntesis y el presente perfecto del subjuntivo para escribir tu frase.

Modelo Un artista maya ____*hizo*____ (*hacer / leer*) este diseño. (no creo)

No creo que un artista maya haya hecho este diseño.
_____

1. Los indígenas _____ (*mover / correr*) estas piedras enormes sin usar animales. (dudo)

_____

2. Los indígenas _____ (*calcular / dibujar*) naves espaciales. (es imposible)

_____

3. Ellos _____ (*trazar / unir*) las piedras sin cemento. (es poco probable)

_____

4. Los arqueólogos _____ (*medir / calcular*) todas las piedras. (no es posible)

_____

5. ¡Nosotros _____ (*descubrir / correr*) el observatorio! (no es cierto)

_____

6. Yo _____ (*pesar / saber*) toda la cerámica. (no creo)

_____

7. Ramón _____ (*excavar / medir*) correctamente la distancia entre estos dos monumentos. (es dudoso)

_____

8. Nosotros _____ (*comprender / pesar*) la función de estos óvalos. (no es verdad)

_____

Realidades ❸

Capítulo 7

Nombre _____

Fecha _____

Hora _____

Core Practice **7-7**

Una joven arqueóloga

Isabel trabajó con unos arqueólogos en México este verano y escribió sobre su experiencia. Lee la carta y luego contesta las preguntas. La primera respuesta ya está escrita.

○

○

○

> *Queridos amigos:*
>
> *Este verano ayudé a unos arqueólogos que estaban excavando unas ruinas en México. Lo primero que quiero decirles es que el trabajo de arqueólogo es muy difícil. Hacía mucho calor y trabajamos durante muchas horas. Pero sólo los arqueólogos podían excavar las ruinas. Lo primero que hicimos fue excavar un observatorio. Parecía muy moderno. Tenía, además, unos dibujos que parecían naves espaciales. Yo dije que quizás los extraterrestres ayudaron a este pueblo a construir el observatorio. Los arqueólogos se rieron y me dijeron que eso era improbable. También encontramos otras estructuras. Pasamos horas midiéndolas y pesándolas. No logramos excavar todas las ruinas, pero los arqueólogos piensan terminar el año que viene. Yo volveré en el verano, antes de que todo esté terminado.*
>
> *Saludos,*
> *Isabel*

1. ¿Crees que hacía frío en México?
No creo que haya hecho frío en México. _____

2. ¿Es verdad que Isabel excavó con los arqueólogos?

_____

3. ¿Estás seguro(a) de que encontraron un observatorio?

_____

4. ¿Creen los arqueólogos que los extraterrestres ayudaron a este pueblo?

_____

5. ¿Es verdad que pasaron meses midiendo y pesando?

_____

6. ¿Es evidente que Isabel volverá el invierno que viene?

_____

Realidades 3

Nombre _____

Hora _____

Capítulo 7

Fecha _____

Core Practice **7-8**

Los aztecas y los mayas

Jorge y Carlos conversan sobre lo que saben de los aztecas y los mayas. Completa las palabras de la conversación para saber lo que dicen.

JORGE: ¿Conoces a los aztecas y los mayas?

CARLOS: Sí. Eran **(1.)** ___ ___ b ___ ___ ___ n ___ ___ ___ de México, ¿no?

JORGE: Sí. Aprendí mucho en mi clase sobre las **(2.)** ___ ___ y ___ ___ d ___ ___ de los

aztecas y los mayas. ¿Sabías que ellos tenían muchos cuentos para explicar el

(3.) ___ r ___ g ___ ___ del universo?

CARLOS: Sí, lo sabía. Además tenían muchas **(4.)** ___ ___ o ___ ___ ___ s para explicar

fenómenos como los eclipses.

JORGE: Es cierto. Una **(5.)** ___ ___ e e ___ ___ ___ ___ que tenían era que cuando los

dioses se enojaban, el sol no **(6.)** ___ r ___ ___ ___ ___ b ___ y por eso ocurría el

eclipse.

JORGE: Creo que el eclipse era algo importante y **(7.)** ___ ___ g ___ ___ d ___ para ellos.

CARLOS: Estas civilizaciones tenían un sistema de **(8.)** ___ ___ c ___ i ___ ___ ___ ___ con

símbolos.

JORGE: Yo creo que **(9.)** ___ ___ n ___ ___ ___ b ___ y ___ ___ ___ ___ mucho a las

civilizaciones del resto del mundo.

CARLOS: Me encantó la clase. Lo que más me gusta son las leyendas y los

(10.) ___ ___ t ___ s de estas culturas.

realidades.com

• Web Code: jed-0706

Realidades ③

Capítulo 7

Nombre _____

Fecha _____

Hora _____

Core Practice **7-9**

Las civilizaciones antiguas

Podemos aprender mucho de las civilizaciones antiguas. Contesta las preguntas, usando las ilustraciones. Escribe frases completas.

Modelo

¿Qué vieron los aztecas en el observatorio?

Los aztecas vieron un planeta en el observatorio.

1. Según la leyenda, ¿qué le arrojaron a la Luna?

_____

2. ¿Qué planeta casi se destruyó, según un mito?

_____

3. ¿Cómo se llaman las personas que se dedican a observar los planetas y las estrellas?

_____

4. ¿En qué creían los aztecas?

_____

5. ¿Qué observaban los mayas?

_____

6. ¿Qué usaban las civilizaciones antiguas para escribir?

_____

Realidades 3

Capítulo 7

Nombre _____

Fecha _____

Hora _____

Core Practice **7-10**

El mundo de los arqueólogos

A. Un arqueólogo habla de los problemas de su trabajo. Completa lo que dice con *pero*, *sino* o *sino que*, según corresponda.

Hemos investigado mucho, **(1.)** _____ no hemos descubierto el origen de esta

cerámica. Parece que tiene mucho en común con la cerámica de los incas, **(2.)** _____

no logramos explicar por qué no se encontraría en Sudamérica, **(3.)** _____ en México.

También empezamos a medir las piedras que se excavaron, **(4.)** _____ no fue posible

terminar. Tendremos que trabajar no solamente mañana, **(5.)** _____ también pasado

mañana. Y no terminaremos este año, **(6.)** _____ tendremos que volver al lugar el año

que viene, **(7.)** _____ no tenemos fondos para seguir excavando. Hemos pedido

dinero a varias universidades, **(8.)** _____ todas nos han dicho que no tienen dinero. No

vamos a dejar de buscar dinero, **(9.)** _____ vamos a hacer un esfuerzo más grande.

B. Usa las frases del recuadro para completar cuatro observaciones sobre el proyecto arqueológico. Une los elementos con *pero*, *sino*, *sino también* o *sino que*, según corresponda.

---

las otras sí   el del sol   el español   rectángulos   eran astrónomos también

---

Modelo   Esos diseños geométricos no son triángulos . . .

sino rectángulos.

1. No sólo eran buenos agricultores . . .

_____

2. No es el templo de la Luna . . .

_____

3. Estos indígenas hablan no sólo el quiché . . .

_____

4. Estas ruinas no son de los mayas . . .

_____

• Web Code: jed-0707

Realidades 3

Nombre _____

Hora _____

Capítulo 7

Fecha _____

Core Practice **7-11**

Un verano arqueológico en México

Lee el siguiente anuncio sobre un proyecto arqueológico. Contesta las preguntas, usando el subjuntivo. La primera respuesta ya está escrita.

Proyecto arqueológico en México

Se va a formar un equipo de profesionales y estudiantes para realizar un proyecto arqueológico. Se buscan personas con los siguientes requisitos:

- El jefe tiene que saber organizar un proyecto arqueológico.
- El arqueólogo debe conocer las culturas indígenas de México.
- El traductor necesita hablar español y quiché.
- La médica debe haber estudiado las enfermedades tropicales.
- El secretario tiene que saber usar el correo electrónico.
- Los estudiantes necesitan estar interesados en la arqueología.
- La enfermera necesita tener experiencia de trabajar con los indígenas.
- Los trabajadores deben ser cuidadosos.

---

1. ¿Qué clase de jefe se necesita?

Se necesita un jefe que sepa organizar un proyecto arqueológico.

2. ¿Qué clase de arqueólogo se busca?

_____

3. ¿Qué clase de traductor se necesita?

_____

4. ¿Qué clase de médica se solicita?

_____

5. ¿Qué clase de secretario se quiere contratar?

_____

6. ¿Qué clase de trabajadores se necesita?

_____

Realidades ③

Capítulo 7

Nombre _____

Fecha _____

Hora _____

Core Practice **7-12**

Problemas en el proyecto arqueológico

A. Daniela contesta las preguntas del jefe. Desafortunadamente, todas sus respuestas son negativas. Escribe lo que responde Daniela. Usa el presente o el presente perfecto del subjuntivo, según corresponda.

Modelo   ¿Alguien hace los dibujos de la cerámica?

No, no hay nadie que haga los dibujos de la cerámica.

_____

1. ¿Alguien habla idiomas indígenas?

_____

2. ¿Algún trabajador tiene experiencia excavando?

_____

3. ¿Les interesó algo a los arqueólogos?

_____

4. ¿Alguien sabe leer los números mayas?

_____

5. ¿Algo aquí sirvió de modelo?

_____

B. Daniela responde más preguntas. Escribe sus respuestas con los elementos dados. Usa *sino*, *sino que*, *pero*, o *sino también*, según corresponda.

Modelo   ¿El Sol no apareció? (se puso)

El Sol no apareció, sino que se puso.

1. ¿Tú quieres sólo estudiar? (trabajar)

_____

2. ¿Los dioses quisieron arrojarse al fuego? (no pudieron)

_____

3. ¿Tu hermano es escritor? (arqueólogo)

_____

4. ¿El astrónomo estudia el mar? (los planetas)

_____

realidades.com ✓
• Web Code: jed-0710

Realidades 3

Capítulo 7

Nombre _____

Fecha _____

Hora _____

Core Practice **7-13**

Organizer

I. Vocabulary

Para hablar de mitos y leyendas

_____

_____

_____

_____

Para hablar de descubrimientos

_____

_____

_____

_____

Para hablar del universo

_____

_____

_____

_____

Para describir objetos

_____

_____

_____

_____

Para hablar de los fenómenos inexplicables

_____

_____

_____

_____

Verbos

_____

_____

_____

_____

Realidades **3**

Nombre _____

Hora _____

Capítulo 7

Fecha _____

Core Practice **7-14**

II. Grammar

1. List five expressions of doubt, uncertainty, or disbelief that are followed by the subjunctive.

   _____

   _____

   _____

   _____

   _____

2. List five expressions of belief or certainty that are followed by the indicative.

   _____

   _____

   _____

   _____

   _____

3. When do you use the subjunctive in adjective clauses?

   _____

   _____

4. Which are the two Spanish equivalents for the word *but*?

   _____

5. When is the conjunction *sino* used?

   _____

6. When is *sino que* used?

   _____

7. What is the Spanish equivalent to the expression *not only . . . but also*?

   _____

realidades.com
• Web Code: jed-0711

Realidades ③

Capítulo 8

Nombre _____

Fecha _____

Hora _____

Core Practice **8-1**

A ver si recuerdas . . .

¿Dónde está?

A. Lee las preguntas sobre la posición de estas cosas y contéstalas con frases completas, según los dibujos.

Modelo

¿Dónde está la calle?

La calle está entre el museo y el teatro.

1. ¿Dónde está la plaza?

_____

2. ¿Dónde está el monumento?

_____

3. ¿Dónde está la iglesia?

_____

4. ¿Dónde está el río?

_____

B. Completa estas conversaciones. Escribe la pregunta para cada respuesta.

Modelo —¿Cuándo vas al museo?

—Voy al museo mañana.

1. —_____

—Fui al museo hace mucho tiempo.

2. —_____

—La escultura está en el edificio histórico.

3. —_____

—Mi amiga Luisa vive en esa cuadra.

4. —_____

—Esa artesanía está hecha de oro.

• Web Code: jed-0801

Realidades 3

Capítulo 8

Nombre _____

Fecha _____

Hora _____

Core Practice **8-2**

A ver si recuerdas . . .

Historia de dos amigos

A. Lee la historia de lo que les pasó a Pedro, Martín y Amalia. Completa el párrafo con palabras del vocabulario del capítulo.

Pedro y Martín son buenos amigos y siempre se llevan **(1.)** _____. Ellos casi

nunca se pelean pero una vez tuvieron un **(2.)** _____ muy serio. Esto pasó

hace poco, o **(3.)** _____. Martín se molestó y se

(4.) _____ cuando vio que su novia Amalia estaba con Pedro. Vio que

fueron a una joyería donde venden **(5.)** _____ hechas de oro y

(6.) _____. Pedro **(7.)** _____ cien dólares por un anillo. Se lo

iba a dar a Amalia, cuando Martín entró a la tienda. Amalia y Pedro tuvieron miedo, o se

(8.) _____ un poco por los gritos de Martín. Martín pensaba que Amalia ya

no lo quería. Pero entonces Amalia le explicó a Martín que Pedro le había prestado dinero

para que ella le pudiera comprar un anillo de amistad. ¡Todo había sido un malentendido!

B. Ahora contesta las preguntas, usando el pretérito del verbo entre paréntesis. La primera respuesta ya está escrita.

1. ¿Qué les pasó a Pedro y a Martín hace poco? *(tener)*
Pedro y Martín tuvieron un conflicto.

2. ¿Cómo reaccionó Martín cuando vio a su novia con Pedro? *(ponerse)*
_____

3. ¿Adónde fueron Amalia y Pedro? *(andar)*
_____

4. ¿Qué quería Amalia que Pedro le diera? *(pedir)*
_____

5. ¿Qué pensó Martín de Amalia? *(creer)*
_____

Realidades 3

Capítulo 8

Nombre _____

Fecha _____

Hora _____

Core Practice **8-3**

Seamos arquitectos

Mira los dibujos, lee las frases y complétalas con las palabras que faltan.

Modelo ¡Qué linda _____*arquitectura*_____ tiene ese edificio!

1. Los romanos construyeron este _____.

2. Este castillo tiene _____ impresionante.

3. Este palacio tiene _____ hermosos.

4. Esta casa tiene seis _____.

5. El patio tiene _____ de varios colores.

6. La ventana tiene una _____.

• Web Code: jed-0802

A primera vista 1 ━ *Vocabulario en contexto* **107**

Realidades ③

Capítulo 8

Nombre _____

Fecha _____

Hora _____

Core Practice **8-4**

Conversación

Completa las frases con las palabras apropiadas para saber lo que Cristina y Patricia dicen de su viaje a Andalucía.

CRISTINA: Sevilla es una ciudad impresionante. Me encanta la catedral. ¿Sabes que en

su lugar había una mezquita cuando los **(1.)** _____

dominaban la península?

PATRICIA: ¿La mezquita ya no está allí?

CRISTINA: No, estaba ahí **(2.)** _____, pero ya no.

PATRICIA: Bueno, pero esa catedral es increíble, es una **(3.)** _____.

CRISTINA: Sí, me alegro de que hayamos venido a Andalucía. Es una región muy

interesante. Se ve el efecto, o la **(4.)** _____ de tres

culturas.

PATRICIA: ¿Qué culturas?

CRISTINA: Pues, la cristiana, la **(5.)** _____ y la musulmana.

PATRICIA: ¿Te refieres a la **(6.)** _____ de los edificios?

CRISTINA: Sí, pero eso no es todo, no es lo **(7.)** _____.

PATRICIA: Entonces, ¿qué más?

CRISTINA: También en la **(8.)** _____, o personas que viven allí.

PATRICIA: Claro, en el **(9.)** _____ que hablan.

CRISTINA: Sí. Todas estas culturas han dejado su **(10.)** _____ en la

ciudad.

PATRICIA: Definitivamente.

Realidades 3

Capítulo 8

Nombre _____

Fecha _____

Hora _____

Core Practice **8-5**

Un viaje por España

Algunas personas de la escuela quieren pasar el verano en España y hablan de lo que harían allí. Escribe frases completas con los elementos dados y el verbo en condicional.

Modelo   tú / visitar Barcelona

Tú visitarías Barcelona.

1. yo / ir a Sevilla

   _____

2. nuestros profesores / comprar libros

   _____

3. nosotros / hacer muchas excursiones

   _____

4. Víctor y Nacho / poder hablar español todo el día

   _____

5. Marta / querer ver ruinas romanas

   _____

6. tú / venir con nosotros a Toledo

   _____

7. Alejandro / salir todas las noches

   _____

8. Valeria y yo / divertirse mucho

   _____

Realidades 3

Capítulo 8

Nombre _____

Fecha _____

Hora _____

Core Practice **8-6**

El viaje perfecto

Mira los dibujos y escribe una frase para decir cómo sería el viaje perfecto por España para estos(as) estudiantes. Usa el condicional de los verbos del recuadro.

estudiar	sacar fotos	visitar	jugar
dibujar	comprar	dormir	comer

Modelo   Susana   *Susana sacaría fotos de las rejas.* _____

1. Sergio _____

2. nosotros _____

3. Eva y Sara _____

4. las estudiantes _____

5. Luis y Ernesto _____

6. yo _____

7. tú _____

realidades.com

• Web Code: jed-0803

Realidades 3

Nombre _____ Hora _____

Capítulo 8

Fecha _____ Core Practice **8-7**

Encuesta: ¿Qué harías en España?

Se hizo una encuesta a la clase de español sobre lo que harían los (las) estudiantes si fueran a España. Lee la encuesta. Luego contesta las preguntas, usando el condicional. La primera respuesta ya está escrita.

Nombre	¿Adónde irías?	¿Qué harías?
Juan	Córdoba	estudiar español, visitar La Mezquita
Marta	Segovia	ver el acueducto, salir con amigos
Pilar	Sevilla	caminar en la plaza, estudiar español
Simón	Córdoba	bailar, comprar azulejos
Beatriz	Toledo	tomar fotos de la arquitectura, comer en restaurantes
Fernando	Madrid	comprar postales, ir al zoológico

1. ¿Qué haría Juan?

Juan estudiaría español y visitaría La Mezquita.

2. ¿Adónde irían Juan y Simón?

_____

3. ¿Quiénes querrían estudiar español?

_____

4. ¿Adónde iría Beatriz y qué haría?

_____

5. ¿Quiénes comprarían cosas y qué cosas comprarían?

_____

6. ¿Qué haría Marta y dónde lo haría?

_____

Realidades 3

Capítulo 8

Nombre _____

Fecha _____

Hora _____

Core Practice **8-8**

El trabajo del (de la) escritor(a)

Tú eres escritor(a) y estás escribiendo un libro para niños sobre la historia y la cultura mexicanas. Tienes que explicar los dibujos del libro. Completa las explicaciones antes de entregar tu libro al redactor. Usa las palabras del vocabulario del capítulo.

Modelo Los _____ *aztecas* _____ lucharon contra los españoles.

1. Los _____ construyeron

_____ para enseñarles su religión a los indígenas.

2. Hubo un _____ de

_____ entre Europa y las Américas.

3. No hubo siempre paz; los aztecas también se dedicaban

a la _____.

4. Hernán Cortés y los _____ españoles

iban montados a caballo y llevaban

_____ de fuego.

5. Los indios y los españoles se enfrentaron en numerosas

_____.

realidades.com

• Web Code: jed-0806

España en las Américas

Estás leyendo un libro sobre la historia del encuentro entre los europeos y los indígenas, pero se borraron algunas palabras. Completa las frases con las palabras del capítulo.

1. Los misioneros _____ las misiones para enseñarles su religión a los indígenas.

2. Sarita Montiel tiene antepasados italianos, españoles y portugueses. Ella es de _____ europea.

3. Los aztecas conquistaron muchos pueblos indígenas. Tenían un _____ muy grande.

4. Cuando los españoles trajeron el chocolate y el maíz a Europa, nadie sabía lo que eran. Eran mercancías _____ en Europa.

5. Los aztecas, los toltecas y los mayas son pueblos _____ de México.

6. Los españoles pudieron conquistar el imperio azteca porque con sus armas de fuego y sus caballos eran más _____ que los indígenas.

7. Francia, España, Inglaterra e Italia son países _____.

8. Cuando los españoles conquistaron el imperio azteca, México llegó a ser una _____ española y parte del imperio español.

9. Los españoles y los indígenas lucharon en muchas _____.

10. Muchas costumbres latinoamericanas _____ de elementos de culturas diferentes.

11. Hoy la mayor parte de los indígenas hispanoamericanos son católicos. Esto quiere decir que _____ la religión de los españoles.

12. En toda Hispanoamérica se empezó a hablar español, la _____ de España.

Realidades 3

Capítulo 8

Nombre _____

Fecha _____

Hora _____

Core Practice **8-10**

Pero todo eso tenía que hacerse

Estás conversando con un(a) amigo(a). Dile que todas estas cosas tenían que hacerse. Usa la frase entre paréntesis y el imperfecto del subjuntivo en tus respuestas. Reemplaza los complementos directos con el pronombre apropiado.

Modelo —Los estudiantes no aprendieron el vocabulario. (el profesor dijo)

—*Pero el profesor dijo que lo aprendieran.*

1. —Yo no traje el guacamole. (yo te pedí)

   _____

2. —Tú no estudiaste los resultados. (nadie me dijo)

   _____

3. —Luis pudo terminar el informe. (creímos que era imposible)

   _____

4. —Paula me dijo la respuesta. (yo no quería)

   _____

5. —Uds. no salieron. (nos prohibieron)

   _____

6. —Mamá no hizo la salsa picante. (nadie le sugirió)

   _____

7. —Yo no sembré las flores. (papá insistió)

   _____

8. —Alberto no escribió las palabras nuevas. (era necesario)

   _____

realidades.com

• Web Code: jed-0807

Realidades ③

Capítulo 8

Nombre _____

Fecha _____

Hora _____

Core Practice **8-11**

¡Qué triste!

Explica cómo las cosas podrían ser diferentes para estas personas. Usa las palabras o expresiones entre paréntesis, el imperfecto del subjuntivo con *si* y el condicional.

Modelo —Marcela no estudia. Por eso no aprende. (triste)

—*¡Qué triste! Si estudiara, aprendería.*

1. —Lorenzo no presta atención. Por eso no comprende. (ridículo)

_____

2. —Claudia no llama a sus amigos. Por eso están enojados. (mal educada)

_____

3. —Pablo no duerme. Por eso está siempre cansado. (lástima)

_____

4. —Luisa no sale con sus amigos. Por eso no se divierte. (aburrido)

_____

5. —Juanito no corre con cuidado. Por eso se lastima. (peligroso)

_____

6. —Carolina no arregla su cuarto. Por eso no encuentra sus libros. (desordenada)

_____

7. —Paco se despierta tarde. Por eso no puede asistir a su clase. (tonto)

_____

8. —Laura tiene miedo de hablar con la gente. Por eso no tiene amigos. (tímida)

_____

Realidades 3

Nombre _____

Hora _____

Capítulo 8

Fecha _____

Core Practice **8-12**

Explicaciones

A. Tu amigo(a) es entrometido(a) y quiere saber qué han dicho otras personas. Contesta sus preguntas con el verbo entre paréntesis. Usa el imperfecto del subjuntivo.

Modelo   ¿Qué te recomendó el médico sobre las vitaminas? (tomar)

El médico me recomendó que tomara vitaminas.

1. ¿Qué te dijo el profesor sobre el idioma español? (aprender)

_____

2. ¿Qué te sugirió el entrenador sobre los ejercicios? (hacer)

_____

3. ¿Qué te recomendó el ingeniero sobre el puente? (construir)

_____

4. ¿Qué te dijo tu madre sobre la paciencia? (tener)

_____

B. Explícale a tu amigo(a) lo que piensas. Usa *como si* y el verbo en paréntesis.

Modelo   ¿Por qué preguntas si están enamorados? (portarse)

Porque se portan como si estuvieran enamorados.

1. ¿Por qué preguntas si él es el jefe? (hablar)

_____

2. ¿Por qué preguntas si ellos conocen España? (planear excursiones)

_____

3. ¿Por qué preguntas si yo tengo prisa? (caminar)

_____

4. ¿Por qué preguntas si los turistas no tienen dinero? (regatear)

realidades.com

• Web Code: jed-0810

Realidades 3

Capítulo 8

Nombre _____

Fecha _____

Hora _____

Core Practice **8-13**

Organizer

I. Vocabulary

Para hablar de construcciones

_____

_____

_____

_____

_____

Para hablar del descubrimiento de América

_____

_____

_____

_____

_____

Para hablar del encuentro de culturas

_____

_____

_____

_____

_____

_____

_____

_____

Verbos

_____

_____

_____

_____

Realidades ❸

Capítulo 8

Nombre _____

Fecha _____

Hora _____

Core Practice **8-14**

II. Grammar

1. How do you form the conditional tense?

_____

2. Which verbs show an irregularity in the conditional?

_____

3. Give the conditional forms of the following verbs:

vivir			tener
_____	_____	_____	_____
_____	_____	_____	_____
_____			_____

4. How do you form the stem to which the endings of the imperfect subjunctive are added?

_____

5. What are the endings of the imperfect subjunctive?

yo _____ tú _____ él/ella/Ud. _____

nosotros(as) _____ vosotros(as) _____ ellos/ellas/Uds. _____

6. When do you use the imperfect subjunctive?

_____

_____

7. What does *como si* mean and what form of the verb follows it?

_____

8. Give the imperfect subjunctive forms of the following verbs:

adoptar			hacer
_____	_____	_____	_____
_____	_____	_____	_____
_____			_____

realidades.com ✔

• Web Code: jed-0811

Realidades ③

Capítulo 9

Nombre _____

Hora _____

Fecha _____

Core Practice **9-1**

A ver si recuerdas . . .

Actividades de la gente

Las siguientes personas hacen diferentes cosas. Mira los dibujos. Completa las frases con las palabras que faltan.

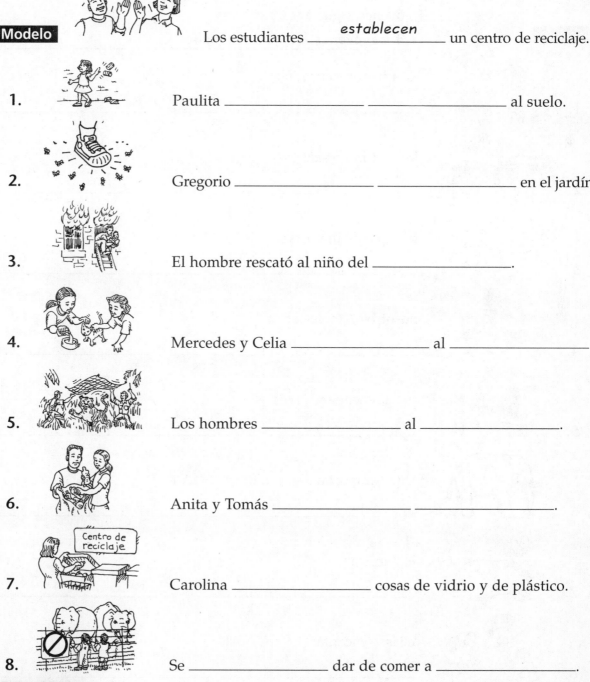

Modelo   Los estudiantes _____*establecen*_____ un centro de reciclaje.

1.   Paulita _____ _____ al suelo.

2.   Gregorio _____ _____ en el jardín.

3.   El hombre rescató al niño del _____ .

4.   Mercedes y Celia _____ al _____ .

5.   Los hombres _____ al _____ .

6.   Anita y Tomás _____ _____ .

7.   Carolina _____ cosas de vidrio y de plástico.

8.   Se _____ dar de comer a _____ .

• Web Code: jed-0901

Realidades 3

Capítulo 9

Nombre _____

Hora _____

Fecha _____

Core Practice **9-2**

A ver si recuerdas . . .

¿Qué te gusta?

Muchas personas se interesan por la naturaleza y el medio ambiente. Mira los dibujos. Escribe frases para hablar de la actitud de estas personas hacia estas cosas.

jóvenes / gustar

Modelo   *A los jóvenes les gusta el valle.* _____

estudiante / encantar

1. _____

Lidia / interesar

2. _____

personas / importar

3. _____

nosotros / molestar

4. _____

tú / preocupar

5. _____

Ud. / importar

6. _____

él / gustar

7. _____

ellas / encantar

8. _____

realidades.com
• Web Code: jed-0901

Realidades 3

Capítulo 9

Nombre _____

Fecha _____

Hora _____

Core Practice **9-3**

Diálogo

Diego y Pablo hablan de la contaminación. Completa las frases con las palabras apropiadas del vocabulario del capítulo para saber lo que dicen Diego y Pablo.

DIEGO: ¿Sabes que algún día usaremos coches eléctricos?

PABLO: Sí, leí un artículo sobre esos coches. Parece que ahorran mucha energía. Son

(1.) __ c __ n __ __ __ c __ __   y limpios.

DIEGO: Mucha gente tiene coches que usan petróleo. Creo que

(2.) __ __ p __ __ d __ __ __ s demasiado del petróleo. Algún día, ya

no habrá petróleo porque se (3.) __ g __ t __ __ __.

PABLO: Sí. Entonces habrá una (4.) __ __ c __ s __ __ de petróleo.

DIEGO: Tenemos que (5.) __ __ m __ __ t __ __ el uso de fuentes de energía

más eficientes y de esa manera conservar nuestros

(6.) __ __ c __ r __ __ __ naturales.

PABLO: Y tenemos que hacerlo (7.) __ a __   __ r __ __ t __

como sea posible.

DIEGO: Otro problema muy (8.) __ r __ v __ es la contaminación de los ríos y de

los mares.

PABLO: Muchas fábricas tienen productos (9.) __ u __ m __ __ __ __.

DIEGO: Sí. Y las fábricas (10.) __ c __ a __ esos productos al agua.

(11.) __ __ b __ d __ a esa práctica, los peces mueren en estas aguas

(12.) __ __ n __ __ m __ __ d __ __.

PABLO: ¡Tantos problemas! El gobierno tiene que tomar

(13.) __ __ d __ d __ __ y (14.) __ __ s __ __ g __ __ con multas

a estas fábricas.

Realidades 3

Capítulo 9

Nombre _____

Fecha _____

Hora _____

Core Practice **9-4**

Nuestro futuro

En el futuro habrá muchos problemas si no protegemos el medio ambiente. Cambia la parte subrayada de cada frase por expresiones o palabras del vocabulario.

Modelo   Estos coches eléctricos <u>ayudan a ahorrar dinero</u>.

Estos coches eléctricos <u>son económicos</u>

1. La población <u>aumenta</u> cada día.

   La población _____ cada día.

2. Hoy tenemos suficiente petróleo, pero en el futuro <u>no habrá suficiente</u> petróleo.

   Hoy tenemos suficiente petróleo, pero en el futuro habrá una _____ de petróleo.

3. Las fábricas <u>arrojan</u> los desperdicios al río.

   Las fábricas _____ los desperdicios al río.

4. Los peces mueren en las aguas <u>sucias</u> por lo que hacen las fábricas.

   Los peces mueren en las aguas _____ por lo que hacen las fábricas.

5. La contaminación del medio ambiente es un problema <u>serio</u>.

   La contaminación del medio ambiente es un problema _____.

6. Nuestro país <u>no puede vivir sin</u> petróleo.

   Nuestro país _____ petróleo.

7. Algún día <u>no habrá más</u> petróleo.

   Algún día _____ petróleo.

8. El gobierno <u>tiene la responsabilidad</u> de hacer leyes para proteger el medio ambiente.

   El gobierno _____ de hacer leyes para proteger el medio ambiente.

realidades.com

• Web Code: jed-0902

Realidades 3

Capítulo 9

Nombre _____

Fecha _____

Hora _____

Core Practice **9-5**

Los estudiantes y el medio ambiente

A. Habla de lo que los estudiantes van a hacer para proteger el medio ambiente. Añade a las frases la persona o las personas que aparecen entre paréntesis.

Modelo   Te veré después de reciclar los periódicos. (tú)
Te veré después de que tú recicles los periódicos.

1. No volveremos a casa hasta limpiar el patio de recreo. (Uds.)

_____

2. Después de visitar el río, escribiremos el informe. (los científicos)

_____

3. El gobierno debe estudiar la situación antes de tomar medidas. (nosotros)

_____

4. No sacaremos la basura hasta separar las botellas de plástico de las de vidrio. (tú)

_____

B. Los estudiantes observan la situación del medio ambiente de su ciudad. Escribe lo que dicen, completando estas frases con los elementos del recuadro.

> mientras las fábricas / seguir contaminando el aire
>
> hasta / estar limpio
>
> hasta que / resolverse el problema
>
> cuando / agotarse el petróleo
>
> cuando el gobierno / castigarla con una multa

Modelo   Hay mucha basura en las calles. Los vecinos no dejarán de quejarse
hasta que se resuelva el problema.

1. El río está muy sucio. No podremos nadar en él _____.

2. Esta empresa dejará de contaminar el medio ambiente _____.

3. No podremos respirar bien _____.

4. No sé cómo vamos a usar nuestros coches _____.

Realidades 3

Nombre _____

Hora _____

Capítulo 9

Fecha _____

Core Practice **9-6**

Hablando del medio ambiente

A. Completa las siguientes frases con uno de los pronombres relativos *que, quien(es)* o *lo que.*

1. El problema del _____ estamos hablando es la contaminación.

2. Es importante poner atención en _____ dicen los científicos.

3. Las personas a _____ les interesa reciclar ayudarán mucho.

4. Los ingenieros _____ están desarrollando el coche eléctrico hacen un trabajo muy importante.

5. Los políticos con _____ hablo dicen que la contaminación es un problema muy grave.

B. Contesta las preguntas de tu amigo(a) sobre el medio ambiente, usando un pronombre relativo.

Modelo ¿Qué medidas fueron necesarias? (tomar / gobierno)
Las medidas que tomó el gobierno

1. ¿Qué petróleo causó problemas? (tirar al mar / las industrias)

   _____

2. ¿Qué científicos lo inventaron? (trabajar con / mi padre)

   _____

3. ¿Qué historias me cuentas? (contarme / mis hermanos)

   _____

4. ¿Qué estudiantes conservan agua? (importarles / el medio ambiente)

   _____

5. ¿Qué fuentes de energía son económicas? (descubrir / los científicos)

   _____

● Web Code: jed-0905

Realidades 3

Capítulo 9

Nombre _____

Fecha _____

Hora _____

Core Practice **9-7**

Por un mundo mejor

Muchos jóvenes trabajan para mejorar el mundo. Completa estos diálogos con el pronombre relativo que falta y con el verbo o la frase que aparece entre paréntesis.

Modelo —Todavía no han cerrado la fábrica _____*que*_____ echa desperdicios al río.

—La cerrarán cuando el gobierno ___*la castigue con una multa*___.
(castigarla con una multa)

1. —¿No te has reunido con el grupo ecológico en el _____ estoy yo?

   —Voy a reunirme con él en cuanto _____.
   (saber más sobre sus actividades)

2. —¿Participaste en la manifestación en la _____ yo participé?

   —Sí, fui a participar en ella tan pronto como yo _____.
   (darse cuenta de lo que se trataba)

3. —¿Han llegado los estudiantes con _____ vamos a trabajar?

   —No, pero te llamaré cuando _____. (llegar)

4. —Es difícil vivir en una ciudad en _____ hay tanta contaminación.

   —Todo seguirá así hasta que el gobierno _____.
   (tomar medidas)

5. —No comprendo _____ dice el profesor.

   —Lo comprenderás cuando _____. (repetirlo)

6. —El petróleo es un recurso natural _____ podría agotarse.

   —No quiero que se agote el petróleo antes de que los ingenieros _____

   _____. (inventar un coche eléctrico)

7. —María y Laura son dos chicas _____ trabajan mucho, ¿verdad?

   —Sí. Dicen que no van a parar hasta _____.
   (resolver el problema)

Realidades ③

Capítulo 9

Nombre _____

Fecha _____

Hora _____

Core Practice **9-8**

Problemas del medio ambiente

Mira los dibujos. Completa las frases con las palabras apropiadas.

Modelo

Algunos científicos dicen que la ___capa de ozono___

tiene ___agujeros___.

1. Se ha producido un _____

_____.

2. El _____ de las _____ cuesta
mucho dinero.

3. La _____ es un animal que hay que proteger.
Si no hacemos algo, vamos a perderla para siempre.

4. El hielo _____ debido al recalentamiento
global.

5. Estos animales se encuentran en peligro de
_____.

6. La _____ _____ ha sido
explotada.

7. La _____ de la _____ está
cubierta de petróleo.

8. El _____ _____ en la atmósfera
hace que las temperaturas aumenten.

realidades.com ✔

• Web Code: jed-0906

Realidades 3

Capítulo 9

Nombre _____

Fecha _____

Hora _____

Core Practice **9-9**

El medio ambiente

Un científico le está explicando a la clase los problemas del medio ambiente. Completa el párrafo para entender lo que dice.

Bueno, jóvenes, hoy les quiero hablar sobre los problemas del medio ambiente.

Es importante que escuchen para poder tomar **(1.)** _____ y entender estos

asuntos. Lo primero que deben saber es que todo lo que ustedes hacen

(2.) _____, o tiene efecto sobre, el medio ambiente. Por ejemplo, el uso de

(3.) _____, como el repelente de insectos, ayuda a crear el agujero de la

capa de ozono. Tenemos que reducir, o **(4.)** _____, su uso.

El aumento de temperatura en el mundo, o el **(5.)** _____, causa

cambios en los **(6.)** _____, como el frío del invierno o el calor del verano.

Por ejemplo, el **(7.)** _____ que está en los polos puede derretirse. Esto

causaría una cantidad de agua **(8.)** _____, o demasiada agua, en los

océanos. A su vez, esto sería un problema para las ballenas. Y las ballenas ya tienen

bastantes problemas cuando las personas tratan de atraparlas y practican la

(9.) _____ de estos animales.

Pero los problemas no sólo ocurren en los océanos, sino también en la

(10.) _____ donde vivimos. Los bosques del trópico, o

(11.) _____, también están en peligro. Y en general, nuestro planeta está

demasiado sucio. Debemos limpiarlo, o realizar una **(12.)** _____. Si todos

colaboramos, viviremos en un mundo mejor.

Realidades 3

Nombre _____

Hora _____

Capítulo 9

Fecha _____

Core Practice **9-10**

Los peligros para el medio ambiente

En una revista lees lo que se puede hacer para resolver los problemas del medio ambiente.
Completa las frases, utilizando las expresiones del recuadro y el subjuntivo.

detenerse su caza	estar en peligro de extinción
aumentar las temperaturas	darles multas a los culpables
conservar las selvas tropicales	haber derrames
disminuirse el uso de aerosoles	tomar conciencia

Modelo   Los barcos de petróleo deben poder viajar sin que
haya derrames _____.

1. Las ballenas azules morirán a menos que

   _____.

2. El agujero de la capa de ozono no aumentará con tal de que

   _____.

3. Hay que evitar la caza excesiva para no tener más animales que

   _____.

4. Las fábricas seguirán echando productos químicos en los ríos a menos que

   _____.

5. No podrá haber recalentamiento global sin que

   _____.

6. No habrá más árboles a menos que

   _____.

7. Pero yo creo que nadie hará nada, a menos que nosotros

   _____.

realidades.com
• Web Code: jed-0908

Realidades 3

Capítulo 9

Nombre _____

Fecha _____

Hora _____

Core Practice **9-11**

Haciendo planes

¿Qué harán estas personas en las siguientes situaciones? Completa los diálogos con el verbo en indicativo o en subjuntivo, según corresponda.

1. —Dicen que mañana lloverá. Yo no quiero salir.

   —Tendrás que salir aunque _____.

2. —¿Y qué pasa si mañana los niveles de ozono están muy altos?

   —Vamos a salir aunque _____ altos.

3. —Este lago me pareció muy limpio.

   —Sí, parece limpio aunque _____ contaminado. Yo sé muy bien que la fábrica de al lado lo está contaminando.

4. —No hay duda que el viaje es muy largo.

   —Tenemos que hacerlo aunque _____ larguísimo.

5. —No podremos terminar este proyecto si nuestros compañeros no vienen a ayudarnos.

   —Tenemos que terminarlo aunque no vengan y no nos _____.

6. —Aquel señor habla español, pero no es español.

   —Sí, él habla español aunque _____ francés.

7. —No sé si quiero ir a casa de Roberto.

   —Tienes que ir aunque no _____.

8. —Perdón. No te di la dirección de la casa de Ángela.

   —No te preocupes. Encontré la casa aunque no me _____ la dirección.

Realidades 3

Capítulo 9

Nombre _____

Fecha _____

Hora _____

Core Practice **9-12**

¿Para qué?

Completa estas frases con el infinitivo o el subjuntivo del verbo que aparece entre paréntesis, según corresponda.

1. Vamos al río para _____ *(ver / castigar)* si está contaminado.

2. Llevaremos una botella de agua del río al laboratorio para que los científicos

_____ *(investigar / agotar)* si el agua está contaminada o no.

3. No saldremos de casa sin _____ *(fomentar / llamarte)*.

4. No nos iremos sin que tú _____ *(llamarnos / conservar)*.

5. Tenemos que hacer un esfuerzo para _____ *(conservar / castigar)* el medio ambiente.

6. Te lo digo para que lo _____ *(disminuir / saber)*.

7. No saldré hasta _____ *(afectar / decirte)* lo que pienso.

8. Estudié hasta _____ *(resolver / derretir)* el problema.

9. El profesor esperará hasta que todo el mundo _____ *(terminar / limitar)*.

10. Tendrán que gastar mucho dinero para _____ *(fomentar / limpiar)* el derrame.

realidades.com

• Web Code: jed-0908

Realidades ③

Capítulo 9

Nombre _____

Fecha _____

Hora _____

Core Practice **9-13**

Organizer

I. Vocabulary

Para hablar de la contaminación

_____

_____

_____

_____

_____

Para hablar sobre los animales

_____

_____

_____

_____

_____

Para hablar del medio ambiente

_____

_____

_____

_____

_____

_____

_____

_____

_____

Para hablar de los recursos naturales

_____

_____

_____

_____

_____

Verbos

_____

_____

_____

_____

_____

_____

Realidades ③

Capítulo 9

Nombre _____

Fecha _____

Hora _____

Core Practice **9-14**

II. Grammar

1. Make a list of six conjunctions that can be followed either by the indicative or subjunctive.

   _____ _____ _____

   _____ _____ _____

2. When are these conjunctions followed by the subjunctive?

   _____

3. What form of the verb always follows *antes (de) que*?

   _____

4. Make a list of four conjunctions that are followed by the subjunctive to express the purpose or intention of an action.

   _____ _____

   _____ _____

5. When are *para* and *sin* followed by the infinitive?

   _____

6. When is *aunque* followed by the subjunctive?

   _____

7. When is *aunque* followed by the indicative?

   _____

8. When do you use the relative pronoun *que*?

   _____

9. When is the relative pronoun *que* replaced by *quien / quienes*?

   _____

10. When do you use the relative phrase *lo que*?

    _____

realidades.com ✔

• Web Code: jed-0911

Realidades ③

Capítulo 10

Nombre _____

Hora _____

Fecha _____

Core Practice **10-1**

A ver si recuerdas . . .

La política y la comunidad

¿Qué está pasando en esta comunidad? Mira los dibujos y completa las frases con las palabras que faltan.

1. El _____ _____ al ladrón.

2. El _____ y los _____ hablan.

3. Las _____ se _____.

4. Hay una _____ en _____ de la guerra.

5. Luisito no _____ a sus _____.

6. No se _____ entrar en el centro de la comunidad.

7. Estas personas están contentas porque se hicieron

   _____ de los Estados Unidos.

Realidades 3

Capítulo 10

Nombre _____

Hora _____

Fecha _____

Core Practice **10-2**

A ver si recuerdas . . .

Cosas que pasaron

¿Qué pasó o qué pasaba? Completa estas frases que hablan de cosas que sucedían o sucedieron en el pasado. Usa los verbos en pretérito o en imperfecto, según el caso.

reunirse	confiar	obtener
obedecer	disfrutar	resolver

Modelo Yo tenía 18 años cuando _____*obtuve*_____ el permiso de manejar.

1. Eran las nueve de la mañana cuando los miembros del grupo _____.

2. Cuando era niño, mis amigos y yo siempre _____ de las vacaciones.

3. El juez nos dijo que nosotros no _____ la ley esa tarde.

4. Era mi mejor amiga y por eso siempre _____ en ella.

5. Hubo un problema grande, pero tú lo _____.

B. Completa el diálogo con el pretérito o el imperfecto de los verbos entre paréntesis para saber qué dicen Marcos y Ángela acerca de la manifestación.

MARCOS: No te vi en la manifestación. Yo creía que **(1.)** _____ *(querer)*

venir.

ÁNGELA: Es que yo no **(2.)** _____ *(saber)* que había una manifestación. Yo

lo **(3.)** _____ *(saber)* después. ¿Fue Ana contigo?

MARCOS: No, Ana **(4.)** _____ *(querer)* ir, pero no **(5.)** _____ *(poder)*.

Su abuela no se sentía bien y Ana no **(6.)** _____ *(querer)* dejarla

sola. Pero vino a la manifestación Javier Rodríguez.

ÁNGELA: ¿Quién es él? Yo no lo conozco.

MARCOS: Es un estudiante nuevo. Yo tampoco lo **(7.)** _____ *(conocer)*. Lo

(8.) _____ *(conocer)* allí, en la manifestación.

realidades.com

• Web Code: jed-1001

Realidades 3

Capítulo 10

Nombre _____

Fecha _____

Hora _____

Core Practice **10-3**

Conversación: Derechos y deberes

Raúl y sus padres, Fernando e Isabel, tienen una discusión porque Raúl ha llegado tarde a la casa. Completa las frases con las palabras apropiadas del recuadro para saber lo que dicen.

liobagn	nattar	bedeser	pesreto
araaldmtto	uijstiianc	ibtaelrd	

PADRE: Es la una de la mañana, Raúl. ¿Olvidaste que tenías que estar en casa para las

doce? Tú ya conoces las reglas de la casa.

RAÚL: Papá, no es justo, es una **(1.)** _____. Trata de comprenderme.

Uds. me **(2.)** _____ como a un niño pequeño. Tengo 17 años y

debo tener la **(3.)** _____ de decidir a qué hora vuelvo a casa.

MADRE: ¡Raúl! ¡No le hables así a tu papá! Te exigimos que nos trates con

(4.) _____. ¡Somos tus padres! A ti nunca te hemos

(5.) _____. Al contrario, siempre te hemos tratado bien.

RAÚL: Pero, mamá, tú y papá me **(6.)** _____ a hacer ciertas cosas y me

prohíben que haga otras. No me gustan estos **(7.)** _____. Creo

que debo tener más derechos. Creo que debemos hablar de estas cosas, porque

yo también tengo algo que decir.

MADRE: Bueno, mañana seguiremos hablando.

• Web Code: jed-1002

Realidades **3**

Capítulo 10

Nombre _____

Fecha _____

Hora _____

Core Practice **10-4**

Expresar en otras palabras

Los estudiantes de la escuela "Simón Rodríguez" están hablando sobre los derechos y los deberes. Completa las frases para que tengan el mismo significado.

1. La escuela no permite que los estudiantes se vistan como quieran.

   La escuela tiene un _____ de _____.

2. Todos son iguales ante la ley.

   Hay _____ ante la ley.

3. Nadie puede maltratar a los niños.

   Los niños no pueden estar _____ a maltratos.

4. No me hagan ir con Uds.

   No me _____ a ir con Uds.

5. Quieren que yo sea feliz.

   Quieren mi _____.

6. Los estudiantes no tienen que pagar sus estudios.

   Los estudiantes reciben una enseñanza _____.

7. En los Estados Unidos las personas piensan y se expresan libremente.

   En los Estados Unidos hay la _____ de _____ y

   expresión.

8. El estudiante les hace caso a sus maestros.

   El estudiante respeta la _____ de sus maestros.

9. Pueden decir lo que quieran sin miedo.

   _____ de libertad de _____.

10. El gobierno tiene que aplicar las leyes.

    El _____ tiene que aplicar las leyes.

realidades.com

• Web Code: jed-1002

Realidades 3

Capítulo 10

Nombre

Fecha

Hora

Core Practice **10-5**

Noticias del día

Alberto nos cuenta algunas noticias que ocurrieron hoy. Usa la voz pasiva y el pretérito para formar frases con los elementos dados.

Modelo   nuevas reglas / establecer / las autoridades

       Nuevas reglas fueron establecidas por las autoridades.

1. las responsabilidades del gobierno / discutir / en los periódicos

2. varios programas de salud / promover / las enfermeras de la ciudad

3. un discurso / leer / el presidente del país

4. varios temas / tratar / en el discurso

5. una nueva tienda de deportes / abrir / en el centro

6. muchos clientes / entrevistar / los reporteros

7. las opiniones de los clientes / escuchar / el público

8. el problema de la contaminación del río / resolver / un grupo de estudiantes

9. una campaña de limpieza / organizar / ellos

Realidades 3

Nombre _____

Hora _____

Capítulo 10

Fecha _____

Core Practice **10-6**

Ya no

Tú y tu amiga están hablando de cómo eran las cosas antes y cómo son ahora. Primero, completa la pregunta en el presente. Luego, contesta la pregunta en el pasado.

Modelo — ¿Los profesores insisten en que los muchachos _____*lleven*_____
(*llevar* / *aplicar*) una camisa blanca?

— *Antes insistían en que llevaran una camisa blanca. Ya no.*

1. —¿Los profesores piden que los estudiantes _____ (*sufrir* / *hacer*) tarea durante las vacaciones?

   —_____

2. —¿La escuela permite que las reglas no _____ (*aplicarse* / *maltratar*) con igualdad?

   —_____

3. —¿La escuela deja que los profesores _____ (*votar* / *abrir*) los armarios de los estudiantes?

   —_____

4. —¿El director insiste en que _____ (*haber* / *gozar*) un código de vestimenta?

   —_____

5. —¿Es posible que los estudiantes _____ (*sufrir* / *participar*) en todas las decisiones del colegio?

   —_____

6. —¿Es necesario que los estudiantes _____ (*quedarse* / *saber*) hasta las cinco de la tarde?

   —_____

7. —¿Se prohíbe que los estudiantes _____ (*sacar* / *tratar*) libros de la biblioteca?

   —_____

8. —¿Exigen que los estudiantes _____ (*votar* / *levantarse*) cuando entra el profesor?

   —_____

realidades.com
• Web Code: jed-1005

Realidades 3

Capítulo 10

Nombre _____

Hora _____

Fecha _____

Core Practice **10-6**

Conversando

Ahora tu amiga y tú hablan de lo que ha pasado en el colegio. Completa las conversaciones, usando el imperfecto del subjuntivo o el presente perfecto del subjuntivo.

Modelo
— Bárbara no vino.
— Pero yo le dije _____*que viniera*._____

— Bárbara no ha venido.
— Me sorprende *que no haya venido*._____

1. —Los estudiantes no estudiaron.

   —Pero el profesor les había pedido _____.

2. —Luisa no ha votado.

   —Me sorprende que _____.

3. —Los chicos se divirtieron.

   —Me alegro _____.

4. —Pedro no se puso una corbata.

   —Yo sé que su madre le dijo _____.

5. —Estos adolescentes se trataban con respeto.

   —El director del colegio les exigió _____.

6. —Este informe fue escrito por José Antonio.

   —Pero yo no creo _____.

7. —Estas reglas han sido establecidas por el director.

   —No nos gusta _____.

8. —Han prohibido las manifestaciones.

   —Me parece injusto _____.

Realidades 3

Capítulo 10

Nombre _____

Fecha _____

Hora _____

Core Practice **10-8**

Vivir en una democracia

¿Qué sabes de la democracia? Completa estas frases, escribiendo las palabras que correspondan de acuerdo a las letras en los espacios.

1. El — c — — — d —, o la persona que se cree cometió un crimen,

   tiene derecho a tener un — u — — i — rápido y público.

2. La libertad de palabra es algo importante en la democracia, y es un

   — — l — r que mucha gente respeta.

3. Unos chicos tienen ideas y — r — — — n — — soluciones a los

   conflictos del planeta, o problemas — — n — — — l — —.

4. Las personas que vieron el accidente son los t — — — — g — —

   y ellos pueden ayudar a decidir si el acusado es — — l — — b — — —

   o inocente.

5. La policía no puede arrestar ni — — t — n — — a una persona sin

   acusarla de un crimen específico.

6. Nosotros creemos y — p — n — — — — que todos tienen

   derecho a hacer las cosas que desean hacer y lograr sus

   — — p — r — — — — — e —.

7. Los jóvenes hablan entre ellos para — — t — — c — — b — — —

   sus ideas y dar sus — r o — u — — — — — para resolver los

   problemas del medio ambiente.

Realidades 3

Capítulo 10

Nombre _____

Fecha _____

Hora _____

Core Practice **10-9**

Club de la Democracia

Estos estudiantes han formado un club. Para saber de qué se trata, completa las frases, usando las palabras en paréntesis como pistas.

HILDA: Nuestro Club de la Democracia ya tiene 100 miembros. Es muy importante

que fomentemos las ideas y valores **(1.)** _____ (*de la democracia*).

MARCO: En muchos países del mundo la gente no goza de la libertad, la

(2.) _____ (*ser iguales*) y la justicia.

PEDRO: Sí, son cosas que hay en una sociedad **(3.)** _____ (*con libertad*)

como la nuestra.

CHELO: Es cierto. No todos tienen la suerte de tener estos derechos

(4.) _____ (*principales*).

TERESA: También hay muchas personas que no gozan de la libertad de

(5.) _____ (*periódicos y revistas*).

MARÍA: Cierto. Y ése es un derecho que nos da acceso a diferentes

(6.) _____ (*opiniones*).

MARCO: Ojalá que todo el mundo viviera en una sociedad sin

(7.) _____ (*falta de igualdades*) y oportunidad.

ROBERTO: Sí. **(8.)** _____ (*En vez de*) pelearse, todos podrían vivir

en armonía.

LUIS: Siempre hay que buscar soluciones **(9.)** _____ (*que evitan la guerra*).

CARLOS: Creo que ése va a ser el **(10.)** _____ (*la meta*) de nuestro

nuevo club.

Realidades 3

Capítulo 10

Nombre _____

Fecha _____

Hora _____

Core Practice **10-10**

Hacia una sociedad mejor

Marta habla del progreso que ve en su sociedad cuando vuelve del extranjero. Usa los elementos sugeridos para escribir lo que dice. Usa el pluscuamperfecto del subjuntivo.

| Modelo | Se había garantizado la libertad de expresión. (Me alegré) |

Me alegré de que se hubiera garantizado la libertad de expresión.

1. Las mujeres habían exigido la igualdad de derechos. (Me pareció bien)

_____

2. Los trabajadores habían pedido mejor acceso a los hospitales. (Me gustó)

_____

3. Habían decidido tratar mejor a los extranjeros. (Me pareció importante)

_____

4. El gobierno había prometido proteger la libertad de prensa. (No pude creer)

_____

5. Habían garantizado los derechos del acusado. (Me alegré)

_____

6. Habían propuesto soluciones pacíficas a los conflictos con otros países. (Dudaba)

_____

7. El gobierno había empezado a luchar contra el desempleo. (Fue bueno)

_____

8. El país había mejorado tanto. (¡Cuánto me alegré!)

_____

realidades.com

• Web Code: jed-1007

Realidades 3

Capítulo 10

Nombre _____

Fecha _____

Hora _____

Core Practice **10-11**

Nadie habría hecho eso

Di, en cada caso, que la persona mencionada habría actuado de otra manera en esa situación.

Modelo Juan se sentía mal, pero corrió dos horas. ¿A ti te parece bien eso?

No, yo no habría corrido dos horas.

1. Marta estaba enferma, pero salió. ¿A Luisa le parece bien eso?

   _____

2. El agua del lago estaba muy fría, sin embargo nadé. ¿A ti te parece bien eso?

   _____

3. A Pablo no le cae bien Susana, pero él la invitó. ¿A Francisco le parece bien eso?

   _____

4. A mí no me gustó la decisión, pero la acepté. ¿A ti te parece bien eso?

   _____

5. Sarita tenía prisa y no respetó las reglas. ¿A Uds. les parece bien eso?

   _____

6. Marcos no preguntó y no se enteró del problema. ¿A los otros les parece bien eso?

   _____

7. No encontraron la evidencia porque no buscaron en la casa. ¿A Uds. les parece bien eso?

   _____

8. Ellos no comprendían el problema y no lo resolvieron. ¿A ti te parece bien eso?

   _____

9. Alfredo no puso atención y no propuso una solución. ¿A nuestros amigos les parece bien eso?

Las cosas habrían podido ser diferentes

Di cómo estas situaciones habrían podido ser diferentes. Usa frases completas con el condicional perfecto y el pluscuamperfecto del subjuntivo.

Modelo   Yo no estudié todos los días. No saqué buenas notas.
Si hubiera estudiado todos los días, habría sacado buenas notas.

1. Tú condujiste tan rápidamente. Te detuvo la policía.

   _____

2. Pedro dejó abierta la puerta de su coche. Su coche desapareció.

   _____

3. No hubo traductores. No comprendimos la conferencia.

   _____

4. Esas personas no conocían sus derechos. No pudieron defenderse.

   _____

5. No respetaron sus derechos. Lo arrestaron.

   _____

6. Alicia no corrió bien en la carrera. No ganó el premio.

   _____

7. Él no vio el accidente. No pudo ser testigo.

   _____

8. No manejaron con cuidado. Tuvieron un accidente.

   _____

● Web Code: jed-1010

Realidades 3

Capítulo 10

Nombre _____

Fecha _____

Hora _____

Core Practice **10-13**

Organizer

I. Vocabulary

Para hablar de derechos y responsabilidades

_____

_____

_____

_____

_____

Para hablar de los derechos de los ciudadanos

_____

_____

_____

_____

_____

Para hablar del hogar

_____

_____

_____

_____

_____

Para hablar de la escuela

_____

_____

_____

_____

_____

Para hablar de los derechos de todos

_____

_____

_____

_____

_____

Adjetivos y expresiones

_____

_____

_____

_____

_____

Realidades 3

Capítulo 10

Nombre _____

Fecha _____

Hora _____

Core Practice **10-14**

II. Grammar

1. How do you form the passive voice?

   _____

2. Does the past participle form change in the passive voice? Explain.

   _____

   _____

3. After what tenses do you use the present subjunctive?

   _____   _____

   _____   _____

4. After what tenses do you use the imperfect subjunctive?

   _____   _____

   _____   _____

5. What forms can be used after *como si?*

   _____

   _____

6. How do you form the conditional perfect?

   _____

7. In sentences with *si* clauses referring to the past, what form of the verb is used in the *si* clause?

   _____

8. In sentences with *si* clauses referring to the past, what form of the verb is used in the main clause?

   _____

9. Give the conditional perfect of *ir:*

   _____   _____

   _____   _____

   _____   _____

realidades.com

• Web Code: jed-1011

Notes

Notes

Strategy:

- Remind your child that class participation and memorization are very important in a foreign language course.
- Tell your child that in reading or listening activities, as well as in the classroom, it is not necessary to understand every word. Suggest that your child listen or look for key words to get the gist of what's being communicated.
- Encourage your child to ask questions in class if he or she is confused. Remind the child that other students may have the same question. This will minimize frustration and help your child succeed.

Real-life connection:

- Outside of the regular study time, encourage your child to review words in their proper context as they relate to the chapter themes. For example, when studying the chapter about art and artists, your child can create a short biography about a favorite singer or actor/actress using the vocabulary in Chapter 2.
- Motivate your child with praise for small jobs well done, not just for big exams and final grades. A memorized vocabulary list is something to be proud of!

Review:

- Encourage your child to review previously learned material frequently, and not just before a test. Remember, learning a language is a building process, and it is important to keep using what you've already learned.
- To aid vocabulary memorization, suggest that your child try several different methods, such as saying words aloud while looking at a picture of the items, writing the words, acting them out while saying them, and so on.
- Suggest that your child organize new material using charts, graphs, pictures with labels, or other visuals that can be posted in the study area. A daily review of those visuals will help keep the material fresh.
- Help your child drill new vocabulary and grammar by using the charts and lists in the **Manos a la obra 1** and **2** and **Repaso del capítulo** sections.

Resources:

- Offer to help frequently! Your child may have great ideas for how you can facilitate his or her learning experience.
- Ask your child's teacher, or encourage your child to ask, about how to best prepare for and what to expect on tests and quizzes.
- Ask your child's teacher about the availability of audio recordings and videos that support the text. The more your child sees and hears the language, the greater the retention. There are also on-line and CD-ROM based versions of the textbook that may be useful for your child.
- Visit www.realidades.com with your child for more helpful tips and practice opportunities, including downloadable audio files that your child can play at home to practice Spanish. Enter the appropriate Web Code from the list on the next page for the section of the chapter that the class is working on and you will see a menu that lists the available audio files. They can be listened to on a computer or on a personal audio player.

Capítulo	A primera vista	Manos a la obra	Repaso
Para empezar			jed-0099
Capítulo 1	1. jed-0161 2. jed-0171	1. jed-0162 2. jed-0172	jed-0199
Capítulo 2	1. jed-0261 2. jed-0271	1. jed-0262 2. jed-0272	jed-0299
Capítulo 3	1. jed-0361 2. jed-0371	1. jed-0362 2. jed-0372	jed-0399
Capítulo 4	1. jed-0461 2. jed-0471	1. jed-0462 2. jed-0472	jed-0499
Capítulo 5	1. jed-0561 2. jed-0571	1. jed-0562 2. jed-0572	jed-0599
Capítulo 6	1. jed-0661 2. jed-0671	1. jed-0662 2. jed-0672	jed-0699
Capítulo 7	1. jed-0761 2. jed-0771	1. jed-0762 2. jed-0772	jed-0799
Capítulo 8	1. jed-0861 2. jed-0871	1. jed-0862 2. jed-0872	jed-0899
Capítulo 9	1. jed-0961 2. jed-0971	1. jed-0962 2. jed-0972	jed-0999
Capítulo 10	1. jed-1061 2. jed-1071	1. jed-1062 2. jed-1072	jed-1099

Above all, help your child understand that a language is not acquired overnight. Just as for a first language, there is a gradual process for learning a second one. It takes time and patience, and it is important to know that mistakes are a completely natural part of the process. Remind your child that it took years to become proficient in his or her first language, and that the second one will also take time. Praise your child for even small progress in the ability to communicate in Spanish, and provide opportunities for your child to hear and use the language.

Don't hesitate to ask your child's teacher for ideas. You will find the teacher eager to help you. You may also be able to help the teacher understand special needs that your child may have, and work together with him or her to find the best techniques for helping your child learn.

Learning to speak another language is one of the most gratifying experiences a person can have. We know that your child will benefit from the effort, and will acquire a skill that will serve to enrich his or her life.

Realidades 3

Para empezar

Nombre _____

Hora _____

Fecha _____

Vocabulary Flash Cards, Sheet 1

Copy the word or phrase in the space provided.

comer	ir de compras	llegar
	_____ _____	
_____	_____	_____
estudiar	hacer la tarea	navegar en la Red
	_____	_____
	_____	_____ _____
_____	_____	_____
ver la tele	hablar por teléfono	ir a la escuela
_____	_____	_____
_____	_____	_____
_____	_____	_____

Realidades 3

Para empezar

Nombre _____

Hora _____

Fecha _____

Vocabulary Flash Cards, Sheet 2

Copy the word or phrase in the space provided.

inolvidable	**bello, bella**	**talentoso, talentosa**
_____	_____, _____	_____, _____
una película policíaca	**un drama**	**una película romántica**
_____ _____	_____ _____	_____ _____
típico, típica	**divertido, divertida**	**emocionante**
_____, _____	_____, _____	_____

Realidades 3

Para empezar

Nombre _____

Hora _____

Fecha _____

Vocabulary Check, Sheet 1

Tear out this page. Write the English words on the lines. Fold the paper along the dotted line to see the correct answers so you can check your work.

comer _____

estudiar _____

hablar por teléfono _____

hacer la tarea _____

ir de compras _____

llegar _____

navegar en la Red _____

practicar deportes _____

tener una cita _____

ver la tele _____

típico, típica _____

divertido, divertida _____

emocionante _____

exagerado, exagerada _____

inolvidable _____

un drama _____

una película de horror _____

una película policíaca _____

una película romántica _____

Fold In →

Realidades **3**

Para empezar

Nombre _____

Hora _____

Fecha _____

Vocabulary Check, Sheet 2

Tear out this page. Write the Spanish words on the lines. Fold the paper along the dotted line to see the correct answers so you can check your work.

to eat _____

to study _____

to talk on the phone _____

to do homework _____

to go shopping _____

to arrive _____

to surf the Web _____

to play sports _____

to have a date _____

to watch TV _____

typical _____

fun _____

touching _____

exaggerated _____

unforgettable _____

a drama _____

a horror movie _____

a police movie _____

a romance (movie) _____

Fold In

realidades.com
• Web Code: jed-0099

Realidades 3

Para empezar

Nombre _____

Hora _____

Fecha _____

Guided Practice Activities, Sheet 1

Verbos irregulares (p. 3)

- Remember that some verbs in Spanish have irregular **yo** forms. Look at the following list of common verbs that are irregular in the **yo** form only—the other forms of these verbs follow the regular conjugation rules.

dar: **doy**	poner: pon**go**	saber: **sé**
salir: sal**go**	caer: cai**go**	conocer: cono**zco**
traer: trai**go**	hacer: ha**go**	ver: **veo**

- Other verbs you have learned with irregular **yo** forms include **obedecer**, **ofrecer** and **parecer**, which are conjugated like **conocer**.

A. Answer each question by writing the irregular **yo** form of the verb given.

Modelo ¿Sabes esquiar? Sí, (yo) _____*sé*_____ esquiar muy bien.

1. ¿Haces la tarea siempre? Sí, _____ la tarea todos los días.

2. ¿Dónde pones tus libros? _____ mis libros en mi mochila.

3. ¿Le das la tarea a la maestra? Sí, le _____ la tarea siempre.

4. ¿Traes tu libro de texto a casa? Sí, _____ mi libro a casa para estudiar.

5. ¿Ves la foto de José y María? Sí, _____ la foto. Es muy bonita.

6. ¿Obedeces a tus padres? Sí, siempre _____ a mis padres.

7. ¿Conoces a alguna persona famosa? Sí, (yo) _____ a Enrique Iglesias.

- Other verbs are irregular not only in the **yo** form but in all the forms. Look at the following list of important verbs that are irregular in all forms of the present tense.

ser		ir		decir	
soy	somos	voy	vamos	digo	decimos
eres	sois	vas	vais	dices	decís
es	son	va	van	dice	dicen

estar		oír		tener		venir	
estoy	estamos	oigo	oímos	tengo	tenemos	vengo	venimos
estás	estáis	oyes	oís	tienes	tenéis	vienes	venís
está	están	oye	oyen	tiene	tienen	viene	vienen

Verbos irregulares (continued)

B. Complete the following sentences with the correct forms of the verbs in parentheses. Follow the model.

Modelo (salir) María _____*sale*_____ a las 7.30 pero yo _____*salgo*_____ a las 8.

1. **(ir)** Yo _____ a mi casa después de mis clases pero mis amigos _____ al gimnasio.

2. **(tener)** Mi padre _____ cuarenta y cinco años, pero yo _____ diecisiete.

3. **(saber)** Nosotros _____ que hay un examen mañana, pero yo no _____ si va a ser difícil.

4. **(decir)** José _____ que la clase de química es aburrida, pero yo _____ que es muy interesante.

5. **(traer)** Yo _____ mis libros de texto a casa cada noche, pero mi mamá _____ muchos papeles de su trabajo.

C. Write complete sentences to describe what happens in a Spanish class. Follow the model.

Modelo Los estudiantes / tener / un examen / el viernes
_____*Los estudiantes tienen un examen el viernes.*_____

1. Yo / saber / todas las respuestas del examen

_____

2. Javier / ser / un estudiante muy serio

_____

3. Nosotros / salir / de la clase / a las once

_____

4. Yo / oír / una canción / en español

_____

5. Ellas / conocer / a unos estudiantes de Puerto Rico

_____

• Web Code: jed-0001

Realidades ③

Para empezar

Nombre _____

Hora _____

Fecha _____

Guided Practice Activities, Sheet 3

Presente de los verbos con cambio de raíz (p. 5)

- Remember that, in the present tense, stem-changing verbs have stem changes in all forms <u>except</u> the **nosotros/nosotras** and **vosotros/vosotras** forms.

- The types of stem changes are: O→UE, U→UE, E→IE, and E→I. Look at the chart below to see how **volver** (*ue*), **pensar** (*ie*), and **servir** (*i*) are conjugated. Their stem changes have been underlined:

volver		pensar		servir	
v<u>ue</u>lvo	volvemos	p<u>ie</u>nso	pensamos	s<u>i</u>rvo	servimos
v<u>ue</u>lves	volvéis	p<u>ie</u>nsas	pensáis	s<u>i</u>rves	servís
v<u>ue</u>lve	v<u>ue</u>lven	p<u>ie</u>nsa	p<u>ie</u>nsan	s<u>i</u>rve	s<u>i</u>rven

- Here is a list of common verbs with each type of stem change:

  O→UE   poder, dormir, morir, volver, devolver, almorzar, recordar, encontrar, contar, costar, acostarse

  U→UE   jugar

  E→IE   perder, empezar, querer, preferir, pensar, divertirse, despertarse, sentirse, mentir, cerrar, comenzar, entender

  E→I   pedir, servir, repetir, reír, sonreír, seguir, vestirse

A. Complete the sentences about Santiago's activities using the verbs in parentheses. Follow the model.

Modelo   (despertarse) Santiago _se despierta_ muy temprano porque es un chico activo.

1. **(querer)**   Santiago _____ leer el periódico antes de salir para la escuela.

2. **(recordar)**   Santiago _____ su tarea y sus libros cuando sale.

3. **(comenzar)**   Santiago _____ su clase de francés a las ocho de la mañana.

4. **(sentarse)**   Santiago ____ _____ cerca de la maestra para escuchar bien lo que ella dice.

5. **(pedir)**   Santiago _____ una ensalada y pollo.

6. **(volver)**   Santiago _____ a casa a las tres de la tarde.

7. **(jugar)**   y _____ un poco de fútbol con su hermano.

Realidades **3**

Para empezar

Nombre _____

Hora _____

Fecha _____

Guided Practice Activities, Sheet 4

B. Ana is writing a letter to her pen pal. Look at the lines from her letter and underline the subject for each verb in the sentence. Then, complete the sentence with the correct forms of the verb given.

Modelo (**preferir**) <u>Yo</u> ___*prefiero*___ pasar tiempo con mi amiga Tere. Y <u>tú</u>, ¿con quién ___*prefieres*___ pasar tiempo?

1. (**contar**) Mis amigos y yo siempre _____ chistes. Y Uds., ¿_____ chistes?

2. (**poder**) Yo _____ hablar un poco de francés. Y tú, ¿_____ hablar otras lenguas?

3. (**almorzar**) Los otros estudiantes y yo _____ en la cafetería. Y Uds., ¿_____ en casa o en la escuela?

4. (**reír**) Mis amigos y yo _____ mucho cuando vemos películas cómicas. Y tú, ¿_____ mucho cuando vas al cine?

5. (**pensar**) Yo _____ estudiar biología en la universidad. Y tú y tus amigos, ¿qué _____ estudiar?

6. (**dormir**) Mis hermanos y yo _____ ocho horas todas las noches. Y tú, ¿_____ más de ocho horas o menos?

C. Write complete sentences to describe what the people in the sentences do for activities. Follow the model.

Modelo Este fin de semana / mis amigos y yo / querer / jugar al vóleibol.

   Este fin de semana, mis amigos y yo queremos jugar al vóleibol.

1. Nadia y Bárbara / siempre / perder / las llaves

   _____

2. La cafetería de la escuela / servir / comida saludable

   _____

3. Tú / poder / hablar ruso y jugar al ajedrez / ¿no?

   _____

4. La primera clase del día / empezar / a las ocho de la mañana

   _____

5. Yo / no entender / la tarea de matemáticas

   _____

Los verbos reflexivos (p. 7)

- Remember that reflexive verbs are usually used to talk about things people do to or for themselves. Each verb has two parts: a reflexive pronoun and a conjugated verb form.

  Look at the example of the reflexive verb **despertarse**:

despertarse	
me despierto	**nos** despertamos
te despiertas	**os** despertáis
se despierta	**se** despiertan

- Notice that the reflexive pronoun *se* is used for both the **él/ella/Ud.** and **ellos/ellas/Uds.** forms.

A. Underline the reflexive pronoun in each of the following sentences.

> **Modelo**   Rafaela y Silvia <u>se</u> lavan el pelo por la mañana.

1. Yo me levanto a las nueve y media los sábados.

2. Mis amigos y yo nos ponemos las chaquetas cuando hace frío.

3. ¿Tú te cepillas los dientes después de almorzar?

4. Mi madre se viste con ropa elegante para la cena formal.

5. Los jugadores de béisbol van a acostarse temprano porque tienen un partido importante mañana.

B. Write the reflexive pronoun in each sentence to finish the descriptions of the Navarro household's daily preparations.

> **Modelo**   El Sr. Navarro ___se___ afeita antes de bañarse.

1. Laurena _____ ducha por media hora.

2. Ramón y Nomar _____ arreglan juntos.

3. Tú _____ cepillas los dientes dos veces cada día.

4. La Sra. Navarro _____ pinta las uñas por la noche.

- When a conjugated verb is followed by an infinitive, in expressions such as **ir a** + infinitive or **pensar** + infinitive, the reflexive pronoun can come before the first verb or be attached at the end of the infinitive.

  Voy a cepillarme los dientes.   *I am going to brush my teeth.*

  Me voy a cepillar los dientes.   *I am going to brush my teeth.*

- In the above example, both ways of writing the sentence are correct and, as you can see, have the same meaning.

C. Complete each sentence using both ways to write the infinitive of the reflexive verbs in the box below. ¡Recuerda! You will need to change the reflexive pronouns to fit the subject. Follow the model.

| acostarse | lavarse | cepillarse | ~~secarse~~ | afeitarse | ponerse |

Modelo

Nosotras __*nos*__ pensamos __*secar*__ el pelo. /
Nosotras pensamos __*secarnos*__ el pelo.

1. Los niños _____ piensan_____ los dientes. /
   Los niños piensan _____ los dientes.

2. Yo _____ pienso_____ los jeans. /
   Yo pienso _____ los jeans.

3. Tú _____ piensas_____ la cara. /
   Tú piensas _____ la cara.

4. Uds. _____ piensan _____ las manos. /
   Uds. piensan _____ las manos.

5. Carla _____ piensa _____ por la noche. /
   Carla piensa _____ por la noche.

realidades.com

• Web Code: jed-0003

Verbos que se conjugan como gustar (p. 11)

• Remember that the verb **gustar** is conjugated a bit differently from most other verbs in Spanish. In sentences with **gustar**, the subject of the sentence is the thing or things that are liked. In the present tense, we use **gusta** before the thing that is liked (singular noun or infinitive) and **gustan** before the things that are liked (plural noun). For example:

Me gusta el vóleibol. *I like volleyball.*
Me gustan los deportes. *I like sports.*

To show *who* likes the thing or things mentioned you place an *indirect object pronoun* before the form of **gustar**:

me gusta(n)	*I like*	**nos** gusta(n)	*we like*
te gusta(n)	*you like*	**os** gusta(n)	*you all (informal) like*
le gusta(n)	*he/she/you (formal) likes*	**les** gusta(n)	*they/you all like*

A. Complete the following sentences with the correct indirect object pronoun.

Modelo A mis padres _____*les*_____ gustan las notas buenas en la escuela.

1. A mí _____ gusta el fútbol americano.

2. A nosotros _____ gustan las ciencias, como la biología y la física.

3. A Manuel _____ gusta el chocolate; ¡es delicioso!

4. A ella _____ gusta la familia y por eso visita a su abuela con frecuencia.

5. ¿A ti _____ gustan los animales como los perros y los gatos?

6. A Uds. _____ gusta el programa nuevo en la televisión.

B. Now look back at the sentences in exercise A. Each verb ends in **-a** or **-an**. Draw a box around these endings. Then, circle the noun in the sentence that determines whether the verb is singular or plural.

Modelo A mis padres _____*les*_____ gust⬚an (las notas) buenas en la escuela.

Verbos que se conjugan como *gustar* (*continued*)

- There are several other verbs that work like **gustar**. Some important ones are:

  importar *to matter*   **encantar** *to love*   **interesar** *to interest*

  Al director le importan las reglas.   *The rules are important to the principal.*
  A mí me encanta comer helado.   *I love to eat ice cream.*
  A Jennifer le interesa la música.   *Jennifer is interested in music.*

C. Find the subject in each of the following sentences and underline it. Then, use the subject you underlined to help you determine the correct form of the verb. Circle your choice. Follow the model.

Modelo   A mí me ((encantan) / encanta) <u>las telenovelas</u>.

1. A Carolina Herrera le (**interesan** / **interesa**) la ropa.

2. A ti te (**importan** / **importa**) reunirte con amigos.

3. A Pablo le (**encantan** / **encanta**) las fiestas de verano.

4. A Uds. les (**importan** / **importa**) el béisbol.

D. Complete each sentence with the correct indirect object pronoun on the first line and the correct form of the verb in parentheses on the second line.

Modelo   A ti ___*te*___ ___*encanta*___ (**encantar**) la música folklórica.

1. A nosotros _____ _____ (**interesar**) los artículos del periódico.

2. A ellas _____ _____ (**importar**) la política.

3. A mí _____ _____ (**gustar**) los refrescos de frutas.

4. A Joaquín _____ _____ (**interesar**) la historia europea.

5. A nosotras _____ _____ (**encantar**) la nueva canción de Shakira.

6. A los estudiantes _____ _____ (**importar**) las tareas para sus clases.

7. ¿A ti _____ _____ (**gustar**) la comida de la cafetería?

8. A mi hermano _____ _____ (**encantar**) los deportes.

9. A nosotros _____ _____ (**interesar**) ir al cine.

10. A Uds. _____ _____ (**encantar**) hablar por teléfono.

realidades.com ✔
- Web Code: jed-0004

Realidades 3

Para empezar

Nombre _____

Hora _____

Fecha _____

Guided Practice Activities, Sheet 9

Adjetivos posesivos (p. 12)

- Possessive adjectives describe an object by indicating who owns it. Remember that in Spanish, the possessive adjectives agree in number with the object being possessed, not with the person who owns it. For example:

  Mis clase de español es divertida.   *My Spanish class is fun.*
  Mis clases de español son divertidas.   *My Spanish classes are fun.*

- The following possessive adjectives are used in Spanish. Note that the **nosotros** and **vosotros** adjectives must also agree in gender (feminine or masculine) with the item possessed.

mi/mis *my*	nuestro/nuestra/nuestros/nuestras *our*
tu/tus *your (informal)*	vuestro/vuestra/vuestros/vuestras *your (group-informal)*
su/sus *his/her/your (formal)*	su/sus *their/your (group)*

A. In the following sentences a line is drawn under the item possessed to help you determine the correct possessive adjective. Circle one of the two options. Follow the model.

Modelo   Quiero ir al partido de básquetbol con (**mi** /(**mis**)) amigos esta noche.

1. Consuelo necesita traer (**su / sus**) libro de texto a clase.

2. Nosotros vamos a (**nuestra / nuestras**) casas después de la escuela.

3. Enrique y Sara van a preparar (**su / sus**) cena ahora.

4. ¿Tú tienes (**tu / tus**) sombrero y (**tu / tus**) guantes?

5. Mi papá prefiere leer (**su / sus**) revistas en el sofá.

6. ¿Cuándo es (**nuestro / nuestros**) examen de español?

7. (**Mi / Mis**) clases comienzan a las ocho y media de la mañana.

B. Read each possessive statement below. Then, write the corresponding possessive adjective in the second sentence. Follow the model.

Modelo   Es la mochila de Alicia. Es ___su___ mochila.

1. Son las tijeras de nosotros. Son _____ tijeras.

2. Son los gatos de la Sra. Barbosa. Son _____ gatos.

3. Es el televisor de Pilar. Es _____ televisor.

4. Son los libros de nosotras. Son _____ libros.

C. Complete the following conversation between two people at a party with the correct possessive adjectives from the box. You will use each possessive adjective only once.

nuestros	mi	mis	tu	su	~~sus~~

Modelo **Teresa:** Las botas de Luisa son bonitas, ¿no?

  Sonia: Sí, _____*sus*_____ botas son muy elegantes.

Teresa: Esta fiesta es fantástica. La mamá de Raúl prepara unas comidas muy sabrosas, ¿no?

Sonia: Sí, me encanta _____ tortilla española. ¿Tus padres saben cocinar algo especial?

Teresa: Sí, _____ padre sabe preparar unas enchiladas fenomenales, pero siempre tiene que preparar muchas porque tengo cinco hermanos y _____ hermanos pueden comerse un millón de enchiladas.

Sonia: ¡_____ familia es muy grande! Sólo tengo una hermana. En nuestra casa, mi hermana y yo preparamos la comida los fines de semana y _____ padres la preparan durante la semana. Es una buena costumbre.

D. You need to answer some questions from an exchange student at your school. In the first blank, fill in the appropriate possessive adjective. In the second blank, finish the sentence so that it is true for you.

Modelo ¿A qué hora empieza tu clase de español?

  _____*Mi*_____ clase de español empieza a _____*las dos*_____.

1. ¿Cuáles son tus clases favoritas?

   _____ clases favoritas son _____.

2. ¿Cuál es el nombre de tu profesor(a) de español?

   _____ nombre es _____.

3. Tú y tus amigos escuchan música interesante. ¿Cuál es su grupo favorito?

   _____ grupo favorito es _____.

4. ¿En qué ciudad vive tu familia?

   _____ familia vive en _____.

5. ¿Cuáles son las comidas favoritas de tu mejor amigo/a?

   _____ comidas favoritas son _____.

6. Tú y tus amigos hacen muchas actividades divertidas. ¿Cuál es su actividad favorita?

   _____ actividad favorita es _____.

Realidades **3**

Capítulo 1

Nombre _____

Hora _____

Fecha _____

AVSR, Sheet 1

El pretérito de los verbos (p. 17)

- Remember that the preterite is used to talk about past events. To conjugate regular -**ar**, -**er**, and -**ir** verbs in the preterite, use the following endings:

cant**ar**		beb**er**		sal**ir**	
cant**é**	cant**amos**	beb**í**	beb**imos**	sal**í**	sal**imos**
cant**aste**	cant**asteis**	beb**iste**	beb**isteis**	sal**iste**	sal**isteis**
cant**ó**	cant**aron**	beb**ió**	beb**ieron**	sal**ió**	sal**ieron**

A. Complete the sentences about what students did last summer with the correct preterite endings of each -**ar** verb. Pay attention to the regular endings in the chart above and to the accent marks.

Modelo (**nadar**) Marcos y Raúl nad*aron*_____ en el lago.

1. (**caminar**) Yo camin_____ por la playa.

2. (**montar**) Tú mont_____ a caballo en las montañas.

3. (**pasear**) Mis primos pase_____ en bicicleta.

4. (**tomar**) Nosotros tom_____ el sol en la playa.

5. (**usar**) Esteban us_____ la computadora.

B. Complete the sentences by writing the correct preterite form of each -**er** or -**ir** verb. Follow the model. Pay attention to the regular endings and accent marks in the chart above.

Modelo (**aprender**) Marta __*aprendió*__ un poco de francés antes de ir a París.

1. (**comer**) Nosotros _____ helado de fresa.

2. (**decidir**) Ellos _____ visitar Puerto Rico.

3. (**correr**) Yo _____ por el río con mi padre.

4. (**escribir**) Tú me _____ una carta el mes pasado.

5. (**abrir**) Mamá _____ la ventana.

Realidades ③

Capítulo 1

Nombre _____

Fecha _____

Hora _____

AVSR, Sheet 2

- Some verbs have irregular conjugations in the preterite. Three of them, **hacer**, **dar**, and **ver**, are conjugated below:

hacer		dar		ver	
hice	hicimos	di	dimos	vi	vimos
hiciste	hicisteis	diste	disteis	viste	visteis
hizo	hicieron	dio	dieron	vio	vieron

- Note that unlike the regular preterite conjugations, these conjugations do **not** have written accent marks.

C. Complete each sentence with the correct form of the irregular preterite verb. Remember that these verb forms do not use written accent marks.

Modelo (**dar**) Nosotros ____*dimos*____ una caminata por las montañas.

1. (**ver**) Yo _____ unos animales exóticos en el bosque.

2. (**hacer**) Mis hermanos _____ camping una noche.

3. (**ver**) ¿Tú _____ unas flores bonitas?

4. (**dar**) Mi hermana y yo _____ un paseo por la playa.

5. (**hacer**) La familia _____ muchas cosas divertidas.

D. First, circle the verb. If it is regular in the preterite tense, write **R**. If it is irregular in the preterite tense, write **I**. Then, use the preterite to write complete sentences about activities people did in the past. Follow the model.

Modelo __*I*__ Mis primos / (hacer) surf de vela / el verano pasado

Mis primos hicieron surf de vela el verano pasado.

1. _____ Yo / montar en bicicleta / el fin de semana pasado

_____

2. _____ Nosotros / dar una caminata por el parque / anoche

_____

3. _____ Mis amigos / comer en un restaurante / el martes pasado

_____

4. _____ Tú / ver una película / hace dos semanas

_____

5. _____ Mi mejor amigo y yo / hacer una parrillada / el mes pasado

_____

realidades.com

• Web Code: jed-0101

El pretérito de los verbos *ir* y *ser* (p. 19)

- The verbs **ir** and **ser** have the same conjugations in the preterite. You need to use context to determine whether the verb means *went* (**ir**) or *was/were* (**ser**). Look at the conjugations below:

ir		ser	
fui	fuimos	fui	fuimos
fuiste	fuisteis	fuiste	fuisteis
fue	fueron	fue	fueron

A. Determine whether **ir** or **ser** is used in the following sentences by indicating the meaning of the underlined preterite verb.

<u>Modelo</u>   Nosotras <u>fuimos</u> a la biblioteca para estudiar.

    ☑ went (**ir**)   □ were (**ser**)

1. La clase <u>fue</u> muy interesante.

     □ went (**ir**)   □ was (**ser**)

2. Las jugadoras <u>fueron</u> al estadio para competir.

     □ went (**ir**)   □ were (**ser**)

3. Los equipos de fútbol <u>fueron</u> excelentes.

     □ went (**ir**)   □ were (**ser**)

4. Yo <u>fui</u> al parque ayer para montar en monopatín.

     □ went (**ir**)   □ was (**ser**)

B. Read each sentence and decide if **ir** or **ser** is needed. Underline the correct infinitive. Then, write the correct preterite form in the blank.

<u>Modelo</u>   (<u>ir</u> / ser)   Pablo _____*fue*_____ a la playa con sus amigos.

1. (ir / ser)   Nosotros _____ al gimnasio para hacer ejercicio.

2. (ir / ser)   Los partidos de béisbol _____ muy divertidos.

3. (ir / ser)   Yo _____ al centro comercial el fin de semana pasado.

4. (ir / ser)   Ellos _____ los estudiantes más serios de la clase.

5. (ir / ser)   Benito se rompió el brazo. _____ un accidente terrible.

6. (ir / ser)   ¿Adónde _____ (tú) ayer?

Realidades ③

Capítulo 1

Nombre _____

Hora _____

Fecha _____

AVSR, Sheet 4

El pretérito de los verbos que terminan in *-car*, *-gar* y *-zar* (p. 19)

- Remember that some verbs have spelling changes in the **yo** forms of the preterite to preserve the correct pronunciation. Look at the chart below to see how verbs that end in **-car**, **-gar**, and **-zar** change spelling in the preterite.
- Note that the other forms of the verb are conjugated normally:

tocar		**llegar**		**empezar**	
toqué	tocaste	**llegué**	llegamos	empe**cé**	empezamos
tocaste	tocasteis	llegaste	llegasteis	empezaste	empezasteis
tocó	tocaron	llegó	llegaron	empezó	empezaron

C. First, look at the infinitives below and underline the ending (**-car**, **-gar**, or **-zar**) in each. Then, conjugate each verb in the preterite tense for the forms provided. Notice that the first column has the **yo** form. Remember that only the **yo** forms have a spelling change!

| Modelo | bus<u>car</u> | yo bus*qué*____ | él bus*có*____ |

1. jugar   yo ju_____   nosotros ju_____

2. navegar   yo nave_____   él nave_____

3. sacar   yo sa_____   Uds. sa_____

4. almorzar   yo almor_____   nosotros almor_____

5. investigar   yo investi_____   ella investi_____

6. cruzar   yo cru_____   los niños cru_____

D. Complete the following paragraph about Carmen's activities last week by conjugating the verbs in the preterite. The first one has been done for you.

La semana pasada, mis amigas, Julia y Cristina, y yo ____*fuimos*____ (ir) al gimnasio.

Nosotras _____ (hacer) mucho ejercicio. Yo _____ (correr) y mis amigas

_____ (nadar) en la piscina. Después yo _____ (practicar) baloncesto

y ellas _____ (dar) una caminata por un parque que está cerca del gimnasio.

Yo _____ (llegar) a mi casa a las cinco y media y _____ (comenzar) a

hacer mi tarea. Mi papá _____ (preparar) la cena y después mis padres

_____ (ver) una película y yo _____ (jugar) unos videojuegos. Y tú,

¿qué _____ (hacer)?

realidades.com ⊘
• Web Code: jed-0101

Realidades ③

Capítulo 1

Nombre _____

Fecha _____

Hora _____

Vocabulary Flash Cards, Sheet 1

Write the Spanish vocabulary word or phrase below each picture. Be sure to include the article for each noun.

_____

_____

_____

_____

_____

_____

_____

_____

_____

_____

_____

_____

_____

_____

_____

Write the Spanish vocabulary word or phrase below each picture. Be sure to include the article for each noun.

_____
_____

_____
_____

_____

_____
_____

_____
_____

_____
_____

_____
_____

_____
_____

_____
_____

Copy the word or phrase in the space provided. Be sure to include the article for each noun.

acercarse a _____ _____	**andar** _____	**aparecer** _____
así _____	**asustar** _____	**dar un paseo** ____ ____ _____
dejar de _____ _____	**el granizo** _____ _____	**hermoso, hermosa** _____ , _____

Copy the word or phrase in the space provided. Be sure to include the article for each noun. The blank cards can be used to write and practice other Spanish vocabulary for the chapter.

impresionar _____	**la naturaleza** ____	**pasarlo bien/mal** _____
refugiarse _____	**el refugio** ____	**un rato** _____
suceder _____	**el trueno** ____	**una vez allí** ____ ____

Realidades 3

Nombre _____

Hora _____

Capítulo 1

Fecha _____

Vocabulary Check, Sheet 1

Tear out this page. Write the English words on the lines. Fold the paper along the dotted line to see the correct answers so you can check your work.

el bosque _____

el desierto _____

hermoso, hermosa _____

la naturaleza _____

el paisaje _____

el refugio _____

la roca _____

la sierra _____

el valle _____

acercarse (a) _____

andar _____

asustar _____

dar un paseo _____

dejar de _____

escalar _____

perderse _____

refugiarse _____

Fold In →

Realidades 3

Capítulo 1

Nombre _____

Fecha _____

Hora _____

Vocabulary Check, Sheet 2

Tear out this page. Write the Spanish words on the lines. Fold the paper along the dotted line to see the correct answers so you can check your work.

wood, forest   _____

desert   _____

beautiful   _____

nature   _____

landscape   _____

refuge, shelter   _____

rock   _____

sierra, mountain range _____

valley   _____

to approach   _____

to walk, to move   _____

to scare   _____

to take a walk, to stroll _____

to stop (doing something) _____

to climb (a rock or   _____
mountain)

to get lost   _____

to take shelter   _____

Fold In

Tear out this page. Write the English words on the lines. Fold the paper along the dotted line to see the correct answers so you can check your work.

los binoculares _____

la brújula _____

la linterna _____

el repelente de insectos _____

el saco de dormir _____

la tienda de acampar _____

caer granizo _____

el granizo _____

el relámpago _____

el trueno _____

suceder _____

tener lugar _____

al amanecer _____

al anochecer _____

Fold In →

Realidades 3

Capítulo 1

Nombre _____

Hora _____

Fecha _____

Vocabulary Check, Sheet 4

Tear out this page. Write the Spanish words on the lines. Fold the paper along the dotted line to see the correct answers so you can check your work.

binoculars   _____

compass   _____

flashlight   _____

insect repellent   _____

sleeping bag   _____

tent   _____

to hail   _____

hail   _____

lightning   _____

thunder   _____

to occur   _____

to take place   _____

at dawn   _____

at dusk   _____

Fold In ◂

realidades.com

• Web Code: jed-0102

El pretérito de los verbos con el cambio ortográfico i→y (p. 30)

- Remember that verbs ending in **-uir**, such as the verb **construir**, have a spelling change in the preterite. The **i** from the **él/ella/Ud.** and the **ellos/ellas/Uds.** forms becomes a **y**. Other verbs, such as **oír** and **creer**, also have this change. Look at the verbs **creer** and **construir** below as examples:

creer		construir	
creí	creímos	construí	construimos
creíste	creísteis	construiste	construisteis
creyó	creyeron	construyó	construyeron

A. The events below took place in the past. Circle the correct preterite form to complete each sentence.

Modelo   La semana pasada, Ernesto (lee /(leyó)) un libro sobre los bosques tropicales.

1. Recientemente unas tormentas violentas (**destruyeron / destruyen**) gran parte de un bosque.

2. ¿Tú (**oyes / oíste**) algo sobre ese evento desastroso?

3. Ernesto y sus amigos (**leyeron / leen**) algo sobre el paisaje hermoso del bosque.

4. Nosotros (**creímos / creemos**) que esa parte del mundo era interesante.

5. Rafael (**oyó / oye**) un anuncio sobre un viaje a los bosques de Chile.

6. Cuando nosotros fuimos al bosque, yo (**me caigo / me caí**) pero no me lastimé.

B. Complete the preterite verb forms by adding the correct endings.

Modelo   (creer) Mari y Toni cre _yeron_

1. (**destruir**) el oso destru_____   5. (**caerse**) ellos se ca_____

2. (**leer**) yo le_____   6. (**leer**) mi madre le_____

3. (**creer**) nosotros cre_____   7. (**oír**) el oso o_____

4. (**oír**) tú o_____   8. (**caerse**) nosotros nos ca_____

- Web Code: jed-0103

El pretérito de los verbos con el cambio ortográfico i→y (*continued*)

C. Complete each sentence with the preterite forms of the verb in parentheses. Each sentence has two different forms of the same verb.

Modelo (destruir) El granizo *destruyó* las flores y los relámpagos *destruyeron* varios árboles.

1. (leer) Nosotros _____ el mismo mapa que ustedes _____ cuando pasaron por aquí hace diez años.

2. (oír) Mis padres _____ el trueno. Luego, yo lo _____ también.

3. (caerse) Andrés _____ _____ cuando bajó del coche y sus amigos _____ _____ cuando salieron de la tienda de acampar.

4. (construir) Ayer, yo _____ un edificio de bloques para mi sobrino y después, él _____ su propio edificio de bloques.

D. Write complete sentences using the preterite of the indicated verbs. Follow the model.

Modelo Los vecinos / no / **oír** / nada / sobre el accidente

Los vecinos no oyeron nada sobre el accidente. _____

1. Ellos / **leer** / las instrucciones para usar la brújula

_____

2. Tú / **creer** / que / la tormenta / fue muy peligrosa

_____

3. Los relámpagos / **destruir** / los árboles del bosque

_____

4. Nosotros / **oír** / el sonido del granizo cayendo

_____

5. Yo / **leer** / una novela al anochecer

_____

realidades.com

• Web Code: jed-0103

El pretérito de los verbos irregulares (p. 31)

- Several verbs have irregular stems in the preterite. Look at the chart below.

Verb	Stem	Verb	Stem
tener	tuv...	poner	pus...
estar	estuv...	saber	sup...
andar	anduv...	venir	vin...
poder	pud...		

- The irregular verbs share the same endings. The verbs **tener** and **saber** have been conjugated for you as examples.

tener		**saber**	
tuve	tuv**imos**	supe	sup**imos**
tuv**iste**	tuv**isteis**	sup**iste**	sup**isteis**
tuv**o**	tuv**ieron**	sup**o**	sup**ieron**

- Notice that none of these irregular forms has a written accent mark.
- The verbs **decir** and **traer** also have irregular stems and have different endings in the **ellos/ellas/Uds.** form. Look at the conjugations below:

   decir: dije, dijiste, dijo, dijimos, dijisteis, dij**eron**;
   traer: traje, trajiste, trajo, trajimos, trajisteis, traj**eron**

A. Underline the correct form of the irregular preterite verb in each sentence.

Modelo María (dije / <u>dijo</u>) que se perdió en el bosque.

1. Nosotros (**trajiste / trajimos**) los binoculares y la brújula.

2. Yo no (**pude / pudo**) encontrar mi saco de dormir.

3. Los muchachos (**anduvo / anduvieron**) por el bosque.

4. ¿Tú (**viniste / vino**) al bosque para hacer camping?

B. Complete Paco's story of his day with the correct irregular preterite **yo** form of each verb.

Modelo (**poner**) Yo _____*puse*_____ mis libros y tarea en mi mochila.

1. (**decir**) Yo le _____ "Buenos días" a mi maestra de español.

2. (**tener**) Yo _____ un examen de física.

3. (**estar**) Yo _____ en la escuela por 6 horas más.

4. (**venir**) Yo _____ a mi casa a las cuatro y media.

• Web Code: jed-0104

C. A teacher asks her students about their weekend activities. Complete her questions with the **Uds.** form of the verb and the students' answers with the **nosotros** form. Follow the model.

Modelo   (**andar**)   Uds. ___*anduvieron*___ por el bosque, ¿no?
                 Sí, ___*anduvimos*___ por el bosque.

1. (**poder**) Uds. _____ jugar unos deportes, ¿no?

           Sí, _____ jugar al bésibol y al hockey.

2. (**tener**) Uds. _____ que limpiar sus cuartos, ¿no?

           Sí, _____ que limpiarlos.

3. (**venir**) Uds. _____ a ver la obra de teatro estudiantil, ¿no?

           Sí, _____ a verla.

4. (**saber**) Uds. _____ lo que le pasó a Jorge ayer, ¿no?

           Sí, lo _____.

5. (**decir**) Uds. me _____ todo lo que hicieron, ¿no?

           Sí, se le _____ todo.

D. First, identify the pictures. Then, use the pictures and verbs in the preterite to create complete sentences about what people did in the past. Follow the model.

Modelo   Mario / estar / _____ / por tres horas
           Mario estuvo en la tienda de acampar por tres horas.

1.   mis amigos y yo / poder ver / _____ / impresionante / anoche

_____

2.   Ana y Felipe / andar por / _____ / durante todo el día

_____

3.   tú / poner / _____ / en la mochila

_____

4.   Yo / traer / _____ / para ver el sendero

_____

El pretérito de los verbos con los cambios e→i, o→u en la raíz (p. 33)

- Stem changing **-ar** and **-er** verbs, such as **pensar**, have <u>no stem changes</u> in the preterite. However, **-ir** verbs that have a stem change in the present tense also have a stem change in the preterite.
- If the **-ir** verb has an **e→ie** or **e→i** stem change in the present tense, such as **servir**, in the preterite the **e** will change to an **i** in the **él/ella/Ud.** and **ellos/ellas/Uds.** forms.
- If the **-ir** verb has an **o→ue** stem change in the present tense, such as **dormir**, in the preterite the **o** will change to a **u** in the **él/ella/Ud.** and **ellos/ellas/Uds.** forms.

servir	**(e→i)**	**dormir**	**(o→u)**
serví	servimos	dormí	dormimos
serviste	servisteis	dormiste	dormisteis
sirvió	sirvieron	durmió	durmieron

A. The following sentences are all in either the **él/ella/Ud.** or **ellos/ellas/Uds.** form. Fill in the missing vowel to tell what happened on a recent camping trip. Follow the model.

Modelo   (sentirse) Ana y Sofía se s_*i*_ntieron muy cansadas después de escalar las rocas.

1. (**dormir**)   Francisco d___rmió todo el día en su saco de dormir.

2. (**servir**)   El restaurante s___rvió hamburguesas y perros calientes.

3. (**divertirse**)   Mis amigos se div___rtieron mucho en el viaje.

4. (**morirse**)   Un animal se m___rió en el bosque. ¡Qué triste!

B. What Sara did last weekend was different from what her best friends did. Complete the sentences with the correct preterite forms of the verbs in parentheses. Be sure to include the stem change when describing what Sara's friends did. Follow the model.

Modelo   (sugerir) Yo ___*sugerí*___ un fin de semana tranquilo; mis amigas ___*sugirieron*___ un viaje al bosque.

1. (**preferir**)   Yo _____ ir al cine; mis amigas _____ ir a un café.

2. (**dormir**)   Yo _____ en mi casa; mis amigas _____ en un hotel.

3. (**vestirse**)   Yo _____ _____ con jeans y una camiseta; mis amigas _____ _____ con chaquetas, guantes, gorros y botas.

4. (**pedir**)   Yo _____ pollo frito en un restaurante; mis amigos _____ perros calientes preparados en la fogata.

5. (**divertirse**) Yo no _____ _____ mucho; mis amigas _____ _____ bastante.

• Web Code: jed-0105

C. Complete each sentence with the correct preterite verb form to tell what people did on a recent nature hike. Remember that only the **él/ella/Ud.** and **ellos/ellas/Uds.** forms have stem changes.

Modelo (vestirse) Tere __se__ __vistió__ con botas para andar por la montañas.

1. (**dormir**) Yo _____ varias horas la noche antes de salir.

2. (**sugerir**) Mis padres _____ un paseo en canoa.

3. (**pedir**) Mi hermano _____ usar los binoculares.

4. (**sentirse**) Nosotros _____ _____ muy cansados por la caminata.

5. (**preferir**) Tú _____ usar la linterna para ver mejor.

6. (**divertirse**) Los chicos _____ _____ mucho cuando vieron unos animales pequeños.

7. (**morirse**) ¡Casi _____ _____ de hambre cuando perdimos la comida para el almuerzo!

D. Write complete sentences by conjugating each stem-changing **-ir** verb in the preterite tense. Follow the model.

Modelo al anochecer / los niños / divertirse / jugando con las linternas
Al anochecer los niños se divirtieron jugando con las linternas.

1. los insectos / morir / al principio del invierno

_____

2. Ángel y Estela / vestirse / de ropa elegante / para salir anoche

_____

3. el camarero / sugerir / la sopa del día

_____

4. nosotros / dormir / por tres semanas en el saco de dormir

_____

5. yo / sentirse triste / después de ver la película

_____

realidades.com ✔
• Web Code: jed-0105

Realidades 3

Capítulo 1

Nombre _____

Fecha _____

Hora _____

Vocabulary Flash Cards, Sheet 5

Write the Spanish vocabulary word or phrase below each picture. Be sure to include the article for each noun.

_____

_____

_____

_____

_____

_____

_____

_____

_____

Write the Spanish vocabulary word or phrase below each picture. If there is a word or phrase, copy it in the space provided. Be sure to include the article for each noun.

alcanzar _____	**al principio** _____ _____	**la ceremonia** _____ _____
darse cuenta de _____ _____	**desafortunadamente** _____	**duro, dura** _____ _____
 _____ _____	**contra** _____	**eliminar** _____

Realidades 3

Capítulo 1

Nombre _____

Fecha _____

Hora _____

Vocabulary Flash Cards, Sheet 7

Copy the word or phrase in the space provided. Be sure to include the article for each noun.

emocionarse	**el entrenamiento**	**estar orgulloso, orgullosa de**
¡Felicitaciones!	**hacer un esfuerzo**	**hacia**
inscribirse	**la inscripción**	**la meta**

Realidades 3

Capítulo 1

Nombre _____

Fecha _____

Hora _____

Vocabulary Flash Cards, Sheet 8

Copy the word or phrase in the space provided. Be sure to include the article for each noun. The blank cards can be used to write and practice other Spanish vocabulary for the chapter.

el/la participante	el/la representante	obtener
_____ _____	_____ _____	_____
sin embargo	tener lugar	vencer
_____ _____	_____ _____	_____

Tear out this page. Write the English words on the lines. Fold the paper along the dotted line to see the correct answers so you can check your work.

el entrenamiento _____

entrenarse _____

hacer un esfuerzo _____

inscribirse _____

la inscripción _____

alcanzar _____

la carrera _____

el certificado _____

contra _____

eliminar _____

la entrega de premios _____

la medalla _____

la meta _____

obtener _____

el/la participante _____

el/la representante _____

Fold In

Tear out this page. Write the Spanish words on the lines. Fold the paper along the dotted line to see the correct answers so you can check your work.

training _____

to train _____

to make an effort _____

to register _____

registration _____

to reach _____

race _____

certificate, diploma _____

against _____

to eliminate _____

awards ceremony _____

medal _____

goal _____

to obtain, get _____

participant _____

representative _____

Fold In ←

Realidades ③

Capítulo 1

Nombre _____

Hora _____

Fecha _____

Vocabulary Check, Sheet 7

Tear out this page. Write the English words on the lines. Fold the paper along the dotted line to see the correct answers so you can check your work.

salir campeón
(campeona)   _____
                             _____

el trofeo   _____

vencer   _____

animado,
animada   _____

desafortunadamente   _____

desanimado,
desanimada   _____

duro, dura   _____

emocionarse   _____

estar orgulloso(a) de   _____

impresionar   _____

hacia   _____

perder el equilibrio   _____

tener lugar   _____

al principio   _____

Fold In

Realidades 3

Nombre _____

Hora _____

Capítulo 1

Fecha _____

Vocabulary Check, Sheet 8

Tear out this page. Write the Spanish words on the lines. Fold the paper along the dotted line to see the correct answers so you can check your work.

to become the champion
_____
_____

trophy
_____

to beat
_____

excited
_____
_____

unfortunately
_____

discouraged
_____
_____

hard
_____

to be moved
_____

to be proud of
_____

to impress
_____

toward
_____

to lose one's balance
_____

to take place
_____

at the beginning
_____

Fold In

realidades.com

• Web Code: jed-0106

Realidades 3

Capítulo 1

Nombre _____

Fecha _____

Hora _____

Guided Practice Activities, Sheet 7

El imperfecto (p. 42)

- The imperfect tense is used to talk about habitual or repeated events in the past. Look at the conjugations of regular -**ar**, -**er**, and -**ir** verbs in the imperfect tense:

montar		comer		salir	
mont**aba**	mont**ábamos**	com**ía**	com**íamos**	sal**ía**	sal**íamos**
mont**abas**	mont**abais**	com**ías**	com**íais**	sal**ías**	sal**íais**
mont**aba**	mont**aban**	com**ía**	com**ían**	sal**ía**	sal**ían**

- Notice that the **yo** and **él/ella/Ud.** forms of each verb are the same.
- Notice that -**er** and -**ir** verbs have the same endings in the imperfect.

A. Write the imperfect endings of the -**ar** verbs in the first column, and the imperfect endings of the -**er** and -**ir** verbs in the second column.

Modelo ellos (**cantar**) cant _aban_____   (**vivir**) viv _ían_____

1. yo   (**entrenar**) entren_____   (**hacer**) hac_____

2. nosotros (**andar**) and_____   (**correr**) corr_____

3. tú   (**caminar**) camin_____   (**preferir**) prefer_____

4. él   (**jugar**) jug_____   (**querer**) quer_____

5. Uds.   (**eliminar**) elimin_____   (**obtener**) obten_____

- There are only three irregular verbs in the imperfect: **ser**, **ir**, and **ver**. Look at the conjugations of these verbs below:

ser		ir		ver	
era	éramos	iba	íbamos	veía	veíamos
eras	erais	ibas	ibais	veías	veíais
era	eran	iba	iban	veía	veían

B. Complete each sentence with the correct form of the verb in parentheses.

Modelo Marisol _era_ (**ser**) una muchacha atlética.

1. Marisol y sus amigas _____ (**ir**) al gimnasio para entrenarse todos los días.

2. Yo _____ (**ver**) a Marisol y sus amigas en el gimnasio con frecuencia.

3. Nosotras _____ (**ser**) muy dedicadas y nuestra meta _____ (**ser**) participar en una carrera importante de la ciudad.

4. Mis padres siempre _____ (**ver**) los partidos deportivos en la tele.

realidades.com ✔
- Web Code: jed-0107

Realidades 3

Capítulo 1

Nombre _____

Fecha _____

Hora _____

Guided Practice Activities, Sheet 8

El imperfecto (*continued*)

C. A group of adults remembers their high school experiences. Complete each sentence with the correct imperfect verb form.

Modelo (ganar) Nuestros equipos siempre ___*ganaban*___ los campeonatos.

1. **(estar)** Los estudiantes de nuestra escuela siempre _____ muy animados por los partidos deportivos.

2. **(entrenarse)** Yo _____ _____ en el gimnasio todos los días.

3. **(ir)** Mi mamá _____ a todos los partidos de béisbol porque le encantaba ese deporte.

4. **(jugar)** Tú _____ al béisbol cada primavera, ¿no?

5. **(hacer)** Yo siempre _____ un gran esfuerzo para alcanzar mis metas.

6. **(tener)** Los partidos de fútbol americano _____ lugar cerca de la escuela.

7. **(vencer)** Nosotros siempre _____ a nuestros rivales.

8. **(ser)** Mi amigo Javier _____ el muchacho más atlético de nuestra escuela.

D. Write sentences describing your childhood memories by conjugating the verbs in the imperfect tense and completing the sentences with information that applies to you. Follow the model.

Modelo Mis amigos y yo / siempre querer ir a...

Mis amigos y yo siempre queríamos ir a la piscina.

1. Yo / vivir en...

_____

2. Mi mejor amigo(a) / jugar...

_____

3. Mis amigos y yo / ver el programa...

_____

4. Mis padres / siempre decir...

_____

realidades.com
• Web Code: jed-0107

Usos del imperfecto (p. 44)

The imperfect is used:

- to describe events that happened regularly or habitually in the past
- to describe people and places in the past (for example: physical descriptions of what people or places looked like, or people's emotions)
- to describe past events that were ongoing or continuous (including things that "were happening" before being interrupted)
- to give the date, time, and someone's age in the past
- to talk about the weather in the past

A. Each sentence below provides a description in the past. Determine what is being described and write the corresponding letter next to the sentence. Then, underline the imperfect verb form in each sentence. Follow the model.

a. person, place   b. continuous action   c. date, time, age, weather

Modelo   _c_ Eran las nueve y media de la noche.

1. ____ Martín era alto, moreno y atlético.   **4.** ____ Los niños tenían cinco años.

2. ____ Joaquín corría por las montañas.   **5.** ____ La casa era roja y vieja.

3. ____ Hacía mucho frío por la noche.   **6.** ____ La maestra enseñaba la lección.

B. Each statement below indicates what a situation was or how a person was when something happened. Based on the verbs in parentheses, write the correct imperfect verb form.

Modelo   (Llover) ___Llovía___ mucho cuando los atletas salieron del estadio.

1. (estar)   Nosotros _____ en el gimnasio para ver la ceremonia de entrega de premios.

2. (Hacer)   _____ mucho frío cuando caminé a la escuela.

3. (entrenarse) Carlos ____ _____ en el gimnasio cuando sus amigos llegaron.

4. (Ser)   _____ las nueve cuando empezó el concurso.

5. (tener)   Nacho _____ cinco años cuando empezó a jugar al fútbol.

6. (estar)   Las chicas _____ desanimadas porque perdieron el partido.

Realidades ③

Capítulo 1

Nombre _____

Hora _____

Fecha _____

Guided Practice Activities, Sheet 10

- As you have just learned, the imperfect is used to talk about habitual events and to give descriptions in the past. The preterite, in contrast, is used to talk about events that happened once, or events that happened at a specific time in the past. Look at the examples below:

I	Yo **me entrenaba** en el gimnasio todos los días.	*I trained in the gym every day (habitual).*
I	Yo **me entrené** en el gimnasio ayer.	*I trained in the gym yesterday (once).*
I	Yo **estaba** cansada porque eran las once de la noche.	*I was very tired (description) because it was 11pm (time in the past).*
P	Yo **fui** al gimnasio el martes pasado.	*I went to the gym last Tuesday (once).*

C. Look at the following statements and circle the verb. Write **H** if the action is habitual (imperfect) and **O** if the action occurred one time (preterite). Follow the model.

Modelo ___O___ Yo (corrí) en la carrera ayer.

1. ____ Nosotros vencimos al equipo de la escuela San Luis Obispo la semana pasada.

2. ____ El verano pasado yo participé en una carrera muy dura.

3. ____ Los estudiantes practicaban el vóleibol cada semana.

4. ____ Los atletas hacían un esfuerzo increíble todos los días.

D. In the following sentences, a group of students remembers events that happened once (preterite) and how they felt or were when things took place (imperfect). Complete each sentence with the correct preterite or imperfect verb form.

Modelo Federico ___estaba___ (**estar**) orgulloso porque su equipo de fúbol americano ___ganó___ (**ganar**) el campeonato.

1. Nosotros _____ (**perder**) el partido porque no _____ (**ser**) muy atléticos.

2. Los jugadores _____ _____ (**sentirse**) muy felices cuando _____ (**recibir**) el trofeo.

3. Todos los estudiantes _____ (**tener**) mucho frío porque el partido de fútbol _____ (**tener**) lugar en noviembre.

4. Martina _____ (**obtener**) un premio porque _____ (**tener**) mucho talento.

5. Yo _____ (**participar**) en un campeonato de básquetbol cuando _____ (**tener**) catorce años.

6. Nosotros _____ (**estar**) muy desanimados porque no _____ (**alcanzar**) nuestra meta.

realidades.com ✔

• Web Code: jed-0108

Realidades ③

Capítulo 1

Nombre _____

Fecha _____

Hora _____

Reading Activities, Sheet 1

Puente a la cultura *(pp. 48-49)*

A. The reading talks about **peregrinos**, or "pilgrims" who travel for days, even weeks to get to their destination. Imagine that, like the **peregrinos**, you had to plan a trip that would involve at least three days of traveling. Answer the questions below about such a journey.

1. What would you take with you to be prepared for your journey? _____

_____

2. Explain why you would bring each of the items above.

_____

_____

_____

3. How might you feel at the end of your journey? _____

_____

B. Read the following two passages from page 48 in your textbook. Look at the highlighted words and, using the sentence structure to guide you, decide whether the words are **personas** (people) or **lugares** (places). Mark your answer in the table below.

> *Hace más de mil años, en el extremo noroeste de España, se descubrió la **tumba** del **apóstol** Santiago, una figura fundamental de la religión católica.*
>
> *A lo largo de la **ruta** construyeron **iglesias** y **albergues** para recibir a los **peregrinos**.*

	personas	lugares
la tumba		
el apóstol		
la ruta		
las iglesias		
los albergues		
los peregrinos		

C. This article explains several possible reasons for visiting Santiago de Compostela. Put an **X** next to the reasons that are mentioned in the article.

1. _____ Puedes conocer a nuevas personas de todo el mundo.

2. _____ Puedes ver un sitio de importancia cultural e histórica.

3. _____ Puedes encontrar un buen trabajo allí.

4. _____ Puedes ver un lugar de importancia religiosa.

5. _____ Puedes comprar buena comida en los albergues.

realidades.com ✓
• Web Code: jed-0110

Realidades 3

Capítulo 1

Nombre _____

Fecha _____

Hora _____

Reading Activities, Sheet 2

Lectura (pp. 54–56)

A. Look at the title of the reading in your textbook. It contains two names in náhuatl (the language of the Aztecs). Based on this information, which subject do you think would best describe what the reading will be about?

a. modern Mexicans   b. the Mexican landscape   c. a Native Mexican legend

B. Now, look at the captions on page 55 of your textbook. Answer the questions below.

1. What do you think the words **príncipe** and **princesa** mean?

_____

2. What do you think is the relationship between the two people pictured?

_____

C. This story focuses on a powerful king who seeks a suitable husband for his daughter, the princess. Read the following excerpt from the story. Circle the words or phrases that describe the characteristics the king is looking for.

Muchos príncipes ricos y famosos venían de todas partes de la región tolteca para ganar el amor de la princesa, pero ella no se enamoraba de ninguno. El rey, que quería para su hija un esposo rico de buena posición en la sociedad tolteca, ya estaba impaciente. A veces le preguntaba a la princesa qué esperaba.

D. Now, read the excerpt that describes the different cultural backgorunds of the Chichimec prince and Toltec princess, who fall in love.

Los chichimecas no tenían una civilización tan espléndida como la de los toltecas. Vivían de la caza y la pesca en las montañas. Los toltecas pensaban que los chichimecas vivían como perros, y se reían de ellos.

Does the Chichimec prince fit the description of what the Toltec king is looking for? Why or why not?

_____

_____

Realidades **3**

Capítulo 1

Nombre _____

Fecha _____

Hora _____

Reading Activities, Sheet 3

E. The love that the prince and princess have for each other causes a series of events to take place. Put in order the following details of the story in your textbook.

_____ La princesa tolteca y el príncipe chichimeca se casan.

_____ La princesa tolteca y el príncipe chichimeca sólo comen hierbas y frutas.

_____ La princesa tolteca es expulsada de Teotihuacán.

_____ La princesa tolteca y el príncipe chichimeca se duermen para siempre.

_____ El príncipe chichimeca es expulsado de su tribu.

F. This reading, like many legends, ends with what happened to the protagonists of the tale. Read the excerpt below and answer the questions that follow.

> La princesa subió la montaña Iztaccíhuatl y el príncipe subió la montaña Popocatépetl. Cuando la princesa llegó a la cumbre (summit) de su montaña, se durmió y la nieve la cubrió (covered). El príncipe se puso de rodillas, mirando hacia la princesa y la nieve también lo cubrió.

1. Does this story have a happy or tragic ending? _____

2. How does this resemble fairy tales that you are used to? How is this story similar or different?

_____

_____

3. How does nature figure into the end of this tale? Is it a hostile environment or gentle? Explain.

_____

_____

_____

Realidades 3

Capítulo 2

Nombre _____

Hora _____

Fecha _____

AVSR, Sheet 1

Concordancia y comparación de adjetivos (p. 63)

Remember that, in Spanish, adjectives must agree in gender (masculine or feminine) and number (singular or plural) with the nouns they describe. Look at the following rules for types of adjectives:

- For most adjectives, the masculine form ends in **-o** and the feminine form ends in **-a.**

     *el hombre viej**o*** *la mujer viej**a***

- Adjectives that end in **-e** or in a consonant (such as **-s** or **-l**), as well as those that end in **-ista,** may be either masculine or feminine.

     *el palacio **real*** *la ciudad **real***

     *el hombre deport**ista*** *la mujer deport**ista***

- If the masculine form of an adjective ends in **-or,** add an **-a** at the end to make the feminine form.

     *el hijo trabajad**or*** *la hija trabajad**ora***

- Remember that if you have a group of both masculine and feminine nouns, you will use the plural, masculine form of the adjective.

     *el hombre y la mujer alt**os***

A. Circle the correct form of the adjective given, depending on the gender and number of what is being described.

Modelo Prefiero el cuadro ((moderno) / moderna).

1. El arte de Picasso es muy (**interesante** / **interesantes**).

2. Salvador Dalí fue un artista (**surrealista** / **surrealistas**).

3. La profesora de arte de nuestra escuela es muy (**trabajador** / **trabajadora**).

4. Las pinturas de Frida Kahlo son muy (**personal** / **personales**).

5. Los colores de ese dibujo son muy (**vivas** / **vivos**).

B. Complete each sentence with the correct form of the adjective in parentheses. Some adjectives will not require changes!

Modelo (sencillo) Las flores de esa pintura de Picasso son _____*sencillas*_____.

1. (realista) Esos cuadros de Frida Kahlo no son muy _____.

2. (divertido) El museo del Prado en Madrid es un lugar muy _____ para visitar.

3. (exagerado) Las figuras de Botero tienen unas características _____.

4. (oscuro) Los cuadros de Goya muchas veces son muy _____.

realidades.com
- Web Code: jed-0201

- To compare two things that are the same, use **tan** + *adjective* + **como**.

    Los cuadros de Picasso son **tan interesantes como** *los cuadros de Dalí.*

- To compare two things that are different, use **más / menos** + *adjective* + **que**.

    El retrato de Botero es **más cómico que** *el retrato de Velázquez.*

    Remember that the adjective must agree in gender and number with the noun it describes.

C. Use the signs provided to complete each of Juan's opinions using either **más...que**, **menos...que**, or **tan...como**. Then, circle the correct form of the adjective in parentheses based on the corresponding noun. Follow the model.

Modelo (+) Creo que el arte de Picasso es __más__ (interesantes / (interesante)) __que__ el arte de Velázquez.

1. (–) El color rosado es _____ (**vivo** / **viva**) _____ el color rojo.

2. (=) Creo que los museos son _____ (**divertido** / **divertidos**) _____ los cines.

3. (+) Ese mural de Diego Rivera es _____ (**grande** / **grandes**) _____ aquel retrato de Frida Kahlo.

4. (=) El pintor es _____ (**trabajador** / **trabajadora**) _____ la pintora.

5. (–) El papel y el plástico son _____ (**caros** / **caro**) _____ el oro y la plata.

- With the adjectives **bueno(a)**, **malo(a)**, **viejo(a)** and **joven**, you do not use the **más** or **menos** + *adjective* structure. Instead, use one of the following irregular comparative forms:

bueno(a)	**mejor (que)**	(*pl.* **mejores**)	*better (than)*
malo(a)	**peor (que)**	(*pl.* **peores**)	*worse (than)*
viejo(a)	**mayor (que)**	(*pl.* **mayores**)	*older (than)*
joven	**menor (que)**	(*pl.* **menores**)	*younger (than)*

D. Use the irregular comparative adjectives to create accurate comparisons.

Modelo Susana tiene 16 años y Martina tiene 18 años. Martina es __mayor__ que Susana.

1. Ana tiene 13 años y Luz tiene 17 años. Ana es _____ que Luz.

2. Pedro saca una "A" en la clase de inglés y Jorge saca una "C." La nota de Pedro es _____ que la nota de Jorge.

3. Paco tiene 16 años y su abuelo tiene 83. El abuelo es _____ que Paco.

4. Los cuadros de Carla no son muy buenos, pero los cuadros de Tomás son excelentes. Los cuadros de Carla son _____ que los cuadros de Tomás.

Realidades **3**

Capítulo 2

Nombre _____

Hora _____

Fecha _____

AVSR, Sheet 3

Comparación de sustantivos y el superlativo (p. 65)

- To make a comparison of quantity between two nouns that are equal in number, use **tanto (tanta/tantos/tantas)** + *noun* + **como**. Be sure to pay attention to gender and number agreement.

   *Hay **tantos** actores **como** actrices en la obra de teatro.*

- To make a comparison of quantity between two nouns that are not equal, use **más/menos** + *noun* + **que**.

   *Hay **más** actores **que** músicos en la obra de teatro.*

   *Hay **menos** personas en el teatro **que** anoche.*

A. Use **menos...que** or **más...que** to create logical sentences.

Modelo   Hay tres actores y dos actrices. Hay ___*más*___ actores ___*que*___ actrices.

1. Hay dos directores y diez actores. Hay _____ directores _____ actores.

2. Hay doce personas en el coro y veinte personas en la orquesta. Hay _____ personas en la orquesta _____ en el coro.

3. Este año se van a presentar veinticinco conciertos y diez obras de teatro en el Teatro Santiago. Se van a presentar _____ obras de teatro _____ conciertos.

4. La actriz principal tiene mucho talento pero los otros actores no tienen mucho talento. Ellos tienen _____ talento _____ la actriz principal.

5. En la ciudad hay cuatro cines y dos teatros. Hay _____ cines _____ teatros.

B. Use **tanto, tanta, tantos** or **tantas** to complete each sentence.

Modelo   Hay dos guitarras y dos pianos en la orquesta. Hay ___*tantas*___ guitarras como pianos.

1. La actriz principal tiene mucho talento y el actor principal tiene mucho talento. El actor tiene _____ talento como la actriz.

2. Se presentan dos obras dramáticas y dos obras musicales en el teatro este fin de semana. Se presentan _____ obras dramáticas como obras musicales.

3. Ayer asistieron doscientas personas a la obra y hoy asisten doscientas. Hoy hay _____ gente como ayer.

4. Hay diez músicos y diez bailarines en la obra. Hay _____ músicos como bailarines.

5. Hoy las entradas cuestan $15 y anoche las entradas costaron $15. Las entradas cuestan _____ dinero hoy como ayer.

50 *A ver si recuerdas* ━ 2-3

- Web Code: jed-0201

Comparación de sustantivos y el superlativo (*continued*)

- To say something is the "most" or the "least," you use a structure called the superlative. To form the superlative, use **el/la/los/las + noun + más/menos +** *adjective*.

  Celia Cruz es **la cantante más talentosa.**

  Creo que Roger Ebert es **el crítico más inteligente.**

- To compare one thing within a large group, use **de** + the group or category.

  Marta es la más alta **de** *todas las actrices.*

C. Complete the following superlatives with the missing elements. Follow the model.

Modelo (+) La clase de español es la ___*más*___ divertida de mi escuela.

1. Andrés es el más alto _____ mi clase de español.

2. (+) El domingo es el día _____ tranquilo de la semana.

3. (+) Mariana tiene la voz _____ bella del coro.

4. (–) Ésa es la escena _____ emocionante del drama.

5. Las hermanas Cruz son las músicas más talentosas _____ la escuela.

- Use the adjectives **mejor(es)** and **peor(es)** + noun to express *best* and *worst*.

  Plácido Domingo es **el mejor** *cantante.*

  Esos son **los peores** *efectos especiales.*

D. Read the description of the following theater, art, and music students. Use the context of the sentence to decide whether to use **mejor / mejores** or **peor / peores**. Complete the sentences with your choice.

Modelo Maricarmen tiene una voz muy bonita. Es la ___*mejor*___ cantante del coro.

1. Ramón no puede bailar muy bien. Es el _____ bailarín del grupo.

2. Sonia y Teresa actúan muy bien. Son las _____ actrices de su escuela.

3. El director de la obra es muy antipático y grita mucho. ¡Es el _____ director del mundo!

4. Nuestra orquesta toca perfectamente. Es la _____ orquesta de la ciudad.

5. Los argumentos de estas dos obras son muy aburridos. Son los _____ argumentos.

realidades.com
- Web Code: jed-0201

Realidades 3

Nombre _____   Hora _____

Capítulo 2

Fecha _____   **Vocabulary Flash Cards, Sheet 1**

Write the Spanish vocabulary word or phrase below each picture. Be sure to include the article for each noun.

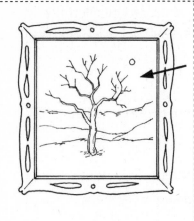
_____

_____

_____

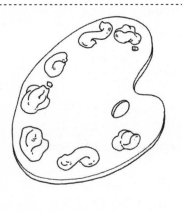
_____

_____

_____

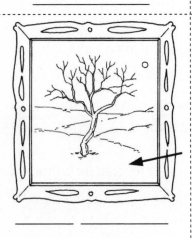
_____

_____

_____

52 *Guided Practice Activities* — *Vocabulary Flash Cards 2*

Realidades ③

Capítulo 2

Nombre _____

Fecha _____

Hora _____

Vocabulary Flash Cards, Sheet 2

Write the Spanish vocabulary word below each picture. If there is a word or phrase, copy it in the space provided. Be sure to include the article for each noun.

_____

_____

_____

_____
_____

_____

_____

_____
_____

a través de

_____
_____

abstracto, abstracta

_____
_____

Realidades 3

Capítulo 2

Nombre _____

Hora _____

Fecha _____

Vocabulary Flash Cards, Sheet 3

Copy the word or phrase in the space provided. Be sure to include the article for each noun.

expresar(se)	la figura	la fuente de inspiración
_____	___ _____	___ _____ ___ _____
influir	inspirar	representar
_____	_____	_____
el sentimiento	el siglo	volverse
___ _____	___ _____	_____

Realidades 3

Capítulo 2

Nombre _____

Fecha _____

Hora _____

Vocabulary Check, Sheet 1

Tear out this page. Write the English words on the lines. Fold the paper along the dotted line to see the correct answers so you can check your work.

abstracto, abstracta _____

a través de _____

el autorretrato _____

la cerámica _____

el escultor,
la escultora _____

la escultura _____

expresar(se) _____

famoso, famosa _____

la figura _____

el fondo _____

la fuente de
inspiración _____
_____

la imagen _____

influir (i➜y) _____

inspirar _____

mostrar(ue) _____

el mural _____

Fold In

Tear out this page. Write the Spanish words on the lines. Fold the paper along the dotted line to see the correct answers so you can check your work.

abstract _____

through _____

self-portrait _____

pottery _____

sculptor _____

_____

sculpture _____

to express (oneself) _____

famous _____

figure _____

background _____

source of inspiration _____

_____

image _____

to influence _____

to inspire _____

to show _____

mural _____

Fold In →

Realidades 3

Capítulo 2

Nombre _____

Hora _____

Fecha _____

Vocabulary Check, Sheet 3

Tear out this page. Write the English words on the lines. Fold the paper along the dotted line to see the correct answers so you can check your work.

la naturaleza muerta _____

la obra de arte _____

la paleta _____

parado, parada _____

el pincel _____

la pintura _____

el primer plano _____

representar _____

el retrato _____

sentado, sentada _____

el sentimiento _____

el siglo _____

el taller _____

el tema _____

volverse (ue) _____

Fold In →

Realidades 3

Capítulo 2

Nombre _____

Hora _____

Fecha _____

Vocabulary Check, Sheet 4

Tear out this page. Write the Spanish words on the lines. Fold the paper along the dotted line to see the correct answers so you can check your work.

still life _____

work of art _____

palette _____

standing _____

brush _____

painting _____

foreground _____

to represent _____

portrait _____

seated _____

feeling _____

century _____

workshop _____

subject _____

to become _____

Fold In ←

• Web Code: jed-0202

Realidades 3

Capítulo 2

Nombre _____

Fecha _____

Hora _____

Guided Practice Activities, Sheet 1

Pretérito vs. imperfecto (p. 76)

- Remember that you have learned two past tenses: the preterite and the imperfect. Look at the information below for a summary of when to use each tense:

Preterite

- actions that happened once or were completed in the past
- to relate a series of events that happened

Imperfect

- habitual or repeated actions in the past
- descriptions such as background information, physical appearance, emotions, time, date, age, and weather

When you have two verbs in one sentence, use the following rules:

- If two actions were going on simultaneously and did not interrupt each other, put both verbs in the imperfect:

  *Yo **leía** mientras mi hermana **pintaba**.*

- If one action that is in progress in the past is interrupted by another action, put the action in progress in the imperfect and the interrupting action in the preterite:

  *Los estudiantes **pintaban** cuando su maestro **salió** de la clase.*

A. Read each of the following statements about Picasso's life and career. Then decide if the statement is about something Picasso *used to do* or if it is something he *did once*. Place a checkmark in the box of your choice.

Modelo   Pablo Ruiz Picasso **nació** en Málaga el 25 de octubre de 1881.

　　　　□ used to do　　　　☑ did once

1. **Hizo** un viaje a París en 1900.

   □ used to do　　　　□ did once

2. **Pasaba** mucho tiempo con el artista André Breton y la escritora Gertrude Stein.

   □ used to do　　　　□ did once

3. **Hacía** cuadros monocromáticos.

   □ used to do　　　　□ did once

4. **Quería** expresar la violencia y la crueldad de la Guerra Civil Española.

   □ used to do　　　　□ did once

5. **Pintó** el cuadro *Guernica* para ilustrar los horrores de la guerra.

   □ used to do　　　　□ did once

B. Javier recently visited his friend Domingo's art studio. Read each part of the story and decide if it gives *description/background information* or if it tells *what happened* in the story. Circle your choice.

Modelo	Eran las tres y hacía buen tiempo.	**What happened**	⬭**Description**
1.	Llegué al taller de Domingo a las tres y media.	**What happened**	**Description**
2.	Llamé a la puerta, pero nadie contestó.	**What happened**	**Description**
3.	La puerta estaba abierta.	**What happened**	**Description**
4.	Entré en el taller.	**What happened**	**Description**
5.	Encontré a Domingo.	**What happened**	**Description**
6.	No tenía ganas de trabajar más.	**What happened**	**Description**

C. Choose the correct form of each verb to complete these sentences about an artist.

1. Cuando (**era / fui**) niña, me (**gustaba / gustó**) mucho el arte.

2. Siempre (**tomaba / tomé**) clases de arte y (**dibujaba / dibujé**) en mi tiempo libre.

3. La semana pasada, (**empezaba / empecé**) una pintura nueva.

4. Primero, (**pintaba / pinté**) el fondo con colores oscuros y después, (**incluía / incluí**) unas figuras de animales.

D. Complete the following sentences with the preterite or the imperfect form of the verb.

Modelo	___*Eran*___ (**ser**) las dos cuando la clase de arte ___*empezó*___ (**empezar**).

1. Los estudiantes ya _____ (**trabajar**) cuando su profesor _____ (**entrar**).

2. El profesor les _____ (**decir**), «Uds. son muy trabajadores».

3. Luego, el profesor _____ (**hacer**) una demostración de una técnica artística nueva.

4. Mientras los estudiantes _____ (**practicar**), el profesor _____ (**caminar**) por la clase para observar sus avances.

5. El profesor _____ (**estar**) contento porque sus estudiantes _____ (**aprender**) la técnica muy bien.

Estar + participio (p. 79)

• To form the past participle of **-ar** verbs, add **-ado** to the root of the verb. For **-er** and **-ir** verbs, add **-ido** to the root. See the examples below.

lav**ar** lav**ado** *(washed)*	com**er** com**ido** *(eaten)*	serv**ir** serv**ido** *(served)*

A. Write the past participle form for each verb. Follow the model.

Modelo   (crear) ___creado___

1. (inspirar) _____
2. (vestir) _____
3. (representar) _____
4. (vender) _____

5. (influir) _____
6. (pintar) _____
7. (tomar) _____
8. (mover) _____

• It is common to use the past participle with the verb **estar** to give descriptions. Remember that since the past participle is being used as an adjective in these cases, it must agree in gender and number with the noun it describes:

> *El pintor **está cansado**.*   ***Las** pintoras **están cansadas**.*

B. Read the following descriptions of famous paintings. Underline the noun in the sentence. Then, circle which form of the past participle best completes each sentence.

Modelo   Las dos <u>chicas</u> están (**sentada** /(**sentadas**)).

1. La ventana del fondo está (**cerrado** / **cerrada**).
2. El fondo está (**pintado** / **pintados**) con colores oscuros.
3. Dos gatos están (**dormidos** / **dormidas**) en el sofá.
4. La cena está (**preparada** / **preparado**).
5. La pintura está (**basado** / **basada**) en los sueños del artista.
6. El pintor está (**incluido** / **incluida**) en la pintura.
7. Unos temas importantes están (**representadas** / **representados**).

• Some verbs have irregular past participles. Look at the list below:

| poner: **puesto** | decir: **dicho** | hacer: **hecho** | escribir: **escrito** | ver: **visto** |
| abrir: **abierto** | morir: **muerto** | romper: **roto** | volver: **vuelto** | resolver: **resuelto** |

C. Read the following description of an artist's workshop. First, write the past participle of the verb in parentheses. Next, complete the sentences with the correct form of this past participle. Be careful to make its ending match the noun in the sentence in number and gender.

Modelo (poner:_*puesto*_) Cuando entré en el taller, las luces no estaban _*puestas*_ .

1. (abrir:_____) La ventana estaba _____ y hacía frío.

2. (romper:_____) Una pintura grande estaba _____ en el suelo.

3. (poner:_____) Los pinceles y la paleta estaban _____ en la mesa.

4. (escribir:_____) Unas notas para pinturas futuras estaban _____ en el cuaderno del artista.

5. (hacer:_____) Una escultura de un animal estaba _____ .

6. (morir:_____) Un ratón estaba _____ en el taller. ¡Qué horror!

D. The classroom was a mess when the students arrived Monday morning. Use the verbs in parentheses to write a sentence using **estar** + *past participle*. Follow the model.

Modelo Las ventanas _*estaban*_ _*abiertas*_ (**abrir**).

1. Unas palabras _____ _____ (**escribir**) en la pared.

2. Las paletas _____ _____ (**poner**) en el suelo.

3. Las botellas de agua de la maestra _____ _____ (**beber**).

4. La computadora _____ _____ (**romper**).

5. Los libros de texto _____ _____ (**perder**).

6. Unos insectos habían entrado por la ventana y _____ _____ (**morir**) en el suelo.

realidades.com
• Web Code: jed-0205

Write the Spanish vocabulary word or phrase below each picture. Be sure to include the article for each noun.

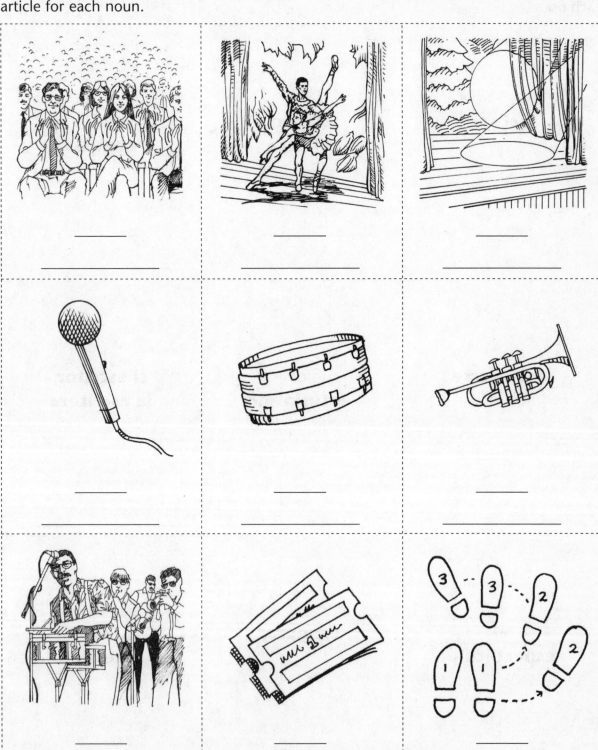

Realidades 3

Nombre _____

Hora _____

Capítulo 2

Fecha _____

Vocabulary Flash Cards, Sheet 5

Copy the word or phrase in the space provided. Be sure to include the article for each noun.

actuar	**clásico, clásica**	**el compás**
_____	_____	_____
destacarse	**el entusiasmo**	**el escritor, la escritora**
_____	_____	_____
el espectáculo	**exagerar**	**el gesto**
_____	_____	_____

Realidades 3

Capítulo 2

Nombre _____

Hora _____

Fecha _____

Vocabulary Flash Cards, Sheet 6

Copy the word or phrase in the space provided. Be sure to include the article for each noun.

identificarse con _____ _____	**interpretar** _____	**la interpretación** _____
la letra _____ _____	**la melodía** _____ _____	**pararse** _____
parecerse a _____ _____	**el poema** _____ _____	**el/la poeta** _____ _____

Copy the word or phrase in the space provided. Be sure to include the article for each noun. The blank cards can be used to write and practice other Spanish vocabulary for the chapter.

realizar	**la reseña**	**el ritmo**
_____	_____	_____
sonar a	**el tema**	
_____	_____	_____

Realidades 3

Capítulo 2

Nombre _____

Fecha _____

Hora _____

Vocabulary Check, Sheet 5

Tear out this page. Write the English words on the lines. Fold the paper along the dotted line to see the correct answers so you can check your work.

actuar _____

el aplauso _____

clásico, clásica _____

el compás _____

el conjunto _____

la danza _____

destacar(se) _____

la entrada _____

el entusiasmo _____

el escenario _____

el escritor,
la escritora _____

el espectáculo _____

exagerar _____

el gesto _____

identificarse con _____

Fold In

Tear out this page. Write the Spanish words on the lines. Fold the paper along the dotted line to see the correct answers so you can check your work.

to perform   _____

applause   _____

classical   _____

rhythm   _____

band   _____

dance   _____

to stand out   _____

ticket   _____

enthusiasm   _____

stage   _____

writer   _____

   _____

show   _____

to exaggerate   _____

gesture   _____

to identify oneself with   _____

Fold In ←

Tear out this page. Write the English words on the lines. Fold the paper along the dotted line to see the correct answers so you can check your work.

la interpretación _____

interpretar _____

la letra _____

la melodía _____

el micrófono _____

el movimiento _____

pararse _____

el paso _____

el/la poeta _____

realizar _____

la reseña _____

el ritmo _____

sonar(ue) (a) _____

el tambor _____

la trompeta _____

Fold In

Realidades 3

Capítulo 2

Nombre _____

Hora _____

Fecha _____

Vocabulary Check, Sheet 8

Tear out this page. Write the Spanish words on the lines. Fold the paper along the dotted line to see the correct answers so you can check your work.

interpretation _____

to interpret _____

lyrics _____

melody _____

microphone _____

movement _____

to stand up _____

step _____

poet _____

to perform, accomplish _____

review _____

rhythm _____

to sound (like) _____

drum _____

trumpet _____

Fold In

realidades.com
• Web Code: jed-0206

Realidades 3

Capítulo 2

Nombre _____

Hora _____

Fecha _____

Guided Practice Activities, Sheet 5

Ser y estar (p. 88)

- Remember that Spanish has two verbs that mean "to be": **ser** and **estar**. Look at the rules below to review the circumstances in which each verb should be used:

  Ser is used . . .
  - to describe permanent physical and personal characteristics
  - to describe nationality or origin
  - to describe someone's job or profession
  - to tell where and when an event will take place
  - to tell whom something belongs to

  Estar is used . . .
  - to describe temporary physical conditions or emotions
  - to give location
  - as part of the progressive tenses, such as *está escuchando* or *estaba escuchando*

A. Use **es** or **está** to describe the director of a show.

El director...

1. nació en Madrid. _____ español.

2. trabaja mucho todos los días. _____ muy serio.

3. cree que los actores están trabajando muy bien esta noche. _____ contento.

4. Tiene mucho dinero. _____ rico.

5. Lleva un traje elegante esta noche. _____ muy guapo.

6. _____ músico también.

B. Complete the paragraph with the appropriate present tense forms of **ser** or **estar**.

Nuestra escuela _____ preparando una presentación de la obra de teatro *Romeo y Julieta*. *Romeo y Julieta* _____ la historia de dos jóvenes que _____ enamorados, pero sus familias _____ enemigas. Marta Ramos _____ la actriz principal: interpreta el papel de Julieta. Marta _____ una chica muy talentosa que _____ de Puerto Rico. Ella _____ muy entusiasmada porque este viernes _____ la primera representación de la obra. _____ en el teatro de la escuela a las siete de la noche. Todos los actores _____ trabajando mucho esta semana para memorizar el guión. Los acontecimientos de las vidas de Romeo y Julieta _____ muy trágicos, pero la obra _____ magnífica.

• Web Code: jed-0207

Realidades ③

Capítulo 2

Nombre _____

Hora _____

Fecha _____

Guided Practice Activities, Sheet 6

Ser y estar (continued)

- Sometimes using **ser** or **estar** with the same adjective causes a change in meaning:

El café *es bueno*.	Coffee is good. (in general).
El café *está bueno*.	The coffee tastes good. (today).
El actor *es aburrido*.	The actor is boring. (in general)
El actor *está aburrido*.	The actor is bored. (today)
La directora *es bonita*.	The director is pretty. (in general)
La directora *está bonita*.	The director looks pretty. (today)
Los actores *son ricos*.	The actors are rich. (in general)
La comida *está rica*.	The food is tasty. (today)

C. Decide if the following statements refer to what the people in a show are like in general, or if they describe what they are like in today's show.

1. La cantante...

   a. es bonita.   **hoy**   **en general**

   b. está nerviosa.   **hoy**   **en general**

   c. es cómica.   **hoy**   **en general**

   d. es colombiana. **hoy**   **en general**

2. Los actores...

   a. están elegantes. **hoy**   **en general**

   b. son ricos.   **hoy**   **en general**

   c. están contentos. **hoy**   **en general**

   d. son talentosos. **hoy**   **en general**

D. You and a friend are commenting on a variety show. Read each statement and decide which response best states the situation. The first one has been done for you.

1. La actriz tiene un vestido especialmente bonito esta noche.

   a. Es guapa.   **b.** Está guapa.

2. Los músicos no tocan mucho y quieren irse.

   a. Son aburridos.   **b.** Están aburridos.

3. Esos hombres tienen mucho dinero y coches lujosos.

   a. Son ricos.   **b.** Están ricos.

4. Las cantantes se sienten bien porque cantaron muy bien la canción.

   a. Son orgullosos.   **b.** Están orgullosas.

5. El camarero nos preparó un café especialmente delicioso esta noche.

   a. El café es rico.   **b.** El café está rico.

realidades.com

- Web Code: jed-0207

Verbos con distinto sentido en el pretérito y en el imperfecto (p. 90)

- Some verbs have different meanings in the preterite and the imperfect. Look at the following chart to understand these changes in meaning:

Verbo	Imperfecto	Pretérito
saber	knew a fact or how to do something	found out
conocer	knew a person or place	met for the first time
querer	wanted to	tried to
no querer	didn't want to	refused to
poder	could, was able to	tried and succeeded in doing

A. Choose which idea is being expressed by the underlined verb in each sentence.

Modelo   Los estudiantes <u>conocieron</u> al actor famoso.
☑ met   ☐ knew

1. Jorge <u>quería</u> ser el galán de la obra de teatro.

   ☐ tried to   ☐ wanted to

2. Lupe <u>quiso</u> sacar fotos del espectáculo.

   ☐ tried to   ☐ wanted to

3. Yo <u>sabía</u> el título del poema.

   ☐ found out   ☐ knew

4. Mi mamá <u>supo</u> que nuestro vecino es artista.

   ☐ found out   ☐ knew

5. <u>No quería</u> aprender la melodía de esta canción aburrida.

   ☐ refused to   ☐ didn't want to

6. <u>No quise</u> entrar al teatro.

   ☐ refused to   ☐ didn't want to

7. <u>Pudimos</u> realizar el baile sin problemas.

   ☐ managed to, succeeded in   ☐ were able to, could

8. <u>Podíamos</u> identificarnos con el protagonista.

   ☐ managed to, succeeded in   ☐ were able to, could

• Web Code: jed-0209

B. Ana tells the story of how she finally got to meet a famous salsa singer. Complete the following sentences with the correct preterite or imperfect form of the verb in parentheses.

Modelo Yo _____*conocí*_____ (**conocer**) a Carlos, mi mejor amigo, hace dos años.

1. Hacía muchos años que Carlos _____ (**conocer**) a una cantante de salsa.

2. Yo _____ (**saber**) bailar salsa y me gustaba ir a los clubes de salsa.

3. Una noche Carlos y yo decidimos ir al club donde trabajaba la cantante pero luego yo _____ (**saber**) que tenía que trabajar y no pude ir.

4. Carlos _____ (**saber**) que yo quería conocer a su amiga y la invitó a mi casa al día siguiente.

5. Yo _____ (**conocer**) a la cantante y fue el día más fantástico de mi vida.

C. Complete the following sentences with the correct preterite or imperfect **yo** form of the verb in parentheses.

Modelo Yo _____*quise*_____ (**querer**) aprender los pasos de la salsa, pero no sé bailar bien y la clase fue un desastre.

1. Yo _____ (**querer**) leer en un café. Por eso le pregunté al dueño del café si era posible.

2. Yo _____ (**querer**) leer la poesía en el café, pero me puse nerviosa y no pude terminar el poema.

3. Julia no _____ (**querer**) salir con Pepe, pero salieron porque él es el mejor amigo de su novio.

4. Julia no_____ (**querer**) salir con Pepe y por eso él tuvo que ir solo al cine.

5. El director nos dijo que nosotros _____ (**poder**) participar en la obra de teatro.

6. Nosotros no teníamos mucho dinero, pero _____ (**poder**) comprar las entradas porque sólo costaban $5. Las compramos ayer.

Realidades **3**

Capítulo 2

Nombre

Fecha

Hora

Reading Activities, Sheet 1

Puente a la cultura (pp. 94–95)

A. Look at the paintings by Francisco de Goya on the pages surrounding the article. Check off all words on the following list that could be used to describe one or more of the works you see.

☐ realistas   ☐ abstractos

☐ retratos   ☐ surrealistas

☐ oscuros   ☐ monocromáticos

B. This reading contains many *cognates*, or Spanish words that look and sound like English words. Can you determine the meanings of the following words? Circle the option that you think represents the correct meaning.

1. la corte	**a.** curtain	**b.** court
2. los triunfos	**a.** triumphs	**b.** trumpets
3. la época	**a.** epoch, age	**b.** epicenter
4. las tropas	**a.** traps	**b.** troops
5. las imágenes	**a.** imaginations	**b.** images
6. los monstruos	**a.** monsters	**b.** monsoons

C. This reading talks about four important events in Goya's life and how each event affected the art he created. Match each event with the painting or type of paintings it led Goya to produce.

1. _____ Se enfermó

2. _____ Llegó a ser Pintor de la Cámara

3. _____ Hubo una guerra entre España y Francia

4. _____ Trabajó para la Real Fábrica de Tapices

a. *El 3 de mayo de 1808*

b. bocetos *(sketches)* de la vida diaria en Madrid

c. las "Pinturas negras"

d. retratos de los reyes y la familia real

Realidades 3

Capítulo 2

Nombre _____

Hora _____

Fecha _____

Reading Activities, Sheet 2

Lectura (pp. 100-103)

A. The reading in your book, *Cuando era puertorriqueña*, is an excerpt from an autobiography. From what you know of autobiographies, check off the items you might find in this reading.

☐ important events in one's life

☐ first person narration

☐ talking animals

☐ real-world settings

☐ analysis of scientific data

B. Read the following excerpt from the story. Based on what you read, write the letter of the teacher who would most likely discuss each topic below with his or her students.

> —Mister Gatti, el maestro de gramática, te dirigirá ... Y Missis Johnson te hablará acerca de lo que te debes de poner y esas cosas.

1. ____ la ropa

2. ____ la pronunciación

3. ____ la fonética

4. ____ el inglés

a. Mr. Gatti

b. Mrs. Johnson

C. The girl in the story, Esmeralda, has her first audition to get into the Performing Arts High School. Circle the best choice below to complete the statements about the events leading up to and including the audition.

1. Esmeralda quería salir muy bien en su audición porque (**quería salir de Brooklyn / quería ser una actriz famosa**).

2. Cuando Esmeralda se enfrentó con el jurado (**se le salió un inglés natural / se le olvidó el inglés**).

3. Antes de presentar su soliloquio, Esmeralda estaba (**tranquila / nerviosa**).

4. Cuando presentó su soliloquio, (**habló con mucha expresión / habló muy rápido**).

5. Las mujeres del jurado sabían que Esmeralda (**estaba nerviosa / tenía talento**).

D. Now, read the statements about the events following the audition, and circle whether they are true (**cierto**) or false (**falso**).

1. La mamá de Esmeralda fue con ella a la audición. **cierto** **falso**

2. Esmeralda tuvo la oportunidad de pronunciar su soliloquio una segunda vez. **cierto** **falso**

3. Bonnie y Esmeralda hicieron el papel de hermanas. **cierto** **falso**

4. En la segunda actuación, Esmeralda imaginó que estaba decorando un árbol de Navidad. **cierto** **falso**

5. Esmeralda no fue admitida a la Performing Arts High School. **cierto** **falso**

E. The end of this autobiography occurs years after the audition of Esmeralda, although it recalls the events as if they had just happened. Read the excerpt and answer the questions that follow.

> Me dijo que el jurado tuvo que pedirme que esperara afuera para poderse reír, ya que les parecía tan cómico ver a aquella chica puertorriqueña de catorce años chapurreando (babbling) un soliloquio acerca de una suegra posesiva durante el cambio de siglo, las palabras incomprensibles porque pasaban tan rápidas.

1. Why, does it turn out, that the jury panel asked Esmeralda to wait outside?

2. What did the jury find funny about Esmeralda?

Realidades 3

Capítulo 3

Nombre _____

Hora _____

Fecha _____

AVSR, Sheet 1

Pronombres de complemento directo (p. 109)

- In Spanish, as in English, direct objects describe who or what directly receives the action of a verb. Direct object pronouns are often used to avoid repeating words in conversation.

  ¿Comes frijoles todos los días?

  *Sí, **los** como todos los días.*

  The direct object pronouns in Spanish are:

me	nos
te	os
lo/la	los/las

- Direct object pronouns are usually placed in front of a conjugated verb.

  ¿Quieres el pan tostado?　　*Sí, **lo** quiero.*

- If a conjugated verb is followed by an infinitive or present participle, the direct object pronoun can also be attached to the end of the infinitive or participle.

  *Sí, **los** voy a comer.*　　*Sí, voy a comer**los**.*
  ***Lo** estoy comiendo.*　　*Estoy comiéndo**lo**.*

A. Everyone is doing different things before dinner. First, underline the direct object pronoun in each sentence. Then, match each statement with the food to which it refers.

1. _____ José María la quiere.

2. _____ La tía de Margarita está comiéndolas.

3. _____ Mis amigos los prueban.

4. _____ Luisa va a prepararlo.

a. el pan tostado

b. la carne de res

c. los espaguetis

d. las salchichas

B. Read the following sentences about who is making what for the family picnic. Underline the direct object in first sentence. Then, write the direct object pronoun that should replace it in the second sentence. Follow the model.

Modelo　Mi tía Anita prepara <u>la ensalada</u>. __*La*__ prepara.

1. Mi tía Donna trae las papas. _____ trae.

2. Mi tío Bill arregla el plato de frutas. _____ arregla.

3. Mi prima Laura prepara unos postres deliciosos. _____ prepara.

4. Mamá pone la mesa. _____ pone.

realidades.com

- Web Code: jed-0301

Realidades 3

Capítulo 3

Nombre _____

Fecha _____

Hora _____

AVSR, Sheet 2

C. You are helping a friend prepare for a dinner party. Respond to each of her questions using direct object pronouns. Remember that you will need to change the verbs to the **yo** form to answer the questions. Follow the model.

| Modelo | ¿Serviste la ensalada? | Sí, _la_ _serví_ . |

1. ¿Cortaste la sandía?   Sí, ____ _____.

2. ¿Probaste los camarones?   Sí, ____ _____.

3. ¿Compraste los dulces?   No, no ____ _____.

4. ¿Preparaste el postre?   No, no ____ _____.

5. ¿Cocinaste las galletas?   Sí, ____ _____.

D. Look at the picture of Pablo and his parents eating breakfast. Then, answer the questions below using **sí** or **no**. Write the correct direct object pronoun in your answer. Follow the model.

| Modelo | ¿Come Pablo yogur? | _Sí, lo come._ |

1. ¿Come salchichas?   _____

2. ¿Bebe leche?   _____

3. ¿Come cereal?   _____

4. ¿Comen tocino los padres de Pablo? _____

5. ¿Comen huevos?   _____

6. ¿Beben café?   _____

7. ¿Comen frutas?   _____

8. ¿Beben jugo de piña?   _____

Pronombres de complemento indirecto (p. 111)

- To indicate *to whom* or *for whom* an action is performed, you use indirect object pronouns in Spanish. The indirect object pronouns are:

me	nos
te	os
le	les

- Indirect object pronouns follow the same rules for placement as direct object pronouns. They usually go before a conjugated verb, but can also be attached to the end of an infinitive or a present participle.

    *María **me** prepara el desayuno.*

    *María **te** va a preparar el desayuno. / María va a prepara**rte** el desayuno.*

- To clarify who the indirect object pronoun refers to, you can add **a** + a noun or the corresponding subject pronoun.

    *El doctor **le** da las pastillas **a José**.*

    *La enfermera **les** pone una inyección **a ellas**.*

- Remember that one common use of the indirect object pronouns is with verbs like **gustar**, **encantar**, and **doler**.

A. Doctors and nurses do a lot of things for their patients. First, read the following statements and circle the direct object pronoun. Then, indicate for whom the action is done by choosing a letter from the box below.

> **a.** for me   **c.** for one other person
> **b.** for us   **d.** for a group of other people

Modelo El médico (me) receta la medicina. ___*a*___

1. A veces la enfermera les da regalos a los niños. _____

2. El doctor nos pone una inyección. _____

3. La enfermera le toma la temperatura al niño. _____

4. La doctora me examina. _____

5. Los doctores les dan recetas a sus pacientes. _____

6. La enfermera le toma una radiografía al paciente. _____

7. La doctora nos recomienda la comida buena. _____

realidades.com

- Web Code: jed-0301

Realidades 3

Capítulo 3

Nombre _____

Hora _____

Fecha _____

AVSR, Sheet 4

Pronombres de complemento indirecto (*continued*)

B. Write the correct indirect object pronouns to complete the sentences about what an assistant does for others in his office.

> **Modelo**   El asistente siempre _____*le*_____ prepara café al jefe.

1. El asistente _____ sirve café a nosotros también.

2. El asistente _____ manda (a mí) documentos por correo electrónico.

3. El asistente _____ trae fotocopias a los trabajadores.

4. ¿El asistente _____ prepara los materiales para la reunión (a ti)?

5. El asistente _____ dice la verdad a su jefe.

C. Help the school nurse understand what's wrong with each student. Using the information provided, write a sentence about each picture. Be sure to include an indirect object pronoun in each sentence.

> **Modelo**   (Ronaldo / doler / el brazo)
> *A Ronaldo le duele el brazo.*

1.   (Catrina / no gustar / medicina)

   _____

2.  (A mí / doler / la espalda)

   _____

3.   (Las chicas / doler / la cabeza)

   _____

4.   (Nosotros / doler / el estómago)

   _____

5.   (Enrique / no gustar / la inyección)

   _____

Nombre _____

Hora _____

Fecha _____

Write the Spanish vocabulary word or phrase below each picture. Be sure to include the article for each noun.

_____

_____

_____

_____

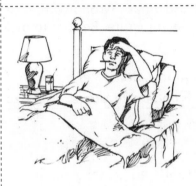

_____

_____

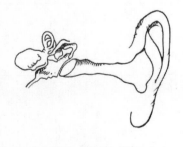

_____

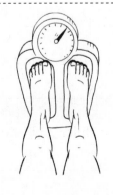

_____

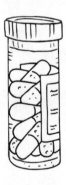

_____

Realidades 3

Capítulo 3

Nombre _____

Hora _____

Fecha _____

Vocabulary Flash Cards, Sheet 2

Write the Spanish vocabulary word below each picture. If there is a word or phrase, copy it in the space provided. Be sure to include the article for each noun.

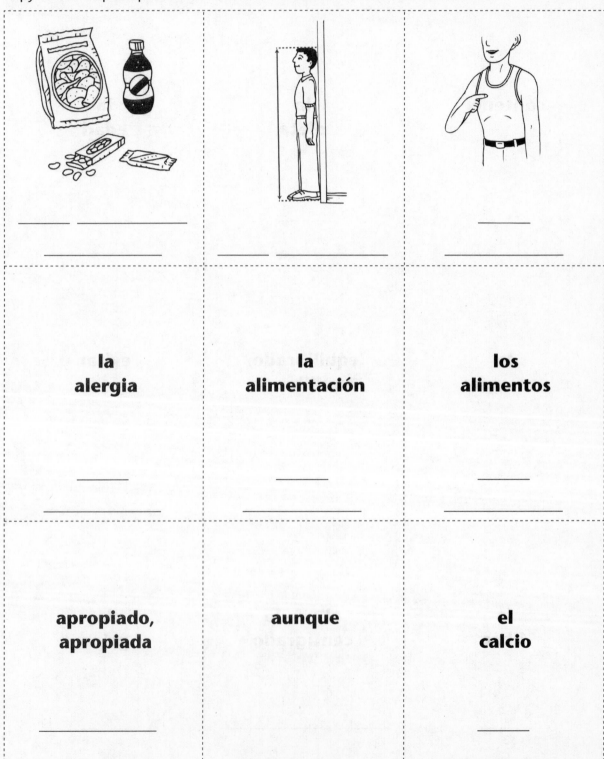

_____ _____	_____	_____
_____	_____	_____
la alergia	**la alimentación**	**los alimentos**
_____	_____	_____
apropiado, apropiada	**aunque**	**el calcio**
_____	_____	_____
_____	_____	_____

Realidades ③

Capítulo 3

Nombre _____

Hora _____

Fecha _____

Vocabulary Flash Cards, Sheet 3

Copy the word or phrase in the space provided. Be sure to include the article for each noun.

contener _____	**la dieta** _____ _____	**la edad** _____ _____
la energía _____ _____	**equilibrado, equilibrada** _____ _____	**evitar** _____
la fibra _____ _____	**el grado centígrado** ____ ____ _____	**la gripe** _____ _____

Realidades 3

Capítulo 3

Nombre _____

Fecha _____

Hora _____

Vocabulary Flash Cards, Sheet 4

Copy the word or phrase in the space provided. Be sure to include the article for each noun.

el hábito alimenticio	**el hierro**	**lleno, llena**
la merienda	**la proteína**	**nutritivo, nutritiva**
saltar (una comida)	**saludable**	**vacío, vacía**

Realidades 3

Nombre _____

Hora _____

Capítulo 3

Fecha _____

Vocabulary Flash Cards, Sheet 5

Copy the word or phrase in the space provided. Be sure to include the article for each noun. The blank cards can be used to write and practice other Spanish vocabulary for the chapter.

el carbohidrato	**tomar**	**la vitamina**
_____		_____
_____	_____	_____
_____	_____	_____
_____	_____	_____

Tear out this page. Write the English words on the lines. Fold the paper along the dotted line to see the correct answers so you can check your work.

la alergia _____

el antibiótico _____

los alimentos _____

apropiado, apropiada _____

aunque _____

el calcio _____

la comida basura _____

contener _____

la dieta _____

la edad _____

la energía _____

equilibrado, equilibrada _____

estar resfriado, resfriada _____

la estatura _____

estornudar _____

evitar _____

la fiebre _____

la fibra _____

Fold In

Tear out this page. Write the Spanish words on the lines. Fold the paper along the dotted line to see the correct answers so you can check your work.

allergy _____

antibiotic _____

food _____

appropriate _____

_____

despite, even when _____

calcium _____

junk food _____

to contain _____

diet _____

age _____

energy _____

balanced _____

_____

to have a cold _____

height _____

to sneeze _____

to avoid _____

fever _____

fiber _____

Fold In ←

Tear out this page. Write the English words on the lines. Fold the paper along the dotted line to see the correct answers so you can check your work.

el grado centígrado _____

la gripe _____

el hábito alimenticio _____

el hierro _____

el jarabe _____

lleno, llena _____

la manera _____

la merienda _____

el nivel _____

nutritivo, nutritiva _____

el oído _____

el pecho _____

la proteína _____

saltar (una comida) _____

saludable _____

tomar _____

la tos _____

vacío, vacía _____

Fold In

Tear out this page. Write the Spanish words on the lines. Fold the paper along the dotted line to see the correct answers so you can check your work.

centigrade degree   _____

flu   _____

eating habit   _____

iron   _____

syrup   _____

full   _____

way   _____

snack   _____

level   _____

nutritious   _____

_____

ear   _____

chest   _____

protein   _____

to skip (a meal)   _____

healthy   _____

to take, to drink   _____

cough   _____

empty   _____

Fold In

realidades.com

• Web Code: jed-0302

Mandatos afirmativos con *tú* (p. 121)

• Affirmative **tú** commands are informal commands telling one person to do something. To form them, you use the present indicative **él/ella/Ud.** form of the verb. Note that this also applies to stem-changing verbs.

Toma vitaminas.	*Take vitamins*
Pide una ensalada.	*Order a salad.*

A. Decide if each of the following statements is an observation the doctor has made about what you normally do, or if it is something the doctor is telling you to do (command).

Modelo	Caminas en el parque.	✔ observación	☐ orden del médico
1.	Practica deportes.	☐ observación	☐ orden del médico
2.	Descansas después de clases.	☐ observación	☐ orden del médico
3.	Levanta pesas.	☐ observación	☐ orden del médico
4.	Saltas el desayuno.	☐ observación	☐ orden del médico
5.	Bebe leche.	☐ observación	☐ orden del médico

B. Write the affirmative **tú** commands of the verbs in parentheses.

Modelo   ___*Duerme*___ (Dormir)

1. _____ (Desayunar)   **4.** _____ (Beber)

2. _____ (Comer)   **5.** _____ (Pedir)

3. _____ (Evitar)   **6.** _____ (Comprar)

• Some verbs have irregular affirmative **tú** command forms. Look at the list below.

hacer: **haz**	tener: **ten**	salir: **sal**	venir: **ven**	decir: **di**
ir: **ve**	ser: **sé**	poner: **pon**	mantener: **mantén**	

C. Change the sentences to affirmative **tú** commands to give a friend health advice.

Modelo   Necesitas hacer ejercicio. ___*Haz*___ ejercicio.

1. Necesitas salir a correr. _____ a correr.

2. Necesitas ser atlético. _____ atlético.

3. Necesitas ir al gimnasio tres veces por semana. _____ al gimnasio.

4. Necesitas venir al parque conmigo para jugar fútbol. _____ al parque conmigo.

5. Necesitas mantener una buena salud. _____ una buena salud.

• Web Code: jed-0303

Mandatos afirmativos con *tú* (*continued*)

- With affirmative commands, any reflexive, direct object, or indirect object pronouns are attached to the end of the verb.

    Cóme*lo*.   *Eat it.*

    Láva*te* las manos.   *Wash your hands.*

- When you attach a pronoun to a verb with two or more syllables, you will need to add a written accent mark to maintain the stress. The accent mark will usually go on the third-to-last vowel of the command.

D. Give the students advice to encourage better eating habits. Write the command form of the verb with the appropriate direct object pronoun for the underlined noun. Don't forget to add the accent mark to the stressed syllable.

Modelo   Ana no come <u>las verduras</u>. ___*Cómelas.*___

1. José no bebe <u>leche</u>. _____

2. Andrés no toma <u>las vitaminas</u>. _____

3. Luci no compra <u>el jugo de naranja</u>. _____

4. Beatriz no evita <u>la comida basura</u>. _____

E. Write the command form of the verb with the reflexive pronoun to give your brother advice about his daily routine. Don't forget to add the accent mark to the stressed syllable as needed.

Modelo   (cepillarse) ___*Cepíllate*___ los dientes dos veces al día.

1. (lavarse)   _____ las manos antes de comer.

2. (despertarse)   _____ temprano por la mañana.

3. (acostarse)   _____ antes de las nueve de la noche.

4. (ducharse)   _____ todos los días.

5. (ponerse)   _____ un sombrero y una chaqueta cuando hace frío.

6. (cortarse)   _____ las uñas una vez por semana.

realidades.com ⓥ
- Web Code: jed-0303

Mandatos negativos con *tú* (p. 122)

- Negative **tú** commands, used to informally tell one person not to do something, are formed differently from affirmative **tú** commands. Use the following rules to form negative **tú** commands:

  1) Put the verb in the **yo** form of the present tense.

  2) Get rid of the **-o** at the end of the verb.

  3) For **-ar** verbs, add the ending **-es**.

  For **-er** and **-ir** verbs, add the ending **-as**.

  caminar: *no camines*   beber: *no bebas*   escribir: *no escribas*

- Following these rules, verbs that have irregular **yo** forms or stem changes in the present tense will have the same stem changes in the negative **tú** commands.

  poner: no pon**gas**   obedecer: no obede**zcas**
  servir: no s**i**rv**as**   contar: c**ue**nt**es**

A. Decide if each of the following statements is an observation the doctor has made about what you normally do, or if it is a suggestion about what you shouldn't do. Check off your choice.

1. No comes frutas.   □ observación   □ orden del médico

2. No comas comida basura.   □ observación   □ orden del médico

3. No descansas mucho.   □ observación   □ orden del médico

4. No tienes energía.   □ observación   □ orden del médico

5. No saltes comidas.   □ observación   □ orden del médico

B. Some students have confessed their bad habits. Tell them not to do it anymore! Be careful to use the correct ending: **-as** or **-es**.

Modelo   Como muchos dulces. _*No*_ _____*comas*_____ muchos dulces.

1. Bebo refrescos con mucho azúcar. _____ _____ esos refrescos.

2. Tomo mucho café todos los días. _____ _____ tanto café.

3. Pido comida basura en los restaurantes. _____ _____ esa comida.

4. Cocino muchas comidas fritas. _____ _____ tantas comidas fritas.

C. José is a student with study habits that need to change. Complete his part with the present tense **yo** form. Then, complete his friend's advice with a negative **tú** command, using the same verb. Follow the model.

Modelo (hacer) —Siempre ___*hago*___ las tareas después de medianoche.

—José, no ___*hagas*___ las tareas tan tarde en la noche.

1. (poner) —Siempre _____ mi tarea debajo de la cama.

—José, no _____ la tarea allí.

2. (escoger) —Siempre _____ las clases más fáciles.

—José, no _____ sólo las clases fáciles.

3. (salir) —Siempre _____ temprano de mis clases.

—José, no _____ temprano de tus clases.

4. (destruir) —Siempre _____ mis exámenes cuando saco malas notas.

—José, no _____ los exámenes. Estúdialos para entender tus errores.

- When including a direct object, indirect object, or reflexive pronoun with a negative command, the pronoun must be placed *in front of* the verb.

  *No **te** acuestes muy tarde.*

  *No comas mucha grasa. No **la** comas.*

D. Rewrite the following commands using direct object pronouns. Follow the model.

Modelo No comas muchos dulces. *No los comas*.

1. No compres esas comidas. _____   **3.** No tomes tanto café. _____

2. No bebas esos refrescos. _____   **4.** No pidas esa comida. _____

- Some verbs have irregular negative **tú** command forms. Look at the list below.

dar: **no des**	ir: **no vayas**	estar: **no estés**	ser: **no seas**	saber: **no sepas**

E. Write the correct negative **tú** command for each sentence to help a mother give commands to her teenage daughter.

Modelo (ir) No ___*vayas*___ a lugares desconocidos sin otra persona.

1. (dar) No le _____ tu número de teléfono a nadie.

2. (ser) No _____ irresponsable.

3. (estar) No _____ enojada conmigo.

4. (ir) No _____ a las fiestas de la universidad.

realidades.com
- Web Code: jed-0304

Mandatos afirmativos y negativos con *Ud.* y *Uds.* (p. 123)

- To give formal commands to one person, you need to use an **Ud.** command. To give commands to a group of people, you need to use an **Uds.** command. Both types of commands are formed in a similar manner to the negative **tú** commands.
- To make an **Ud.** command, remove the final **-s** from the negative **tú** command.

    Estudi**e** (Ud.)   No estudi**e** (Ud.)

- To make an **Uds.** command, replace the **-s** of the negative **tú** command with an **-n.**

    Estudi**en** (Uds.)   No estudi**en** (Uds.)

- As you can see from the examples above, the negative commands have the same verb forms as the affirmative commands. The only difference is that they are preceded by the word *no.*

A. Write the correct endings for commands that students and Sra. Méndez, their teacher, give each other. Pay attention to whether you are writing an **Ud.** or an **Uds.** command.

> **Modelo**   (**hablar**) Sra. Méndez, habl_e____ (Ud.) más despacio, por favor.

1. (**tomar**)   Estudiantes, tom_____ (Uds.) apuntes, por favor.

2. (**repetir**)   Sra. Méndez, repit_____ (Ud.) la frase otra vez, por favor.

3. (**escribir**) Sra. Méndez, escrib_____ (Ud.) las palabras nuevas en la pizarra, por favor.

4. (**hacer**)   Estudiantes, no hag_____ (Uds.) tanto ruido, por favor.

5. (**decir**)   Sra. Méndez, no dig_____ (Ud.) que hay más tarea, por favor.

- Verbs that end in **-car, -gar,** and **-zar** have spelling changes in the **Ud.** and **Uds.** commands. See the examples below.

    Bus**que** (Ud.)   No bus**quen** (Uds.)

    Jue**gue** (Ud.)   No jue**guen** (Uds.)

    No almuer**ce** (Ud.)   Almuer**cen** (Uds.)

B. Write the correct **Ud.** command form for each verb below. Pay attention to verb endings to determine the spelling change. Follow the model.

> **Modelo**   (Practicar) ___*Practique*___ la pronunciación con frecuencia.

1. (**llegar**)   No _____ tarde a la clase.

2. (**Empezar**) _____ a escribir ahora.

3. (**Cruzar**)   _____ la calle aquí.

4. (**sacar**)   No _____ la comida en este momento.

5. (**tocar**)   No _____ la mesa sucia.

Realidades 3

Nombre _____

Hora _____

Capítulo 3

Fecha _____

Guided Practice Activities, Sheet 6

- The same verbs that are irregular in the negative **tú** commands are also irregular in the **Ud.** and **Uds.** commands. See the list below for a reminder.

dar: **dé/den**   ir: **vaya/vayan**   ser: **sea/sean**   estar: **esté/estén**   saber: **sepa/sepan**

C. Provide the correct **Uds.** commands for a group of student athletes.

Modelo   (Ser) _____ *Sean* _____ honrados y trabajadores.

1. **(Ir)** _____ al gimnasio a levantar pesas.

2. **(dar)**   No le _____ la pelota a un jugador del otro equipo.

3. **(Saber)** _____ el horario de partidos.

4. **(ser)**   No _____ descorteses con el otro equipo.

- The rules for placement of direct object, indirect object, and reflexive pronouns for **Ud.** and **Uds.** commands are the same as those for the **tú** commands.
- Pronouns are attached to affirmative commands.

    Tome (Ud.) vitaminas. Tómelas.

    Levántense (Uds.) temprano.

- Pronouns go in front of negative commands.

    No se acueste (Ud.) tarde.

    No coman (Uds.) muchas hamburguesas. No las coman.

- Remember that with reflexive verbs the pronoun will be *se* for both **Ud.** and **Uds.** commands.

D. Provide the **Ud.** commands that Paco gives his father during the day. A "+" indicates you should write an affirmative command; a "–" indicates a negative command. Don't forget the reflexive pronoun!

Modelo   (+ levantarse) _____ *Levántese* _____ ahora.

1.   (– afeitarse)   ____ ____ _____ hoy.

2.   (+ ducharse)   _____ ahora.

3.   (– lavarse)   ____ ____ _____ el pelo con el champú de su mamá.

4.   (+ cepillarse)   _____ los dientes.

5.   (+ ponerse)   _____ ese traje gris.

6.   (– irse)   ____ ____ _____ ahora.

realidades.com

• Web Code: jed-0305

Write the Spanish vocabulary word or phrase below each picture. Be sure to include the article for each noun.

Write the Spanish vocabulary word below each picture. If there is a word or phrase, copy it in the space provided. Be sure to include the article for each noun.

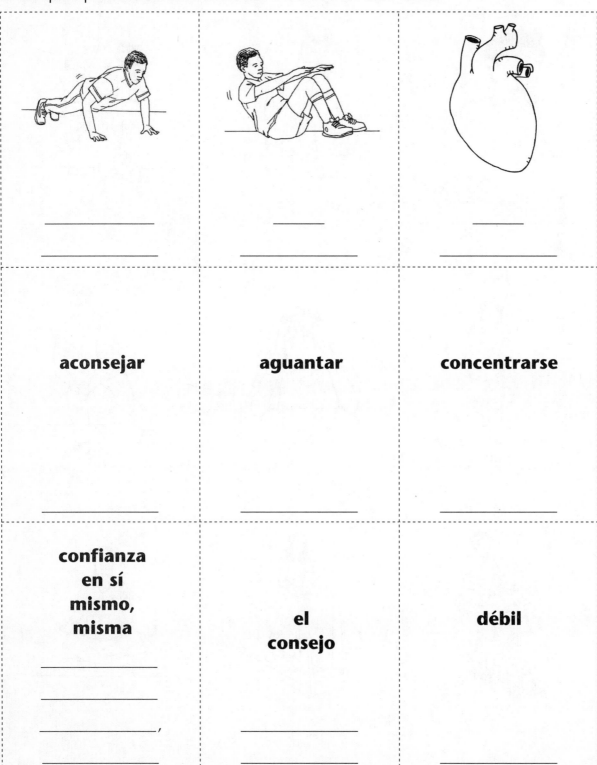

aconsejar

aguantar

concentrarse

confianza en sí mismo, misma

el consejo

débil

Realidades 3

Capítulo 3

Nombre _____

Hora _____

Fecha _____

Vocabulary Flash Cards, Sheet 8

Copy the word or phrase in the space provided. Be sure to include the article for each noun.

desarrollar _____	**estar de buen/mal humor** _____ _____ _____ _____	**el estrés** _____
exigir _____	**fuerte** _____	**la fuerza** _____ _____
incluir _____	**la manera** _____ _____	**el nivel** _____ _____

Realidades 3

Nombre _____

Hora _____

Capítulo 3

Fecha _____

Vocabulary Flash Cards, Sheet 9

Copy the word or phrase in the space provided. Be sure to include the article for each noun. The blank cards can be used to write and practice other Spanish vocabulary for the chapter.

preocuparse	**quejarse**	**relajarse**
_____	_____	_____
respirar	**sentirse fatal**	
_____	_____	_____
_____	_____	_____

Realidades 3

Capítulo 3

Nombre _____

Hora _____

Fecha _____

Vocabulary Check, Sheet 5

Tear out this page. Write the English words on the lines. Fold the paper along the dotted line to see the correct answers so you can check your work.

abdominales _____

aconsejar _____

aguantar _____

caerse de sueño _____

el calambre _____

el consejo _____

concentrarse _____

confianza en sí mismo(a) _____

el corazón _____

débil _____

desarrollar _____

ejercicios aeróbicos _____

estar de buen/
mal humor _____

estar en forma _____

estirar _____

© Pearson Education, Inc. All rights reserved.

Fold In

Guided Practice Activities — *Vocabulary Check 3* **101**

Realidades 3

Capítulo 3

Nombre _____

Fecha _____

Hora _____

Vocabulary Check, Sheet 6

Tear out this page. Write the Spanish words on the lines. Fold the paper along the dotted line to see the correct answers so you can check your work.

crunches _____

to advise _____

to endure; to tolerate _____

to be exhausted, sleepy _____

cramp _____

advice _____

to concentrate _____

self-confidence _____

heart _____

weak _____

to develop _____

aerobics _____

to be in a good/
bad mood _____

_____

to be fit _____

to stretch _____

Fold In ←

Tear out this page. Write the English words on the lines. Fold the paper along the dotted line to see the correct answers so you can check your work.

el estrés _____

estresado, estresada _____

exigir _____

flexionar _____

la fuerza _____

hacer bicicleta _____

hacer cinta _____

hacer flexiones _____

el músculo _____

preocuparse _____

quejarse _____

relajar(se) _____

respirar _____

sentirse fatal _____

el yoga _____

Fold In

Tear out this page. Write the Spanish words on the lines. Fold the paper along the dotted line to see the correct answers so you can check your work.

stress _____

stressed out _____

_____

to demand _____

to flex, to stretch _____

strength _____

to use a stationary bike _____

to use a treadmill _____

to do push-ups _____

muscle _____

to worry _____

to complain _____

to relax _____

to breathe _____

to feel awful _____

yoga _____

Fold In

realidades.com

• Web Code: jed-0306

Realidades 3

Capítulo 3

Nombre _____

Fecha _____

Hora _____

Guided Practice Activities, Sheet 7

El subjuntivo: Verbos regulares (p. 132)

- When someone gives advice, recommendations, suggestions, or demands to another person, Spanish uses the *subjunctive mood.*

- A sentence that includes the subjunctive can be thought of as having two separate halves, which are connected by the word **que**.

  Yo recomiendo que tú *hagas* ejercicio.   *I recommend that you exercise.*

- Notice that the first half (**Yo recomiendo**) includes a verb in the regular present tense and introduces a suggestion, demand, etc. The second half (**tú hagas ejercicio**) includes a verb in the subjunctive and tells what the first person wants the second person to do.

- Verbs in the subjunctive form may look somewhat familiar to you because they follow the same conjugation rules as the **Ud./Uds.** commands. To form verbs in the subjunctive, follow the rules below:

    1) Put the verb in the **yo** form of the present indicative (regular present tense).

    2) Take off the **-o**.

    3) a. For **-ar** verbs, add the following endings: **-e, -es, -e, -emos, -éis, -en**
       b. For **-er** and **-ir** verbs, add the following endings: **-a, -as, -a, -amos, -áis, -an**

- Below are three examples of verbs conjugated in the present subjunctive.

entrenar		correr		tener	
entrene	entrenemos	corra	corramos	tenga	tengamos
entrenes	entrenéis	corras	corráis	tengas	tengáis
entrene	entrenen	corra	corran	tenga	tengan

A. Underline the verbs in the present subjunctive in the following sentences.

Modelo Mis padres recomiendan que yo <u>haga</u> mi tarea.

1. El doctor quiere que los pacientes coman bien.

2. Los profesores exigen que los estudiantes estudien.

3. Yo no permito que tú fumes.

4. Tú prefieres que nosotros tomemos clases de yoga.

5. A nosotros no nos gusta que nuestro padre salte comidas.

6. Recomiendo que nosotros evitemos la comida basura.

Realidades 3

Capítulo 3

Nombre _____

Fecha _____

Hora _____

Guided Practice Activities, Sheet 8

B. Oprah Winfrey is known for her dedication to health and fitness. First, identify if each of the following activities is a custom (**C**) or a recommendation (**R**) of Oprah. Then, choose the correct verb to complete the sentence.

> **Modelo** __R__ Oprah le aconseja a la chica que (**hace** /(**haga**)) cinta.

1. _____ Oprah siempre (**se estira / se estire**) antes de correr.

2. _____ Oprah quiere que los jóvenes (**evitan / eviten**) la comida basura.

3. _____ Oprah recomienda que nosotros (**nos relajamos / nos relajemos**) un poco.

4. _____ Oprah (**come / coma**) alimentos nutritivos cada día.

- You can also use impersonal expressions to give recommendations, suggestions, and demands. These impersonal expressions are followed by **que** and then the subjunctive. Some common expressions are:

  Es importante...   Es necesario...   Es bueno...   Es mejor...

  Es importante que *los atletas* **cuiden** *su corazón.*

C. In each sentence, circle the impersonal expression that indicates a suggestion for healthy living. Then, use the correct present subjunctive form to complete the sentence.

> **Modelo** (Es necesario) que yo _____ *tome* _____ (**tomar**) 8 vasos de agua al día.

1. Es mejor que Miguel _____ (**eliminar**) el estrés.

2. Es importante que Eva y Adán _____ (**comer**) frutas y verduras.

3. Es necesario que Gabriela _____ (**hacer**) ejercicio.

4. Es bueno que los niños _____ (**incluir**) carbohidratos en su dieta.

D. Complete the sentences about a coach's recommendations for his athletes by conjugating the verbs correctly. Remember that your first verb will be in the indicative and your second verb will be in the subjunctive. Follow the model.

> **Modelo** el entrenador / recomendar / que / nosotros / practicar todos los días
> *El entrenador recomienda que nosotros practiquemos todos los días.*

1. es importante / que / nosotros / entregar nuestra tarea

   _____

2. el entrenador / no permitir / que / nosotros / llegar tarde al partido

   _____

3. es bueno / que / nosotros / traer nuestros uniformes / a la escuela

   _____

4. el entrenador / exigir / que / nosotros / tener una buena actitud

   _____

realidades.com
- Web Code: jed-0307

El subjuntivo: Verbos irregulares (p. 135)

- There are six irregular verbs in the present subjunctive. See the chart below for the conjugations of these verbs.

ser	sea, seas, sea, seamos, seáis, sean
estar	esté, estés, esté, estemos, estéis, estén
dar	dé, des, dé, demos, deis, den
ir	vaya, vayas, vaya, vayamos, vayáis, vayan
saber	sepa, sepas, sepa, sepamos, sepáis, sepan
haber	haya, hayas, haya, hayamos, hayáis, hayan

A. Choose the correct form of the subjunctive verb to complete each of the following sentences about healthy living. Circle your choice.

Modelo Te sugiero que tú no ((estés) / estén) tan estresado.

1. Es importante que nosotros (**mantengas / mantengamos**) una buena salud.

2. Quiero que ellos (**vayamos / vayan**) a la práctica de fútbol.

3. El doctor me recomienda que (**sepa / sepas**) tomar buenas decisiones.

4. Es muy bueno que (**haya / hayas**) una clase de yoga este viernes.

5. Los enfermeros no permiten que nosotras (**sean / seamos**) perezosas.

B. A group of students discusses the emphasis on health in their community. Complete the sentences with the correct present subjunctive form.

Modelo (saber) Es importante que nosotros _____sepamos_____ más sobre la buena salud.

1. (estar) Todos recomiendan que nosotros _____ en forma.

2. (dar) Si no te gusta correr, es importante que (tú) _____ un paseo por el parque.

3. (ser) Los padres no deben permitir que sus hijos _____ perezosos.

4. (haber) Es bueno que _____ dos parques en nuestra ciudad.

5. (saber) Los líderes de la ciudad quieren que los jóvenes _____ llevar una vida sana.

6. (estar) Nos gusta que la piscina _____ abierta hasta las diez durante el verano.

El subjuntivo: Verbos irregulares (*continued*)

C. Look at the list of recommendations given by a director of a health club. First, underline the verb that best completes the sentence. Then, write the correct form of the verb using the subjunctive mood. Follow the model.

Modelo   Los doctores prefieren que los jóvenes (<u>ser</u> / saber) _____*sean*_____ activos.

1. Quiero que la gente (**dar / estar**) _____ relajada.

2. Les recomiendo que Uds. (**ir / saber**) _____ al club atlético.

3. Exijo que todos nosotros (**estar / ir**) _____ al gimnasio juntos.

4. Es necesario que (**haber / dar**) _____ clubes atléticos disponibles.

5. Es importante que nosotros (**haber / saber**) _____ algo sobre el cuerpo humano.

D. Complete the following statements about exercise and healthy living.

Modelo   Mis padres / exigir / que / todos nosotros / dar una caminata / en las montañas

   Mis padres exigen que todos nosotros demos una caminata en

   las montañas.

1. Yo / recomendar / que / mis amigos / ser / activos

   _____

2. Es necesario / que / la gente / saber / dónde está el gimnasio

   _____

3. Es bueno / que / haber / clases de ejercicios aérobicos / en nuestra escuela

   _____

4. El entrenador / sugerir / que / yo / ir / al lago para nadar

   _____

• Web Code: jed-0308

Realidades 3

Capítulo 3

Nombre _____

Fecha _____

Hora _____

Guided Practice Activities, Sheet 11

El subjuntivo: verbos con cambio de raíz (p. 137)

- Stem-changing verbs follow slightly different rules than other verbs in the subjunctive. Verbs ending in **-ar** and **-er** have stem changes in all forms except the **nosotros** and **vosotros** forms.

cont**ar**		perd**er**	
cuente	contemos	**pie**rda	perdamos
cuentes	contéis	**pie**rdas	perdáis
cuente	**cue**nten	**pie**rda	**pie**rdan

- The **-ir** stem-changing verbs have stem changes in *all* forms of the subjunctive, but the stem change for the **nosotros** and **vosotros** forms differs slightly.

- If the **-ir** verb has an **o→ue** stem change, such as **dormir**, the **o** will change to a **u** in the **nosotros** and **vosotros** forms. If the **-ir** verb has an **e→ie** stem change, such as **preferir**, the **e** will change to an **i** in the **nosotros** and **vosotros** forms. If the verb has an **e→i** stem change, such as **servir**, it has the same stem change in all forms. Look at the examples below.

dorm**ir**		prefer**ir**		serv**ir**	
d**ue**rma	d**u**rmamos	pref**ie**ra	pref**i**ramos	s**i**rva	s**i**rvamos
d**ue**rmas	d**u**rmáis	pref**ie**ras	pref**i**ráis	s**i**rvas	s**i**rváis
d**ue**rma	d**ue**rman	pref**ie**ra	pref**ie**ran	s**i**rva	s**i**rvan

A. Circle the correct verb form to complete each sentence. Pay attention to whether the statement is trying to persuade someone to do something (subjunctive) or if it is just an observation about someone's lifestyle (indicative).

Modelo   Siempre ((vuelves)/ **vuelvas**) a casa tarde.

1. Te enojas cuando (**pierdes** / **pierdas**) partidos.

2. Es importante que (**te diviertes** / **te diviertas**) cuando practicas deportes.

3. Siempre (**empiezas** / **empieces**) tu tarea muy tarde.

4. Exijo que (**comienzas** / **comiences**) a hacer la tarea más temprano.

5. Con frecuencia (**te despiertas** / **te despiertes**) tarde para tus clases.

6. Es mejor que (**te acuestas** / **te acuestes**) antes de las diez para poder dormir lo suficiente.

B. A talk show host tells her TV audience what she recommends for a healthly lifestyle. Complete each sentence with the **Uds.** form of the verb in the present subjunctive.

Modelo   (entender) Recomiendo que Uds. __*entiendan*__ cómo mantener la salud.

1. **(volver)**   Es mejor que Uds. _____ temprano a casa para cenar.

2. **(divertirse)**   Exijo que Uds. _____ _____ durante el día.

3. **(despertarse)** Es bueno que Uds. _____ _____ temprano todos los días.

4. **(repetir)**   Es necesario que Uds. _____ todas estas reglas.

C. Many people are giving health advice to you and your friends. Complete each sentence with the **nosotros** form of the verb in the present subjunctive. **¡Cuidado!** Remember that only -**ir** verbs have stem changes in the **nosotros** form of the subjunctive.

Modelo   (pedir) Julia nos recomienda que __*pidamos*__ una ensalada.

1. **(dormir)**   Pati nos recomienda que _____ más horas.

2. **(probar)**   Paco nos recomienda que _____ esas comidas nuevas.

3. **(empezar)**   Carmen nos recomienda que _____ lentamente.

4. **(vestirse)** Mateo nos recomienda que _____ _____ con ropa cómoda.

D. Write complete sentences using the words provided. Each sentence should have one verb in the regular present tense and one in the present subjunctive. Don't forget to add the word **que**!

Modelo   Mis padres / querer / yo / seguir / sus consejos
   __*Mis padres quieren que yo siga sus consejos*__.

1. El entrenador / sugerir / los atletas / dormir / ocho horas cada noche

   _____

2. La profesora / recomendar / nosotros / pedir / ayuda

   _____

3. Mi amigo / recomendar / yo / empezar un programa de ejercicio

   _____

4. Él / querer / nosotros / divertirse / en nuestro trabajo

   _____

realidades.com
• Web Code: jed-0309

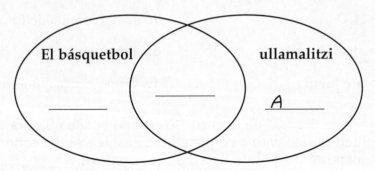

Puente a la cultura (pp. 140–141)

A. You are about to read about an ancient Mexican ball game somewhat similar to basketball. See if you can answer the following questions about the sport of basketball.

1. How many players from each team are on the court at once? _____

2. How many points can a person earn for a basket?

   _____

3. Which of the following *cannot* be considered as a rule of basketball?

   a. no aggressive behavior toward other players

   b. you must dribble the ball using your hands

   c. you must attempt to score within a time limit

   d. you must pass the ball with your feet

B. Use the Venn diagram below to compare *ullamalitzi*, the ancient Aztec ball game with the modern game of basketball. Write the letters of each statement in the appropriate places: the left circle if they apply only to basketball, the right circle if they apply only to the Aztec ball game, or in the middle if they apply to both. The first one is done for you.

El básquetbol   ullamalitzi

___   ___   *A* ___

A. ~~Los nobles juegan.~~

B. Los partidos aparecen en la tele.

C. Hay una pelota bastante grande.

D. La pelota pesa ocho libras.

E. Hay un anillo.

F. Los jugadores usan las manos.

G. Los jugadores no pueden usar las manos.

H. Muchas personas ven los partidos.

I. Los atletas llevan uniformes.

C. Place a check mark next to the adjectives that correspond with the characteristics of Aztec society that the article describes.

☐ aburrida   ☐ desorganizada

☐ religiosa   ☐ atlética

☐ artística

Lectura (pp. 146–149)

A. Use the pictures on pages 146–147 of your textbook to help you determine what the reading will be about. Write two types of advice you think this article will give you, judging by the pictures.

1. _____

2. _____

B. This reading is divided up into six sections. Look at the different sections on pages 146–148 and read each subtitle. Try to anticipate what each section will be about by thinking about the meaning of the subtitle. You can also use the pictures in your textbook to help you. Then, write the letter of the command below that best relates to each subtitle in the reading. The first one has been done for you.

1. __f__ **Aliméntate bien**   **a.** Cepíllate los dientes.

2. _____ **No comas comida basura**   **b.** Mantén la espalda derecha.

3. _____ **Muy limpios**   **c.** Duerme ocho horas al día.

4. _____ **Más H$_2$O**   **d.** Lleva comida de tu casa.

5. _____ **¿Una siesta?**   **e.** Bebe agua.

6. _____ **Siéntate bien.**   **f.** ~~Come el desayuno todos los días.~~

C. Look at the section of the reading entitled "**No comas comida basura.**" Each excerpt contains a highlighted phrase with a cognate in it. First, circle the cognate. Then, try to determine the meaning of the phrase based on the context.

«*Mejor escoge alimentos* **que echen a andar tu motor.**»

1. _____

«*Las palomitas de maíz y* **las frutas deshidratadas** *son una buena opción en lugar de comidas fritas.*»

2. _____

Realidades ③

Capítulo 3

Nombre _____

Fecha _____

Hora _____

Reading Activities, Sheet 3

D. Each section of the reading is divided into goals, steps for reaching the goal, and pieces of advice. Look at the section titled **"Muy limpios"** on p. 147 and check off the answer that best summarizes the content of each part of this section.

1. **Meta**

_____ tener dientes blancos

_____ tener dientes y manos limpios

2. **¡Lógralo!**

_____ cepillarse los dientes antes de comer y lavarse las manos después

_____ lavarse las manos frecuentemente con un gel y cepillarse los dientes después de comer

3. **Nuestros consejos**

_____ traer un cepillo y mentas en tu mochila para tener siempre los dientes limpios

_____ usar mentas todos los días en lugar de cepillarse los dientes

E. Do not get frustrated if you cannot understand every word of the article. Read the sections **"Más H₂0"**, **"¿Una siesta?"**, and **"Siéntate bien"** and write the main point of each section in one sentence. The main point has been done for you for the section **"Más H₂0."**

1. **Más H$_2$O**

It is important to drink water or juice instead of soda to maintain energy and good health.

2. **¿Una siesta?**

_____

_____

3. **Siéntate bien**

_____

_____

Realidades 3

Nombre _____

Hora _____

Capítulo 4

Fecha _____

AVSR, Sheet 1

Otros usos de los verbos reflexivos (p. 155)

- Reflexive verbs in Spanish are often used to talk about actions one does to or for oneself, as opposed to other people. Note that, in the first example below, the woman wakes herself up, but in the second, she wakes her husband up.

    La mujer *se despierta*. (reflexive)   *The woman wakes (herself) up.*

    La mujer *despierta a su esposo*. (non-reflexive)   *The woman wakes her husband up.*

- Many reflexive verbs are associated with elements of one's daily routine:

    - **acostarse** (*to go to bed*)
    - **afeitarse** (*to shave*)
    - **bañarse** (*to bathe*)
    - **despertarse** (*to wake up*)
    - **divertirse** (*to have fun*)
    - **ducharse** (*to shower*)
    - **levantarse** (*to get up*)
    - **ponerse** (*to put on*)
    - **sentirse** (*to feel*)
    - **vestirse** (*to dress oneself*)
    - **lavarse el pelo, las manos**, etc. (*to wash one's own hair, hands, etc.*)
    - **cepillarse el pelo, los dientes,** etc. (*to brush one's own hair, teeth, etc.*)

A. Complete the following sentences by circling the correct reflexive or non-reflexive verb forms. For each sentence, determine who the object of the verb is. If it is the same person who is performing the action, the reflexive verb form is required.

Modelo   El perro siempre ((despierta) / se despierta) a los niños.

1. Marta (**lava / se lava**) el pelo.

2. La mamá (**peina / se peina**) a su hija pequeña.

3. Los hermanos Sánchez (**cepillan / se cepillan**) los dientes.

4. Nosotros (**bañamos / nos bañamos**) el perro.

5. Tú (**levantas / te levantas**) a las seis de la mañana.

B. Write the correct reflexive or non-reflexive present-tense verb form in the space provided. Note: the first space will be left blank if the verb is not reflexive. Follow the model.

Modelo   (vestir/vestirse) Juanito ___se___ ___viste___ en el dormitorio.

1. (cepillar/cepillarse) Nosotros _____ _____ los dientes después de desayunar.

2. (despertar/despertarse) Tú _____ _____ a tu mamá a las seis.

3. (poner/ponerse) Carla y Alicia _____ _____ unas faldas cortas.

4. (sentir/sentirse) Yo _____ _____ mal, pero tengo que ir a la escuela.

realidades.com

• Web Code: jed-0401

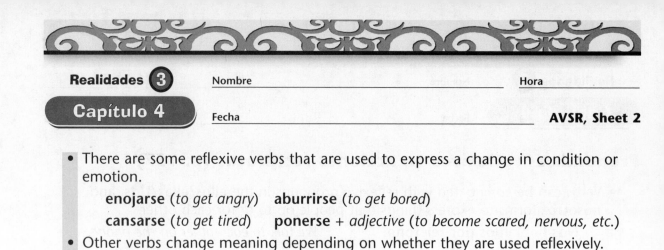

Realidades 3

Capítulo 4

Nombre _____

Fecha _____

Hora _____

AVSR, Sheet 2

- There are some reflexive verbs that are used to express a change in condition or emotion.

  enojarse (*to get angry*)   **aburrirse** (*to get bored*)

  cansarse (*to get tired*)   **ponerse** + *adjective* (*to become scared, nervous, etc.*)

- Other verbs change meaning depending on whether they are used reflexively.

  ir: to go   **irse**: to leave

  quedar: to be located   **quedarse**: to stay in a place

  quitar: to take away   **quitarse**: to take off (clothing)

  perder: to lose   **perderse**: to get lost

  dormir: to sleep   **dormirse**: to fall asleep

  volver: to return   **volverse + adjective (i.e. loco)**: to become (i.e. crazy)

- Some verbs and expressions are always reflexive:

  darse cuenta de: to realize   **quejarse**: to complain

  portarse bien/mal: to behave well/badly

C. Write the correct reflexive or non-reflexive present-tense verb form in the spaces provided. Note: the first space will be left blank if the verb is not reflexive.

Modelo   (**enojar**) Antonio __*se*__ __*enoja*__ cuando su hermano usa sus cosas.

1. (**quejar**) Los profesores _____ _____ de sus estudiantes perezosos.

2. (**quitar**) El camarero _____ _____ la mesa después de la cena.

3. (**cansar**) Yo _____ _____ cuando hago problemas matemáticos difíciles.

4. (**perder**) Nosotros _____ _____ la tarea siempre.

- Reflexive pronouns can either go before the conjugated verb or on the end of a participle or infinitive. If the pronoun is attached to the present participle, add an accent mark.

  Me estoy lavando las manos.   *Estoy lavándome las manos.*

  Te vas a duchar.   *Vas a ducharte.*

D. Write the correct present participle or infinitive of the verbs in parentheses.

Modelo   (**cepillarse**) Estoy __*cepillándome*__ los dientes.

1. (**irse**)   ¿Quieres _____ ahora?

2. (**dormirse**)   Estamos _____ porque estamos muy aburridas.

3. (**enojarse**)   Mis padres van a _____ si no llego a casa a tiempo.

4. (**volverse**)   ¡Estoy _____' loca de tanto trabajar!

Realidades 3

Nombre _____

Hora _____

Capítulo 4

Fecha _____

AVSR, Sheet 3

Pronombres reflexivos en acciones recíprocas (p. 157)

- Verbs can be conjugated with reflexive pronouns in the **ellos/ellas/Uds.** and **nosotros** forms to express things that people do to or for each other.

Nos hablamos por teléfono.	*We talk to each other on the phone.*
Los chicos se escriben frecuentemente	*The boys write to each other often.*

Remember that the reflexive forms are only used if <u>both</u> parties are doing the same thing to or for each other. They are <u>not</u> used if one person is simply doing something to someone else.

Ella y su hermano se ayudan con la tarea.	*She and her brother help each other with homework.*
Ella ayuda a su hermano.	*She helps her brother.*

A. Decide whether the actions in each sentence below are reciprocal or not. Circle the correct completion for the sentences. Follow the model.

Modelo   Jorge y Felipe (**abrazan** / (**se abrazan**)).

1. Margarita y Pilar (**ayudan** / **se ayudan**) en tiempos difíciles.

2. Nacho y Javier (**entienden** / **se entienden**) la lección de matemáticas.

3. Mi mejor amiga y yo (**llevamos** / **nos llevamos**) muy bien.

4. Mis padres y yo (**vemos** / **nos vemos**) muchas películas juntos.

5. Los estudiantes y el profesor (**saludan** / **se saludan**) cuando llegan a clase.

6. Los niños (**pelean** / **se pelean**) por los juguetes.

B. Complete the sentences stating the reciprocal actions that people do based on the pictures. Follow the model.

Modelo   Los novios __se__ __besan__ .

1. Miguel y yo _____ _____ mejor que cualquier persona.

realidades.com ✔

• Web Code: jed-0401

2. Elena y yo _____ _____.

3. Oswaldo y Paco _____ _____.

4. Manolo y Ricardo _____ _____ la mano.

C. Abuelita Cecilia is telling her grandchildren how the family was when she was little. Complete each sentence with the reciprocal verb form in the imperfect tense. Follow the model.

Modelo (abrazar) Mis primos y yo siempre __*nos*__ __*abrazábamos*__ en las reuniones familiares.

1. (pelear) Mis hermanitos _____ _____ frecuentemente cuando jugaban al béisbol.

2. (llevar) Mis padres y yo _____ _____ muy bien generalmente.

3. (conocer) Mis padres y los padres de mis amigos _____ _____ bien.

4. (escribir) Mis amigos que vivían en otras ciudades y yo _____ _____ cartas porque no había correo electrónico.

5. (comprender) Mi hermana mayor y yo _____ _____ muy bien.

6. (leer) Mis padres eran poetas y _____ _____ su poesía con frecuencia.

7. (parecer) Mis hermanos _____ _____ mucho.

8. (contar) Mis primos y yo _____ _____ chistes cómicos.

Realidades 3

Capítulo 4

Nombre _____

Fecha _____

Hora _____

Vocabulary Flash Cards, Sheet 1

Write the Spanish vocabulary word below each picture. If there is a word or phrase, copy it in the space provided. Be sure to include the article for each noun.

**aceptar
tal como**

Copy the word or phrase in the space provided. Be sure to include the article for each noun.

alegrarse (de)	**amable**	**la amistad**
apoyar(se)	**cambiar de opinión**	**la confianza**
confiar (en alguien)	**considerado, considerada**	**contar (con)**

Realidades 3

Nombre _____

Hora _____

Capítulo 4

Fecha _____

Vocabulary Flash Cards, Sheet 3

Copy the word or phrase in the space provided. Be sure to include the article for each noun.

la cualidad	desconfiar	esperar
_____ _____	 _____	 _____
guardar	íntimo, íntima	juntos, juntas
   _____	_____ _____	_____ _____
ojalá	el secreto	sincero, sincera
   _____	_____ _____	_____ _____

Tear out this page. Write the English words on the lines. Fold the paper along the dotted line to see the correct answers so you can check your work.

aceptar tal como (soy)   _____

_____

alegrarse   _____

amable   _____

la amistad   _____

apoyar(se)   _____

_____

cambiar de opinión   _____

cariñoso, cariñosa   _____

celoso, celosa   _____

chismoso, chismosa   _____

comprensivo, comprensiva   _____

la confianza   _____

confiar ($i \rightarrow í$)   _____

considerado, considerada   _____

contar con   _____

la cualidad   _____

desconfiar   _____

Fold In

Nombre _____   Hora _____

Fecha _____   **Vocabulary Check, Sheet 2**

Tear out this page. Write the Spanish words on the lines. Fold the paper along the dotted line to see the correct answers so you can check your work.

to accept (me)
the way (I am)   _____
                        _____

to be delighted   _____

kind   _____

friendship   _____

to support; to back
(one another)   _____

to change one's mind   _____

loving, affectionate   _____

jealous   _____

gossipy   _____

understanding   _____
                         _____

trust   _____

to trust   _____

considerate   _____
                         _____

to count on   _____

quality   _____

to mistrust   _____

Fold In →

Realidades **3**

Capítulo 4

Nombre _____

Fecha _____

Hora _____

Vocabulary Check, Sheet 3

Tear out this page. Write the English words on the lines. Fold the paper along the dotted line to see the correct answers so you can check your work.

egoísta

_____

entrometido,
entrometida

_____

_____

esperar

_____

guardar (un secreto)

_____

honesto, honesta

_____

íntimo, íntima

_____

juntos, juntas

_____

ojalá

_____

el secreto

_____

sincero, sincera

_____

sorprender(se)

_____

temer

_____

tener en común

_____

tener celos

_____

vanidoso, vanidosa

_____

Fold In

Tear out this page. Write the Spanish words on the lines. Fold the paper along the dotted line to see the correct answers so you can check your work.

selfish _____

meddlesome, interfering _____
_____

to hope (for) _____

to keep (a secret) _____

honest _____

intimate _____

together _____

I wish, I hope _____

secret _____

sincere _____

to (be) surprised _____

to fear _____

to have in common _____

to be jealous _____

vain, conceited _____

Fold In ←

realidades.com ✔
• Web Code: jed-0402

El subjuntivo con verbos de emoción (p. 168)

- In Chapter 3, you learned to use the subjunctive in sentences in which someone expresses their desires, requests, or advice for someone else. Another instance in which the subjunctive is used is when one person expresses <u>emotion</u> about someone or something else. Look at the examples below.

Temo que mi amiga se enferme.	*I am afraid my friend will get sick.*
Nos sorprende que el maestro nos dé un examen.	*We are surprised that the teacher gives us an exam.*

  The following list of verbs and expressions are used to indicate emotion:

temer: to be afraid	**ojalá**: I hope or wish
sentir: to regret / be sorry	**es bueno**: it is good
alegrarse de: to be happy	**es malo**: it is bad
esperar: to hope	**es una lástima**: it's a shame/pity
me, te... gusta: I / you . . . like	
me, te... enoja: it angers me, you . . .	

A. Each sentence describes a person's feeling about someone's actions. Circle the logical emotion for each sentence. Then underline the subjunctive verb in each sentence.

Modelo   ((Me molesta) / Me alegro de) que no me <u>aceptes</u> tal como soy.

1. (Es una lástima / Es bueno) que no me comprendas.

2. (Me gusta / Me enoja) que siempre cambies de opinión.

3. (Es malo / Espero) que no tengas celos.

4. (Es triste / Ojalá) que no seas sincera.

5. (Es bueno / Siento) que tu novia y tú no tengan mucho en común.

B. Complete each sentence with the correct subjunctive form of the verb.

Modelo   Espero que mis amigos siempre me _____ (**comprender**)

1. Es una lástima que José _____ egoísta. (**ser**)

2. Me alegro de que Juana _____ conmigo. (**contar**)

3. Me sorprende que Carlos no _____ a su novia. (**apoyar**)

4. Es ridículo que mis padres _____ de mí. (**desconfiar**)

C. Now, go back to exercise B and circle the verb or expression of emotion in each sentence. Follow the model.

Modelo   (Espero) que mis amigos siempre me comprendan.

Realidades 3

Nombre _____

Hora _____

Capítulo 4

Fecha _____

Guided Practice Activities, Sheet 2

• Note that **"que"** marks a change in subject, and thus the subjunctive mood. In impersonal expressions, the verb **es** counts as one subject.

> **Es importante que tú seas honesto.**   *It is important that you be honest.*

D. Combine the elements below to create a sentence using the subjunctive. Remember to use **que** after the first verb in each sentence. Follow the model.

Modelo   Mis padres / temer / yo / no / ser / sincero

Mis padres temen que yo no sea sincero. _____

1. Yo / alegrarse de / mis hermanos / ser / cariñosos

_____

2. Es triste / mis amigos / no guardar / mis secretos.

_____

3. Nosotros / sentir / tus padres / no / apoyar / tus decisiones

_____

4. Es una lástima / tu mejor amiga / tener celos

_____

• If there is only one subject in the sentence, **"que"** is omitted and the infinitive is used after the conjugated verb or expression of emotion.

> **(Yo) Me alegro de tener muchos amigos.**   *I am happy to have (that I have) many friends.*

E. Read each sentence and determine whether to use the infinitive or the present subjunctive. Look for the **"que"** and a change in subject. Follow the model.

Modelo.   (escuchar) Me molesta que mis hermanos _____*escuchen*_____ mis conversaciones con mis amigos.

1. (poder)   Siento no _____ ir a la fiesta. Estoy enfermo.

2. (ser)   Es bueno que nosotros _____ sinceros.

3. (aceptar)   Me alegro de que mis padres me _____ tal como soy.

4. (guardar)   Esperamos _____ los secretos de nuestra familia.

5. (tener)   Es bueno _____ muchos amigos comprensivos.

• Web Code: jed-0403

Los usos de *por* y *para* (p. 171)

- The prepositions **por** and **para** have several distinct uses in Spanish.

  Por is used to indicate:

  - an exchange, such as with money
    *Pago dos dólares **por** una taza de café.*

  - a substitution or replacement
    *Trabajo **por** mi mejor amigo cuando él está enfermo.*

  - the reason for doing something
    *La profesora se enojó **por** las malas notas de sus estudiantes.*

  - an approximate length of time
    *Mi amigo y yo nos hablamos **por** varias horas.*

  - a means of transportation / communication
    *Mi amigo y yo nos comunicamos **por** correo electrónico.*

  - where an action takes place
    *Mis padres corrieron **por** el río.*

  - The following expressions also use **por**:
    **por favor, por eso, por supuesto, por ejemplo, por lo general,
    por primera (segunda, etc.) vez, por la mañana (tarde, noche)**

  Para is used to indicate:

  - deadlines or moments in time
    *Este reportaje es **para** el viernes.*

  - a destination
    *Salimos **para** Madrid a las nueve.*

  - a function or goal
    *Esta cámara digital sirve **para** sacar fotos.*

  - the recipient of an action
    *Este regalo de boda es **para** los novios.*

  - a purpose (in order to)
    *Llamé a mi amigo **para** contarle el secreto.*

  - an opinion
    ***Para** ti, la amistad es muy importante.*

A. Read each of the following statements using the preposition **por** and decide why **por** was used instead of **para**.

_____ 1. Ella se casó **por** dinero.

_____ 2. Pagué $15 **por** el disco compacto.

_____ 3. Dio un paseo **por** el parque.

_____ 4. Corté el césped **por** mi padre.

_____ 5. Leyó el libro **por** muchas horas.

A. length of time

B. where an action takes place

C. an exchange

D. reason or motive

E. action on someone's behalf

B. Read each of the following statements using the preposition **para** and decide why **para** was used instead of **por**. The first one is done for you.

_C_ **1.** Necesito escribir un informe **para** mañana.

____ **2.** Las frutas son buenas **para** la salud.

____ **3.** **Para** mí, es muy importante guardar los secretos.

____ **4.** **Para** ser buen amigo necesitas ser paciente.

____ **5.** Tengo una carta **para** Isabel.

____ **6.** El tren sale **para** México a las siete.

A. purpose, in order to

B. destination

~~**C.** a point in time, deadline~~

D. function, goal

E. opinion

F. recipient of an action

C. Circle **por** or **para** for each of the following sentences. Follow the model.

Modelo   Esta carretera pasa ((**por**) / **para**) Texas.

1. No sé si hay una piscina (**por** / **para**) aquí.

2. Vivimos en Puerto Rico (**por** / **para**) mucho tiempo.

3. Cecilia pagó mucho (**por** / **para**) su vestido de Prom.

4. (**Por** / **Para**) mí, el deporte más divertido es el fútbol.

5. No puedo ir. ¿Puedes ir (**por** / **para**) mí?

6. Compramos un regalo (**por** / **para**) Silvia. Es su cumpleaños.

7. Francisco tomó el avión (**por** / **para**) San Juan.

8. No pudimos acampar (**por** / **para**) la tormenta.

9. Los proyectos son (**por** / **para**) el lunes.

10. Siempre voy (**por** / **para**) el gimnasio antes de ir a la piscina.

11. Quiero ir al parque (**por** / **para**) jugar al fútbol.

12. Prefiero viajar (**por** / **para**) avión.

realidades.com

• Web Code: jed-0404

Realidades ❸

Capítulo 4

Nombre _____

Hora _____

Fecha _____

Vocabulary Flash Cards, Sheet 4

Copy the word or phrase in the space provided. Be sure to include the article for each noun.

acusar	**la armonía**	**atreverse**
_____	_____ _____	_____
colaborar	**el comportamiento**	**el conflicto**
_____	_____ _____	_____
criticar	**la diferencia de opinión**	**estar equivocado, equivocada**
_____	_____ _____ _____	_____ _____

Copy the word or phrase in the space provided. Be sure to include the article for each noun.

la explicación	**hacer las paces**	**hacer caso**
_____	_____	_____
ignorar	**el malentendido**	**mejorar**
_____	_____	_____
pedir perdón	**la pelea**	**pensar en sí mismo, misma**
_____	_____	_____ _____

Copy the word or phrase in the space provided. Be sure to include the article for each noun.

perdonar	**ponerse de acuerdo**	**¡Qué va!**
reaccionar	**reconciliarse**	**reconocer**
resolver	**tener la culpa**	**¡Yo no fui!**

Realidades 3

Nombre _____

Hora _____

Capítulo 4

Fecha _____

Vocabulary Flash Cards, Sheet 7

Copy the word or phrase in the space provided. Be sure to include the article for each noun. The blank cards can be used to write and practice other Spanish vocabulary for the chapter.

sorprenderse	**temer**	**tener celos**
_____	_____	_____
tener en común		
_____	_____	_____
_____	_____	_____

Realidades 3

Capítulo 4

Nombre _____

Fecha _____

Hora _____

Vocabulary Check, Sheet 5

Tear out this page. Write the English words on the lines. Fold the paper along the dotted line to see the correct answers so you can check your work.

acusar _____

la armonía _____

atreverse _____

colaborar _____

el comportamiento _____

el conflicto _____

criticar _____

la diferencia
de opinión _____

estar equivocado,
equivocada _____

la explicación _____

hacer caso _____

hacer las paces _____

ignorar _____

el malentendido _____

Fold In →

Realidades 3

Capítulo 4

Nombre _____

Fecha _____

Hora _____

Vocabulary Check, Sheet 6

Tear out this page. Write the Spanish words on the lines. Fold the paper along the dotted line to see the correct answers so you can check your work.

to accuse _____

harmony _____

to dare _____

to collaborate _____

behavior _____

conflict _____

to criticize _____

difference of _____
opinion _____

to be mistaken _____
_____

explanation _____

to pay attention; to obey _____

to make peace _____

to ignore _____

misunderstanding _____

Fold In

Tear out this page. Write the English words on the lines. Fold the paper along the dotted line to see the correct answers so you can check your work.

mejorar _____

pedir perdón _____

la pelea _____

pensar en sí mismo, misma _____

perdonar _____

ponerse de acuerdo _____

_____

reaccionar _____

reconciliarse _____

_____

reconocer _____

resolver (o→ue) _____

tener la culpa _____

¡Qué va! _____

¡Yo no fui! _____

Fold In →

Realidades ③

Capítulo 4

Nombre _____

Hora _____

Fecha _____

Vocabulary Check, Sheet 8

Tear out this page. Write the Spanish words on the lines. Fold the paper along the dotted line to see the correct answers so you can check your work.

to improve _____

to ask for forgiveness _____

fight _____

to think of oneself _____

_____

to forgive _____

to reach an agreement _____

to react _____

to become friends again _____

to admit; to recognize _____

to resolve _____

to be guilty _____

No way! _____

It was not me! _____

Fold In ←

realidades.com

• Web Code: jed-0406

Mandatos con *nosotros* (p. 182)

- You can express **nosotros** commands two different ways in Spanish. The English equivalent of a **nosotros** command is "*Let's . . .*"

  One way is to use **Vamos** + **a** + infinitive.

  Vamos a bailar.　　　　　*Let's dance.*

  Another way is to use to the **nosotros** form of the subjunctive.

  Bailemos.　　　　　*Let's dance.*

- Remember that **-ir** stem-changing verbs change **o→u** or **e→i** in the **nosotros** form.

  Durmamos aquí.　　　　　*Let's sleep here.*

- Remember that verbs ending in **-car**, **-gar**, and **-zar** change spelling in the subjunctive.

  Juguemos a las cartas.　　　　　*Let's play cards.*

A. Read each of the following statements about Juanita and her best friend. Decide if each statement tells what they normally do, or if it's a suggestion. Follow the model.

Modelo　Guardemos los secretos.

　　　　　☐ normalmente　☑ sugerencia

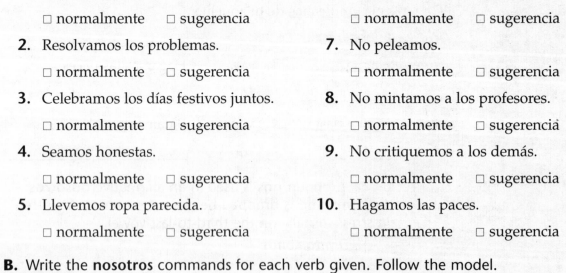

1. Tenemos mucho en común.

　　☐ normalmente　☐ sugerencia

2. Resolvamos los problemas.

　　☐ normalmente　☐ sugerencia

3. Celebramos los días festivos juntos.

　　☐ normalmente　☐ sugerencia

4. Seamos honestas.

　　☐ normalmente　☐ sugerencia

5. Llevemos ropa parecida.

　　☐ normalmente　☐ sugerencia

6. Comamos en un restaurante.

　　☐ normalmente　☐ sugerencia

7. No peleamos.

　　☐ normalmente　☐ sugerencia

8. No mintamos a los profesores.

　　☐ normalmente　☐ sugerencia

9. No critiquemos a los demás.

　　☐ normalmente　☐ sugerencia

10. Hagamos las paces.

　　☐ normalmente　☐ sugerencia

B. Write the **nosotros** commands for each verb given. Follow the model.

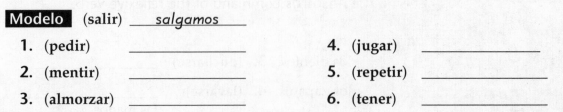

Modelo　(salir) ___*salgamos*___

1. (pedir) _____

2. (mentir) _____

3. (almorzar) _____

4. (jugar) _____

5. (repetir) _____

6. (tener) _____

realidades.com

• Web Code: jed-0407

C. Marisa is suggesting that she and Josefina do the same things. Write the suggestion Marisa gives, using **nosotros** commands. Follow the model.

Modelo Josefina, no _____ la tele hoy.

1. Josefina, _____ la música clásica.

2. Josefina, _____ una explicación cuando tenemos un malentendido.

3. Josefina, _____ en el coro.

4. Josefina, _____ la tarea juntas.

- When you use a direct or indirect object pronoun with an affirmative **nosotros** command, attach it to the end of the verb.

  Resolvamos el problema. Resolvámoslo.

- With a negative **nosotros** command, place the object pronoun in front of the verb.

  No le digamos el secreto al chico chismoso.

D. Each time your parents make a suggestion, respond with an opposite suggestion. Replace the underlined word in each sentence with a direct object pronoun in your answer. Follow the model.

Modelo MAMÁ: Celebremos <u>el cumpleaños</u> de tu abuelita.

  TÚ: *No lo celebremos.*

1. PAPÁ: Limpiemos <u>el garaje.</u>   3. PAPÁ: Hagamos <u>las paces.</u>

   TÚ: _____   TÚ: _____

2. MAMÁ: Escuchemos <u>música clásica.</u>   4. MAMÁ: Pidamos <u>perdón.</u>

   TÚ: _____   TÚ: _____

- When the reflexive or reciprocal pronoun **nos** is used in an affirmative **nosotros** command, the final **-s** of the command is dropped before the pronoun. A written accent is added to maintain stress, usually on the third-to-last vowel.

  Contémonos los secretos.   *Divirtámonos.*

E. Complete each sentence using the **nosotros** command of the reflexive verb.

Modelo (vestirse) _____.

1. (cepillarse) _____ los dientes.   3. (ducharse) _____.

2. (ponerse) _____ los zapatos.   4. (lavarse) _____

                                                        las manos.

Realidades 3

Capítulo 4

Nombre _____

Hora _____

Fecha _____

Guided Practice Activities, Sheet 7

Pronombres posesivos (p. 184)

- Possessive pronouns help you avoid repetition in conversation by replacing nouns. They are usually preceded by a definite article, and must have the same gender and number as the nouns they replace.

    Mi mejor amiga es muy sincera. ¿Cómo es *la tuya*?
    My best friend is very sincere. What is yours *like?*

    El padre de José es tan comprensivo como *el mío*.
    José's father is as understanding as mine.

    Below are the possessive pronouns in Spanish.

    el mío / la mía / los míos / las mías: *mine*

    el tuyo / la tuya / los tuyos / las tuyas: *yours*

    el suyo / la suya / los suyos / las suyas:
    his / hers / yours (sing. formal or plural) / theirs

    el nuestro / la nuestra / los nuestros / las nuestras: *ours*

    el vuestro / la vuestra / los vuestros / las vuestras: *yours (plural)*

A. Write the letter of the question that would most logically follow each statement below. The pronoun in the question should agree in gender and number with the underlined noun. The first one is done for you.

_*B*_ **1.** <u>Mis padres</u> son muy serios.

2. <u>Mi mamá</u> es cariñosa.

3. <u>Mis amigas</u> son deportistas.

4. <u>Nuestro</u> hermano es chismoso.

5. <u>Nuestras amigas</u> no nos hacen caso.

6. <u>Nuestra jefa</u> colabora con nosotros.

A. ¿Y el suyo?

B. ~~¿Y los tuyos?~~

C. ¿Y la suya?

D. ¿Y las tuyas?

E. ¿Y la tuya?

F. ¿Y las suyas?

- When the verb **ser** is used with a possessive pronoun, the definite article is commonly left out.

    *Esos textos son **nuestros**.*   *Esa calculadora es **mía**.*

B. Write the letter of the phrase that is the best completion for each statement. The first one is done for you.

_*B*_ **1.** La corbata...

2. El traje de baño...

3. Los anteojos...

4. Las joyas...

A. ...son suyos.

B. ~~...es mía.~~

C. ...es tuyo.

D. ...son nuestras.

- Web Code: jed-0408

C. The following pairs of statements are opposites. Complete the sentences with the correct form of the possessive pronoun **mío** or **tuyo**. Follow the models.

Modelos Tu familia es unida. _La_ _____ _mía_ es independiente.

Mi casa es pequeña. _La_ _____ _tuya_ es grande.

1. Tus hermanas son divertidas. _____ _____ son aburridas.

2. Mi computadora es vieja. _____ _____ es moderna.

3. Tus libros son grandes. _____ _____ son pequeños.

4. Mis padres son atléticos. _____ _____ son poco atléticos.

5. Mi perro es gordísimo. _____ _____ es flaquito.

6. Tu carro es nuevo. _____ _____ es viejo.

D. Create complete sentences by modifying the possessive pronoun, if necessary, to agree in gender and number with the noun it respresents. Follow the model.

Modelo Los libros / de Cervantes / son / nuestro

Los libros de Cervantes son nuestros. _____

1. Las flores / bonitas / son / mío

_____

2. La culpa / es / tuyo

_____

3. Esas / pinturas / de Velázquez / son / suyo

_____

4. Los / zapatos / son / nuestro

_____

5. El perro / es / suyo

_____

6. La tarea / de / español / es / nuestro

_____

realidades.com

• Web Code: jed-0408

Realidades 3

Capítulo 4

Nombre _____

Hora _____

Fecha _____

Reading Activities, Sheet 1

Puente a la cultura (pp. 186–187)

A. Scan the reading for names of people, and match each of the following artists with the type of art they made or make. (Hint: you will use one letter more than once!)

1. _____ Diego Rivera

2. _____ Judith Francisca

3. _____ Augustín Lara

4. _____ Juana de Ibarbouru

A. la música

B. la pintura

C. la literatura

B. Look at the sentence starters below. Circle the best completion for each sentence based on each section of the reading. Use the reading subtitles to help you.

1. La pintura en murales ha sido otra forma de expresión artística...

   a. del amor.   **b.** de la madre.   **c.** de gente famosa.

2. La fuente de inspiración de la mayoría de sus [de Agustín Lara] canciones fue...

   a. el amor a la pintura.   **b.** el amor a México.   **c.** el amor a la mujer.

3. De todas las formas de expresar el amor en la literatura... la más apropiada es...

   a. la poesía.   **b.** el drama.   **c.** la naturaleza.

C. Look at the poem entitled "*Amor*" from your reading. Circle the words in the poem that have to do with nature.

> *El amor es fragante como un ramo de rosas.*
> *Amando se poseen todas las primaveras.*
> *Eros (god of love) trae en su aljaba (quiver) las flores olorosas*
> *De todas las umbrías (shady areas) y todas las praderas (grasslands).*

Lectura (pp. 192–195)

A. You are about to read several poems about love and friendship. In the spaces provided, write three adjectives in Spanish that you associate with love and friendship. Think of ideals you might expect to see expressed in the poems. Use the models to get you started.

_____ comprensivo _____   _____ íntima _____   _____

_____   _____

B. Match each of the important vocabulary words with its synonym or definition. These words are from the two poems: *Poema No. 15,* on page 192, and *Homenaje a los padres chicanos* on page 193.

1. _____ callarse   **A.** tradición

2. _____ mariposa   **B.** lo que se oye cuando una persona habla

3. _____ voz   **C.** lo que tienes cuando crees en algo

4. _____ melancolía   **D.** no hablar

5. _____ sagrado   **E.** de muchísima importancia

6. _____ costumbre   **F.** respetar mucho y amar

7. _____ fe   **G.** un insecto bonito

8. _____ venerar   **H.** la tristeza fuerte

9. _____ chicano   **I.** mexicano americano

C. Circle the responses in parentheses that best complete the main ideas about the first two poems.

"Poema No. 15"

1. Al poeta le gusta que su novia (hable mucho / no hable mucho) porque (así él la aprecia más / ella no dice muchas cosas importantes).

"Homenaje a los padre chicanos"

2. El poeta quiere ilustrar que (es importante expresar el amor por los padres / los padres deben amar más a sus hijos) aunque en la cultura (gringa / chicana) no es tan común hacerlo.

Realidades 3

Capítulo 4

Nombre _____

Fecha _____

Hora _____

Reading Activities, Sheet 3

D. Look at the following sets of key lines from each poem on page 194 and circle the phrase that best conveys the meaning of each quotation.

"Rimas"

1. *"Poesía ... eres tú."*

    a. La mujer escribe poesía como profesión.

    b. La mujer y la poesía son cosas bellas e imposibles de describir.

"El amor en preguntas"

2. *"¿Qué es necesario para ser amado, para entender la vida y saber soñar?"*

    a. Todos buscan el amor, pero a veces es difícil encontrarlo.

    b. El amor sólo existe en los sueños.

"Como tú"

3. *"Creo que el mundo es bello, que la poesía es como el pan, de todos."*

    a. La poesía es universal y crea conexiones entre las personas.

    b. Hay mucha hambre y pobreza en el mundo, y la poesía no ayuda con los problemas.

E. Roque Dalton named his poem *"Cómo tú"* because it is a comparison of himself with another person. Read the poem on page 194 and check off which of the following are comparisons Dalton actually uses in the poem.

_____ "amo el amor, la vida"

_____ "[amo] el paisaje celeste de los días de enero"

_____ "[amo] la poesía de ti"

_____ "creo que el mundo es bello"

_____ "[creo que] los suspiros son aire"

_____ "[creo que] la poesía es como el pan"

El participio presente (p. 201)

- The present participle is used to talk about actions that are in progress at the moment of speaking. To form the present participle of **-ar** verbs, add **-ando** to the stem. For **-er** and **-ir** verbs, add **-iendo** to the stem.

  cantar: cant**ando** insistir: insist**iendo** tener: ten**iendo**

- The present participle is frequently combined with the present tense of **estar** to talk about what someone *is doing*, or with the imperfect of **estar** to talk about what someone *was doing*.

  Estoy cort*ando* el césped.   *I am mowing the lawn.*

  Los niños estaban hac*iendo* sus quehaceres.   *The kids were doing their chores.*

A. Write the ending of the present participle for each of the following verbs to say what the following people are doing while you're at school. Follow the model.

Modelo (sacar) El fotógrafo está sac*ando* fotos.

1. (trabajar) El agente de viajes está trabaj_____ en su oficina.

2. (beber)   El entrenador está beb_____ agua.

3. (hacer)   El científico está hac_____ un experimento.

4. (escribir) El reportero está escrib_____ un artículo.

- Only **-ir** stem-changing verbs change in the present participle. In the present participle, the **e** changes to **i** and the **o** changes to **u**.

  servir: s*i*rviendo dormir: d*u*rmiendo despedir: desp*i*diendo

B. Write the present participles of the verbs in the chart below. The first row has been done for you. Remember that **-ar** and **-er** stem-changing verbs have <u>no stem changes</u> in the present participle.

-ar, -er	present participle	-ir	present participle
jugar	*jugando*	divertir	*divirtiendo*
sentar	1. _____	sentir	5. _____
contar	2. _____	morir	6. _____
volver	3. _____	preferir	7. _____
perder	4. _____	dormir	8. _____

C. Complete the sentences with the present progressive of the verb given (+ *present participle*) to say what the following people are doing. Follow the model.

Modelo (**decir**) Yo __estoy__ __diciendo__ la verdad.

1. (**dormir**) Tú no _____ _____.

2. (**pedir**) Ellos no _____ _____ una pizza.

3. (**contar**) Nosotros _____ _____ chistes.

4. (**resolver**) Yo _____ _____ problemas de matemáticas.

- A spelling change occurs in the present participle of the verbs **ir**, **oír**, and verbs ending in **-aer**, **-eer**, and **-uir**. The ending becomes **-yendo**.

   creer: cre**yendo**   oír: o**yendo**   caer: ca**yendo**

   construir: constru**yendo**   ir: **yendo**

D. Complete the following sentences with the present progressive. Remember to use the verb **estar** along with the verb provided. Follow the model.

Modelo Mis padres __están__ __trayendo__ (**traer**) el perro al veterinario.

1. El asistente _____ _____ (**oír**) las instrucciones del dentista.

2. La reportera dice que _____ _____ (**caer**) granizo y que _____ _____ (**destruir**) los coches de muchas personas.

3. Las vendedoras _____ _____ (**leer**) las etiquetas de la ropa.

4. Nadie _____ _____ (**creer**) lo que dice el atleta egoísta.

- In the progressive tenses, reflexive or object pronouns can be placed before the verb **estar**, or they can be attached to the end of the present participle. If they are attached to the present participle, a written accent is needed to maintain stress (usually over the third-to-last vowel).

   El bombero está ayudándome.   or   *El bombero me está ayudando.*

E. The sentences below each have a phrase using the present progressive tense and a pronoun. Each phrase is underlined. In the space provided, write the phrase in a different way, using what you learned about placement of pronouns. Follow the model.

Modelo No puedo hablar porque <u>me estoy cepillando</u> los dientes. *estoy cepillándome*

1. Mis abuelos <u>nos están felicitando</u> por la graduación. _____

2. A Juan no le gusta el postre, pero <u>está comiéndolo</u>. _____

3. Mi hermano está en el baño. <u>Está lavándose</u> las manos. _____

4. Mi profesora <u>me está dando</u> este libro para estudiar. _____

Realidades 3

Capítulo 5

Nombre _____

Hora _____

Fecha _____

AVSR, Sheet 3

Dónde van los pronombres reflexivos y de complemento (p. 203)

- Deciding where to put object and reflexive pronouns can sometimes be confusing. Here is a summary of some of these rules.
- When a sentence contains two verbs in a row, as with a present participle or infinitive, the pronoun may be placed either in front of the first verb or be attached to the second verb. Note that the second example is negative.

  Nos vamos a duchar. or *Vamos a ducharnos.*

  *No **nos** vamos a duchar.* or *No vamos a ducharnos.*

- Adding a pronoun to the end of a present participle requires a written accent mark, while adding a pronoun to the end of an infinitive does not.

  Estoy pagándole.   *Voy a pagarle.*

A. Rewrite each phrase using the pronoun in parentheses in two different ways. In column A, place the pronouns before the first verb. In column B, attach them to the second verb. Remember, if you add a pronoun to the end of a present participle, you need to include an accent mark. Follow the model.

	A	**B**
Modelo van a regalar (me)	*me van a regalar*	*van a regalarme*
1. vamos a dar (le)	_____	_____
2. debo encontrar (lo)	_____	_____
3. estamos registrando (nos)	_____	_____
4. van a dormir (se)	_____	_____

- When you give an affirmative command, you must attach any pronouns to the end of the verb and add an accent mark if the verb has two or more syllables.

  Permítelo.   *Ganémoslas.*

  In negative commands, place the pronoun between **no** and the verb. No written accent mark is needed.

  No lo hagan.   *No te laves el pelo ahora.*

B. Combine the following affirmative commands and pronouns. Remember to write an accent mark on the stressed syllable. Follow the model.

Modelo lava + te = _____ *lávate* _____

1. ponga + se = _____

2. vean + los = _____

3. despierten + se = _____

4. ayuden + me = _____

5. consigamos + la = _____

realidades.com

- Web Code: jed-0501

Realidades 3

Capítulo 5

Nombre _____

Hora _____

Fecha _____

AVSR, Sheet 4

C. For each question, write an answer using one of the affirmative **tú** commands with the correct direct object pronoun (**lo, la, los, las**). Use the word bank to help you choose the correct forms. Add accents as needed. Follow the model.

haz	pide	~~cocina~~	enciende	trae	pon

Modelo ¿Cocino el pavo? Sí, _____*cocínalo*_____.

1. ¿Enciendo las velas? Sí, _____.

2. ¿Pido unas flores? Sí, _____.

3. ¿Hago el menú? Sí, _____.

4. ¿Pongo la mesa? Sí, _____.

5. ¿Traigo una botella de vino? Sí, _____.

D. Write the negative command that corresponds to each affirmative command below. Follow the model.

Modelo Córtense las uñas. No __*se*__ __*corten*__ el pelo.

1. Vístanse con la ropa suya. No _____ _____ con la ropa de sus amigos.

2. Pónganse las chaquetas. No _____ _____ las joyas.

3. Báñense por la tarde. No _____ _____ por la mañana.

4. Levántense a las ocho. No _____ _____ tarde.

5. Cepíllense los dientes. No _____ _____ los dedos.

Write the Spanish vocabulary word below each picture. If there is a word or phrase, copy it in the space provided. Be sure to include the article for each noun.

_____ ,

_____

_____ ,

_____

_____

_____ ,

_____

_____

_____

_____

_____

_____

_____

_____ ,

_____

agradable

Copy the word or phrase in the space provided. Be sure to include the article for each noun.

atender _____	**a tiempo completo** ___ _____ _____	**a tiempo parcial** ___ _____ _____
beneficiar _____	**los beneficios** ___ _____	**la compañía** ___ _____
la computación ___ _____	**el consejero, la consejera** ___ _____ ___ _____	**los conocimientos** ___ _____

Realidades ❸

Nombre _____

Hora _____

Capítulo 5

Fecha _____

Vocabulary Flash Cards, Sheet 3

Copy the word or phrase in the space provided. Be sure to include the article for each noun.

cumplir con	dedicado, dedicada	el dueño, la dueña
_____ _____	_____	_____ _____
encargarse (de)	la entrevista	la fecha de nacimiento
_____	_____ _____	_____ _____
flexible	la habilidad	el puesto
_____	_____ _____	_____ _____

Realidades 3

Capítulo 5

Nombre

Hora

Fecha

Vocabulary Flash Cards, Sheet 4

Copy the word or phrase in the space provided. Be sure to include the article for each noun.

puntual	**presentarse**	**reparar**
_____	_____	_____
la referencia	**repartir**	**el salario**
_____	_____	_____
		_____
seguir	**solicitar**	**la solicitud de empleo**
		_____ _____
_____	_____	

Realidades 3

Capítulo 5

Nombre

Fecha

Hora

Vocabulary Flash Cards, Sheet 5

These blank cards can be used to write and practice other Spanish vocabulary for the chapter.

Tear out this page. Write the English words on the lines. Fold the paper along the dotted line to see the correct answers so you can check your work.

a tiempo completo _____

a tiempo parcial _____

agradable _____

el anuncio clasificado _____

atender _____

los beneficios _____

el cliente, la clienta _____

la compañía _____

el consejero,
la consejera _____

los conocimientos _____

cumplir con _____

dedicado, dedicada _____

el dueño, la dueña _____

encargarse (de) _____

la entrevista _____

la fecha de nacimiento _____

el/la gerente _____

la habilidad _____

Fold In

Realidades 3

Capítulo 5

Nombre _____

Hora _____

Fecha _____

Vocabulary Check, Sheet 2

Tear out this page. Write the Spanish words on the lines. Fold the paper along the dotted line to see the correct answers so you can check your work.

full time _____

part time _____

pleasant _____

classified ad _____

to help, assist _____

benefits _____

client _____

firm/company _____

counselor _____

_____

knowledge _____

to carry out, to perform _____

dedicated _____

owner _____

to be in charge (of) _____

interview _____

date of birth _____

manager _____

skill _____

Fold In

Tear out this page. Write the English words on the lines. Fold the paper along the dotted line to see the correct answers so you can check your work.

el mensajero,
la mensajera _____

el niñero, la niñera _____

presentarse _____

repartir _____

el puesto _____

puntual _____

el/la recepcionista _____

reparar _____

el repartidor,
la repartidora _____

el requisito _____

la responsabilidad _____

el salario _____

el/la salvavida _____

seguir (+ *gerund*) _____

soler (*o→ue*) _____

la solicitud de empleo _____

solicitar _____

Fold In

Tear out this page. Write the Spanish words on the lines. Fold the paper along the dotted line to see the correct answers so you can check your work.

messenger   _____
                                  _____

babysitter   _____

to apply for a job   _____

to deliver   _____

position   _____

punctual   _____

receptionist   _____

to repair   _____

delivery person   _____
                                  _____

requirement   _____

responsibility   _____

salary   _____

lifeguard   _____

to keep on (doing)   _____

to usually do something _____

job application   _____

to request   _____

Fold In →

realidades.com ⌄
• Web Code: jed-0502

El presente perfecto (p. 214)

- In Spanish, the *present perfect* tense is used to talk about what someone *has done* in the past without necessarily telling the time when they did it.

  Yo *he trabajado* en una tienda de bicicletas. *I have worked at a bicycle store.*

- The present perfect is formed by using the present tense forms of the irregular verb **haber** plus the *past participle* of another verb. Remember that the past participle is formed by adding **-ado** to the stem of an **-ar** verb or **-ido** to the stem of an **-er** or **-ir** verb. Below is the verb **cantar** conjugated in the present perfect.

cantar	
he cant**ado**	**hemos** cant**ado**
has cant**ado**	**habéis** cant**ado**
ha cant**ado**	**han** cant**ado**

Notice that each conjugation has two parts, and that the second part (in this case, **cantado**) is the <u>same</u> in all forms.

- Remember that direct and indirect object pronouns, reflexive pronouns, and negative words are placed before the first part of the conjugation.

  Me he encargado del trabajo.   or   *No se ha afeitado todavía.*

A. Complete the sentences with the correct form of the verb **haber**. The first one has been done for you.

1. Yo _____*he*_____ comido.

2. Ellas _____ trabajado.

3. Nosotros _____ permitido.

4. José _____ aprendido.

5. Tú te _____ dormido.

6. Yo me _____ lavado.

7. María no se _____ presentado.

8. Nosotros no lo _____ repartido.

B. Complete each sentence with the correct present perfect form of the verb. Follow the model. Note that the past participle always ends in **-o**.

Modelo   Margarita Arroyo ___*ha*___ ___*repartido*___ pizzas. (**repartir**)

1. El Sr. Flores _____ _____ a los niños de sus vecinos. (**cuidar**)

2. Las empleadas _____ _____ experiencia con la computación. (**tener**)

3. Marisol y yo _____ _____ muchas clases de arte. (**tomar**)

4. ¿Uds. _____ _____ un trabajo? (**solicitar**)

5. Yo _____ _____ computadoras. (**reparar**)

6. Y tú, ¿_____ _____ con tu trabajo? (**cumplir**)

El presente perfecto (*continued*)

- Verbs that end in **-aer, -eer,** and **-eír,** as well as the verb **oír,** have a written accent mark on the *i* in the past participle.

  leer: leído   oir: oído

  sonreír: sonreído   caer: caído

  Verbs that end in **-uir** do <u>not</u> get a written accent mark in the past participle.

C. Complete the following sentences with the present perfect of the verb. **¡Cuidado!** Remember that verbs that end in **-uir,** do not require an accent mark. Follow the model.

> **Modelo**   (Yo) ____*he*____ _____*leído*_____ los anuncios clasificados. (**leer**)

1. Tú _____ _____ que esta compañía es buena. (**oír**)

2. Mateo Ortega se _____ _____ de su bicicleta. (**caer**)

3. La jefa _____ _____ dos cartas de recomendación. (**incluir**)

4. Los hermanos García _____ _____ una casa. (**construir**)

- Remember that several Spanish verbs have irregular past participles.

  decir: **dicho**   hacer: **hecho**

  poner: **puesto**   ver: **visto**

  escribir: **escrito**   morir: **muerto**

  abrir: **abierto**   ser: **sido**

  resolver: **resuelto**   romper: **roto**

  volver: **vuelto**

D. Tell what the following job candidates have done by writing the irregular present perfect of the verb given. Follow the model.

> **Modelo**   (**escribir**) Verónica Sánchez _____*ha*____ _____*escrito*_____ una descripción de todos sus trabajos.

1. Héctor Pérez y Miguel Díaz _____ _____ que son muy puntuales. (**decir**)

2. Juanita Sánchez y Lidia Rivera _____ _____ mucha información en sus solicitudes de empleo. (**poner**)

3. Raúl Ramírez y yo _____ _____ un vaso en la oficina. (**romper**)

4. Marcos Ortiz _____ _____ su carta de recomendación. (**abrir**)

5. Ud. _____ _____ un problema importante con su horario. (**resolver**)

realidades.com ✔

- Web Code: jed-0503

El pluscuamperfecto (p. 217)

- In Spanish, the *pluperfect* tense is used to tell about an action in the past that happened *before* another action in the past. It can generally be translated with the words "had done" in English.

    Cuando los empleados llegaron a la oficina, su jefe ya *había empezado* a trabajar.
    When the employees arrived at the office, their boss had already started to work.

- You form the pluperfect tense by combining the imperfect forms of the verb **haber** with the past participle of another verb. Here are the pluperfect forms of the verb **repartir**:

había repartido	**habíamos** repartido
habías repartido	**habíais** repartido
había repartido	**habían** repartido

A. What had everyone done prior to their job interviews? Complete the sentences with the correct imperfect form of the verb **haber**. Follow the model.

> **Modelo**   El gerente _____*había*_____ leído las solicitudes de empleo.

1. El dueño _____ hecho una lista de requisitos.

2. Las recepcionistas _____ copiado las solicitudes de empleo.

3. Elena y yo _____ traído una lista de referencias.

4. (Yo) _____ practicado unas preguntas con mi mamá.

5. Y tú, ¿te _____ preparado antes de la entrevista?

B. Why was Mr. Gutiérrez so nervous before beginning his first day at his new job? Complete each sentence with the correct regular past participles. Follow the model.

> **Modelo**   Había _____*mentido*_____ en su solicitud de empleo. (**mentir**)

1. No había _____ a los otros empleados. (**conocer**)

2. No había _____ si había una cafetería en el edificio. (**preguntar**)

3. Había _____ la dirección incorrecta en su solicitud. (**dar**)

4. No había _____ mucho. (**dormir**)

5. Había _____ sus cartas de recomendación. (**olvidar**)

Realidades 3

Capítulo 5

Nombre _____

Hora _____

Fecha _____

Guided Practice Activities, Sheet 4

C. Complete each sentence with the pluperfect tense of the verb in parentheses to tell what people had done before their first day of work. Follow the model.

¡Cuidado! Some past participles require an accent mark and some have completely irregular forms.

Modelo (escribir) Carlos ___*había*___ ___*escrito*___ en una tarjeta todo lo que quería recordar.

1. (**oír**) Nosotros _____ _____ muchos comentarios positivos sobre la compañía.

2. (**poner**) Yo _____ _____ unos bolígrafos y un calendario en mi mochila.

3. (**leer**) Todos los nuevos empleados _____ _____ el manual de trabajo.

4. (**decir**) La jefa de la compañía _____ _____ "Bienvenidos a nuestra oficina."

5. (**sonreír**) Tú _____ _____ durante la entrevista.

D. Based on the pictures, tell what each person had done before leaving for work. You can use the verbs in the word bank to help you describe the actions.

¡Cuidado! Reflexive pronouns, object pronouns, and negative words go in front of the conjugated form of **haber** in the pluperfect.

| levantarse | ~~secarse~~ | lavarse | afeitarse | cepillarse | ponerse |

Modelo Marta ___*se*___ ___*había*___ ___*secado*___ el pelo.

1. Los gemelos _____ _____ _____ los dientes.

2. Luis _____ _____ _____ temprano.

3. Yo _____ _____ _____ la camisa.

4. Tú _____ _____ _____ .

5. Nosotros _____ _____ _____ las manos.

realidades.com

• Web Code: jed-0504

Realidades 3

Capítulo 5

Nombre

Fecha

Hora

Vocabulary Flash Cards, Sheet 6

Write the Spanish vocabulary word below each picture. If there is a word or phrase, copy it in the space provided. Be sure to include the article for each noun.

_____

_____

_____

_____

_____

_____

a favor de

_____

_____

_____

Copy the word or phrase in the space provided. Be sure to include the article for each noun.

la campaña	**la ciudadanía**	**el ciudadano, la ciudadana**
_____ _____	_____ _____	_____ _____ _____
los derechos	**educar**	**en contra (de)**
_____ _____	_____	_____ _____
garantizar	**la gente sin hogar**	**injusto, injusta**
_____	_____ _____ _____	_____ _____

Realidades 3

Capítulo 5

Nombre

Hora

Fecha

Vocabulary Flash Cards, Sheet 8

Copy the word or phrase in the space provided. Be sure to include the article for each noun.

juntar fondos	**justo, justa**	**la ley**
_____	_____	_____
la manifestación	**el medio ambiente**	**me encantaría**
_____	_____	_____
me es imposible	**me interesaría**	**organizar**
_____	_____	_____

Copy the word or phrase in the space provided. Be sure to include the article for each noun. The blank cards can be used to write and practice other Spanish vocabulary for the chapter.

proteger	**responsable**	**la responsabilidad**
el requisito	**el servicio social**	**la sociedad**
soler		

Nombre _____

Hora _____

Fecha _____

Vocabulary Check, Sheet 5

Tear out this page. Write the English words on the lines. Fold the paper along the dotted line to see the correct answers so you can check your work.

a favor de _____

la campaña _____

el centro de la comunidad _____

el centro de rehabilitación _____

el centro recreativo _____

la ciudadanía _____

el ciudadano, la ciudadana _____

el comedor de beneficencia _____

construir (*i*→*y*) _____

los derechos _____

donar _____

educar _____

en contra (de) _____

garantizar _____

la gente sin hogar _____

Fold In

Realidades ③

Capítulo 5

Nombre _____

Hora _____

Fecha _____

Vocabulary Check, Sheet 6

Tear out this page. Write the Spanish words on the lines. Fold the paper along the dotted line to see the correct answers so you can check your work.

in favor of   _____

campaign   _____

community center   _____

      _____

rehabilitation center   _____

      _____

recreation center   _____

citizenship   _____

citizen   _____

      _____

soup kitchen   _____

      _____

to build   _____

rights   _____

to donate   _____

to educate   _____

against   _____

to guarantee   _____

homeless people   _____

Fold In →

Realidades 3

Capítulo 5

Nombre _____

Fecha _____

Hora _____

Vocabulary Check, Sheet 7

Tear out this page. Write the English words on the lines. Fold the paper along the dotted line to see the correct answers so you can check your work.

el hogar de ancianos   _____

injusto, injusta   _____

juntar fondos   _____

justo, justa   _____

la ley   _____

la manifestación   _____

la marcha   _____

el medio ambiente   _____

me es imposible   _____

me encantaría   _____

me interesaría   _____

organizar   _____

proteger   _____

sembrar (e➜ie)   _____

el servicio social   _____

la sociedad   _____

Fold In

Realidades 3

Capítulo 5

Nombre _____

Fecha _____

Hora _____

Vocabulary Check, Sheet 8

Tear out this page. Write the Spanish words on the lines. Fold the paper along the dotted line to see the correct answers so you can check your work.

home for the elderly _____

unfair _____

to fundraise _____

fair _____

law _____

demonstration _____

march _____

environment _____

It is impossible for me... _____

I would love to... _____

I would be interested... _____

to organize _____

to protect _____

to plant _____

social service _____

society _____

Fold In ←

realidades.com

• Web Code: jed-0506

El presente perfecto del subjuntivo (p. 227)

- The present perfect subjunctive is used to talk about actions or situations that may have occurred before the action of the main verb. The present perfect subjunctive often follows expressions of emotion like those you used for the present subjunctive. To review present subjunctive with emotions, see pages 168–170 of your textbook.

  Es bueno que tú *hayas ayudado* en el comedor de beneficencia.

  It is good that you have helped out at the soup kitchen.

- You form the present perfect subjunctive by combining the present subjunctive of the verb **haber** with the past participle of another verb. The verb **educar** has been conjugated as an example below.

haya educado	**hayamos** educado
hayas educado	**hayáis** educado
haya educado	**hayan** educado

A. Read each sentence and underline the expression of emotion that indicates the subjunctive should be used. Then, circle the correct form of **haber** that is used in the present perfect subjunctive. Follow the model.

Modelo <u>Me alegro</u> de que muchos (**han** / (**hayan**)) participado en la manifestación.

1. Es bueno que estos programas (**han** / **hayan**) ayudado a tantas personas.

2. Me sorprende que los estudiantes (**hayas** / **hayan**) trabajado en el hogar de ancianos.

3. Siento que tú no (**haya** / **hayas**) recibido ayuda.

4. Es interesante que el presidente (**hayan** / **haya**) protegido los derechos de los niños.

5. A mí me gusta que nosotros (**hayamos** / **hayan**) sembrado árboles hoy.

B. Complete each sentence about what volunteers have done, using the present perfect of the subjunctive of the verb. Follow the model.

Modelo Es maravilloso que muchos ___*hayan*___ ___*trabajado*___ en el comedor de beneficencia. (**trabajar**)

1. Estamos orgullosos de que los jóvenes _____ _____ en la marcha. (**participar**)

2. Es una lástima que ese político no _____ _____ el movimiento por los derechos de los ancianos. (**apoyar**)

3. Ojalá que nosotros _____ _____ con nuestras responsabilidades. (**cumplir**)

4. Estamos contentos de que esta organización _____ _____ construir un centro recreativo nuevo. (**decidir**)

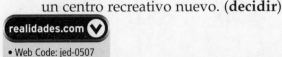

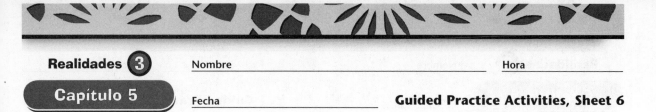

• **¡Recuerda!** Some past participles require an accent mark and some have completely irregular forms. Look back at page 61 of your workbook for a reminder of these verbs.

C. Complete each sentence with the present perfect subjunctive. Follow the model. **¡Cuidado!** The past participles used are irregular.

Modelo (**abrir**) Me alegro de que Uds. les ___*hayan*___ ___*abierto*___ las puertas a esas personas.

1. (**escribir**) Es excelente que tú _____ _____ una composición sobre los derechos humanos.

2. (**hacer**) Nos gusta que los enemigos _____ _____ las paces.

3. (**ver**) Espero que José _____ _____ el nuevo centro de la comunidad.

4. (**resolver**) Me preocupa que el gobierno no _____ _____ los problemas de la contaminación del medio ambiente.

5. (**decir**) Es triste que el presidente _____ _____ que hay tanta gente sin hogar en nuestro país.

D. Create complete sentences by conjugating the verbs in the present perfect subjunctive. Follow the model.

Modelo Es una lástima / que / los estudiantes / no (**donar**) / mucha comida / a la gente pobre

*Es una lástima que los estudiantes no hayan donado mucha comida*
*a la gente pobre.*

1. Es mejor / que / mi amigo / (**aprender**) / más / sobre la campaña

_____

2. Es terrible / que / la comunidad / (**eliminar**) / los servicios sociales

_____

3. Nos sorprende / que / nadie / (**escribir**) / cartas / para apoyar / a los inmigrantes

_____

4. Esperamos / que / los estudiantes / (**hacer**) / proyectos / para beneficiar / a la comunidad

_____

5. El director de escuela / se alegra de / que / nosotros / (**ir**) / al centro recreativo

_____

realidades.com
• Web Code: jed-0507

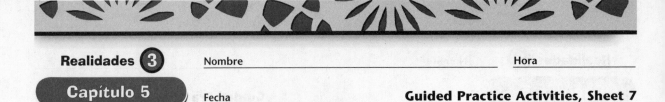

Los adjetivos y los pronombres posesivos (p. 229)

• In Spanish, demonstrative adjectives are used to indicate things that are near or far from the speaker. Demonstrative adjectives are placed in front of a noun and agree with the noun in gender and number.

> **Este** árbol es muy alto.   *This tree is very tall.*

Below is a list of the forms of demonstrative adjectives used to say *this/these (near you)*, *that/those (near the person you're speaking with)*, and *that/those (far away)*.

this: **este, esta**	these: **estos, estas**
that (near): **ese, esa**	those (near): **esos, esas**
that (far): **aquel, aquella**	those (far): **aquellos, aquellas**

A. Your friend is telling you about several of the students below and their accomplishments. Decide which pair of students she is talking about.

1. __A__ Estos estudiantes han construido un centro de donaciones en su escuela.

2. _____ Aquellos jóvenes han hecho mucho trabajo para el centro recreativo.

3. _____ Sé que esos muchachos juntan fondos para el medio ambiente todos los años.

4. _____ Aquellos chicos suelen participar en muchas marchas.

5. _____ ¿Han cumplido estos jóvenes con sus responsabilidades como voluntarios?

B. Circle the demonstrative adjective needed to complete each sentence.

Modelo   (**Esos** /(**Esas**)) donaciones son para el centro de la comunidad.

1. ¿Adónde vas con (**estos** / **estas**) cajas de ropa?

2. (**Aquellas** / **Aquellos**) chicas tienen que solicitar más donaciones.

3. Queremos felicitar a (**ese** / **esos**) voluntarios.

4. Necesitan proteger (**esta** / **estas**) leyes.

- Demonstrative <u>pronouns</u> take the place of nouns. The pronouns must agree in gender and number with the nouns they replace.

  *No quiero este documento. Quiero **ése.***

- Demonstrative pronouns all have written accent marks. Look at the list below:

  this; these: **éste, ésta; éstos, éstas**

  that; those (near the person you're speaking with): **ése, ésa; ésos, ésas**

  that; those (far away): **aquél, aquélla; aquéllos, aquéllas**

C. Underline the correct demonstrative pronoun based on the questions asked. Follow the model.

Modelo   **A:** ¿Qué libro prefieres?   **B:** Prefiero (<u>ése</u> / ésos) porque es para niños.

1. **A:** ¿Quieres una de las camisas?   **B:** Sí, quiero (**éste / ésta**).

2. **A:** ¿Con qué grupo voy a trabajar?   **B:** Vas a trabajar con (**aquél / aquella**).

3. **A:** ¿Qué casas vamos a reparar?   **B:** Vamos a reparar (**aquéllas / aquél**).

4. **A:** ¿Cuál es el documento que vamos a entregar?   **B:** Es (**ése / ésa**).

D. Identify the noun in the first part of the sentence that is being omitted in the second part. Circle the noun. Then, write the correct form of the demonstrative pronoun.

Modelo   Me gusta esta (camisa) pero no me gusta _____*ésa*_____ *(that one).*

1. No voy a comer esas fresas pero sí voy a comer _____ *(these).*

2. No pensamos comprar estos libros pero nos interesan mucho _____
   (those over there).

3. Ellas no quieren marchar por estas calles sino por _____ *(those).*

4. Mis amigos van a llenar esos documentos y yo voy a llenar _____
   (this one).

- There are also three "neutral" demonstrative pronouns that do not have a gender or number. They refer to an idea or to something that has not yet been mentioned.

¿Qué es **eso**?	*What is **that**?*
Esto es un desastre.	***This** is a disaster.*
¿**Aquello** es un centro recreativo?	*Is **that (thing over there)** a rec center?*

  These do not have accent marks and <u>never</u> appear immediately before a noun.

E. Choose whether the demonstrative adjective or the demonstrative pronoun would be used in each of the following situations. Circle your choice.

1. ¿Qué es (**este / esto**)?   3. Traigamos (**aquel / aquello**) libro al centro recreativo.

2. Discutamos (**ese / eso**) más.   4. ¿Quién ha donado (**esa / eso**) computadora?

- Web Code: jed-0508

Realidades 3

Capítulo 5

Nombre _____

Fecha _____

Hora _____

Reading Activities, Sheet 1

Puente a la cultura (pp. 232–233)

A. There are photos of various people mentioned in the reading in your textbook. Match the names of the people with the area of society with which they are paired.

1. _____ Ken Salazar   **A.** los negocios

2. _____ Sonia Sotomayor   **B.** la política

3. _____ Linda Alvarado   **C.** las ciencias

4. _____ Mario Molina

5. _____ Hilda Solís

B. Read the section titled **La población** on page 232 of your textbook. Say whether the following statements are true (**cierto**) or false (**falso**).

1. Más de 50 por ciento de la población de los Estados Unidos es hispano.   **cierto**   **falso**

2. Hay casi 28 millones de hispanohablantes en los Estados Unidos.   **cierto**   **falso**

3. Un diez por ciento de los ciudadanos de los Estados Unidos habla español.   **cierto**   **falso**

4. Hay más hispanohablantes en los Estados Unidos que personas que hablan inglés.   **cierto**   **falso**

5. El español influye en muchos campos de los Estados Unidos.   **cierto**   **falso**

C. Match the three Hispanic women discussed in the sections titled **La política, Los negocios,** and **Las ciencias** with the reason for which they are considered successful.

_____ Sonia Sotomayor   **A.** primera mujer hispana que trabajó para el Senado de California y para el gobierno de Obama

_____ Hilda Solís   **B.** presidenta de su propia compañía y cinco compañías más

_____ Linda G. Alvarado   **C.** primera jueza hispana de la Corte Suprema

• Web Code: jed-0510

Lectura (pp. 238–241)

A. Look at the title of the reading and the four drawings on pages 238 to 240 in order to make predictions about what you will read. Then, place a checkmark next to the type of reading you think this will be.

_____ una biografía realista

_____ una leyenda imaginativa

B. Several key words to understanding the story appear on the first page. Read the excerpts below to help you determine which of the meanings is correct for each highlighted phrase.

> Lo que le molestaba a la viejita es que a aquel que veía el fruto **le daban ganas de** comérselo y sin pedirle permiso se subía a la **mata** y se anolaba las huayas (ate the guavas).

1. "le daban ganas de"   **a.** querían   **b.** sabían

2. "mata"   **a.** árbol   **b.** muerte

> ... un viejito pedía **limosna**, pedía aunque sea le dieran algo para comer en vez de monedas, pero nadie lo **tomaba en cuenta**.

3. "limosna"   **a.** dinero donado   **b.** bebida de frutas

4. "tomaba en cuenta"   **a.** prestaba atención   **b.** conocía

C. In this chapter, you learned about demonstrative pronouns. Look at the following sentence from the reading and circle the demonstrative pronoun. Then, underline the word in the sentence that the demonstrative pronoun replaces.

> En la puerta de su casa había sembrado una mata de huaya, y ésta le daba frutos todo el año.

Realidades 3

Nombre _____

Hora _____

Capítulo 5

Fecha _____

Reading Activities, Sheet 3

D. As you read the story, use the drawings to help you understand what is happening. Circle the letter of the sentence which best describes each drawing.

Dibujo #1 (p. 238)

a. La viejita tiene muchos hijos que la hacen muy feliz.

b. La viejita se preocupa porque unas personas se suben a su árbol para comer las frutas sin permiso.

Dibujo #2 (p. 239)

a. La Muerte quiere matar al árbol de la viejita porque es un árbol viejo.

b. La Muerte viene a matar a la viejita, pero no puede bajarse del árbol.

Dibujo #3 (p. 240)

a. La Muerte no mata a la Pobreza porque ella le permite bajarse del árbol.

b. La Muerte mata a la Pobreza, eliminándola del mundo.

E. This story has four main characters, which are listed in the word bank below. Complete the following lines from the reading in your textbook with one of the character's names.

la viejita (la Pobreza)	el viejito	la Muerte	el doctor

1. —¡Que se cumpla lo que pides! —contestó _____ y se fue satisfecho.

2. Así pasaron muchos años y _____ no llegaba a nadie...

3. Un día, uno de los doctores fue a casa de _____ y lo primero que vio fue la mata llena de frutos.

4. —Entonces, a eso se debe que no mueran las personas —dijo _____.

5. Entonces la gente acordó cortar el árbol para que bajaran _____ y _____.

6. Se fue el señor de _____ y _____ se quedó en la tierra.

Saber vs. conocer (p. 247)

- The verbs **saber** and **conocer** both mean "to know," but they are used in different contexts.

  Saber is used to talk about knowing a fact or a piece of information, or knowing how to do something.

  > Yo **sé** que Madrid es la capital de España.
  >
  > Los bomberos **saben** apagar un incendio.

  Conocer is used to talk about being acquainted or familiar with a person, place, or thing.

  > Yo **conozco** a un policía.
  >
  > Nosotros **conocemos** la ciudad de Buenos Aires.

A. Read each of the following pieces of information. Decide if "knowing" each one would use the verb **saber** or the verb **conocer** and mark your answer. Follow the model.

| Modelo | una actriz famosa | _____ saber | ✓ conocer |

1. reparar coches _____ saber _____ conocer

2. la música latina _____ saber _____ conocer

3. dónde está San Antonio _____ saber _____ conocer

4. la ciudad de Nueva York _____ saber _____ conocer

5. el dentista de tu comunidad _____ saber _____ conocer

6. cuándo es el examen final _____ saber _____ conocer

B. Your school recently hired a new principal. Circle the verb that best completes each statement or question about his qualifications.

Modelo ¿(Sabes /(Conoces)) la Universidad de Puerto Rico?

1. Él (**sabe / conoce**) mucho del mundo de negocios.

2. También (**sabe / conoce**) a muchos miembros de nuestra comunidad.

3. Mis padres lo (**saben / conocen**).

4. Él (**conoce / sabe**) bien nuestra ciudad.

5. Él (**conoce / sabe**) trabajar con los estudiantes y los maestros.

realidades.com

- Web Code: jed-0601

Realidades ③

Capítulo 6

Nombre _____

Fecha _____

Hora _____

AVSR, Sheet 2

C. Complete each sentence with **conozco** or **sé**. Your sentences can be affirmative or negative, based on your own experiences. Follow the model.

Modelo   _Conozco (No conozco)_ bien a Jennifer López.

1. _____ cuándo van a encontrar una cura contra el cáncer.

2. _____ a una mujer de negocios muy inteligente.

3. _____ usar muchos programas en la computadora.

4. _____ Puerto Rico.

D. Complete the sentences below with the correct form of **saber** or **conocer** to discuss jobs and professionals in the community. Follow the model.

Modelo   Patricia, tú _____conoces_____ al veterinario, el Sr. Hernández, ¿no?

1. Sí, nosotros lo _____ (a él) muy bien.

2. Nosotros no _____ cuál es el nombre del gerente de esa compañía.

3. ¿_____ (tú) contar dinero tan rápidamente como ese cajero?

4. ¿_____ (Uds.) un buen sitio Web para encontrar trabajos?

5. Yo _____ al secretario de ese grupo político.

6. Esos mecánicos no _____ reparar los motores de los coches.

- In the preterite, **conocer** means "to meet someone for the first time."

  *Mis padres **conocieron** al veterinario la semana pasada cuando mi gato se enfermó.*

E. Create sentences with the preterite form of **conocer** about when various people met. Follow the model.

Modelo   Mi tío / conocer / al presidente / el año pasado.

   Mi tío conoció al presidente el año pasado.

1. El dependiente / conocer / al dueño / hace dos años

_____

2. Yo / conocer / a mi profesora de español / en septiembre

_____

3. Nosotros / conocer / a una actriz famosa / el verano pasado

_____

4. Mis amigos / conocer / al médico / el miércoles pasado

_____

El *se* impersonal (p. 249)

- When speaking in English, we often say "they do (something)," "you do (something)," "one does (something)," or "people do (something)" to talk about people in general. In Spanish, you can also talk about people in an impersonal or indefinite sense. To do so, you use *se* + the **Ud./él/ella** or the **Uds./ellos/ellas** form of the verb.

Se **venden videos aquí.**	*They sell videos here.*
Se **pone el aceite en la sartén.**	*You put (One puts) oil in the frying pan.*

  In the sentences above, note that you don't know who performs the action. The word or words that come *after* the verb determine whether the verb is singular or plural.

A. First, underline the *impersonal se* expression in each sentence. Then, write the letter of the English translation that might be used for it from the list below. Follow the model.

A. They dance	**C.** They eat	**E.** They sell
B. One finds / You find	**D.** One talks / They talk	**F.** They celebrate

Modelo   En España <u>se cena</u> muy tarde.   _C_

1. En México se celebran muchos días festivos.   _____

2. Se encuentran muchos animales en Costa Rica.   _____

3. En Colombia se habla mucho de los problemas políticos. _____

4. Se baila el tango en Argentina.   _____

5. En Perú se venden muchas artesanías indígenas.   _____

B. Choose the correct verb to complete each description of services offered at the local community center. Follow the model.

Modelo   Se ((habla) / hablan) español.

1. Se (**vende / venden**) refrescos.

2. Se (**ofrece / ofrecen**) información.

3. Se (**mejora / mejoran**) las vidas.

4. Se (**sirve / sirven**) café.

5. Se (**toma / toman**) clases de arte.

6. Se (**construye / construyen**) casas para la gente sin hogar.

realidades.com
- Web Code: jed-0601

Realidades 3

Capítulo 6

Nombre _____

Hora _____

Fecha _____

AVSR, Sheet 4

C. Combine the verbs and objects given to create sentences using **se**. Follow the model.

| Modelo | reparar / televisores 3D | *Se reparan televisores 3D.* |

1. beber / agua _____

2. eliminar / contaminantes _____

3. vender / ropa _____

4. servir / comida _____

5. sembrar / plantas _____

6. leer / poemas _____

- When the word following the conjugated verb in an *impersonal se* expression is an infinitive, the verb form is singular.

   ***Se necesita* encontrar un apartamento.**   *One needs to find an apartment.*

D. Use the *impersonal se* with the two verbs given to create sentences. Use the singular form of the first verb and the infinitive of the second verb. Follow the model.

| Modelo | (necesitar / proteger) la naturaleza |

   Se necesita proteger la naturaleza. _____

1. (**poder / beneficiar**) del aire fresco

   _____

2. (**deber / eliminar**) el estrés

   _____

3. (**acabar de / terminar**) la página web

   _____

4. (**no necesitar / construir**) la casa

   _____

5. (**poder / cambiar**) la vida

   _____

Realidades **3**

Capítulo 6

Nombre _____

Hora _____

Fecha _____

Vocabulary Flash Cards, Sheet 1

Write the Spanish vocabulary word below each picture. Be sure to include the article for each noun.

_____

_____

_____

_____

_____

_____

_____

_____

_____

_____

_____

_____

_____

_____

_____

_____

_____

_____

Realidades **3**

Capítulo 6

Nombre _____

Fecha _____

Hora _____

Vocabulary Flash Cards, Sheet 2

Write the Spanish vocabulary word below each picture. If there is a word or phrase, copy it in the space provided. Be sure to include the article for each noun.

_____	_____ _____	**además de** _____
ahorrar _____	**ambicioso, ambiciosa** _____	**así que** _____
averiguar _____	**capaz** _____	**casado, casada** _____

Realidades 3

Nombre _____

Hora _____

Capítulo 6

Fecha _____

Vocabulary Flash Cards, Sheet 3

Copy the word or phrase in the space provided. Be sure to include the article for each noun.

el contador, la contadora	**cuidadoso, cuidadosa**	**dedicarse a**
_____ _____	_____	_____
_____ _____	_____	_____
desempeñar un cargo	**diseñar**	**eficiente**
_____		
_____ _____	_____	_____
emprendedor, emprendedora	**la empresa**	**las finanzas**
_____	_____	_____
_____ _____	_____	_____

Realidades ③

Capítulo 6

Nombre _____

Hora _____

Fecha _____

Vocabulary Flash Cards, Sheet 4

Copy the word or phrase in the space provided. Be sure to include the article for each noun.

hacerse _____	**haré lo que me dé la gana** ___ ___ ___ ___ ___ ___ ___	**el ingeniero, la ingeniera** _____ _____ _____ _____
el jefe, la jefa _____ _____ _____ _____	**lograr** _____	**maduro, madura** _____ _____
mudarse _____	**la mujer de negocios** _____ _____ _____ _____	**por lo tanto** _____ _____ _____

Realidades 3

Capítulo 6

Nombre _____

Hora _____

Fecha _____

Vocabulary Flash Cards, Sheet 5

Copy the word or phrase in the space provided. Be sure to include the article for each noun. The blank cards can be used to write and practice other Spanish vocabulary for the chapter.

el programador, la programadora _____ _____ _____ _____	**próximo, próxima** _____ _____	**seguir una carrera** _____ _____ _____
soltero, soltera _____ _____	**tomar decisiones** _____ _____	**traducir** _____ _____
el traductor, la traductora _____ _____ _____ _____		

Realidades 3

Capítulo 6

Nombre _____

Fecha _____

Hora _____

Vocabulary Check, Sheet 1

Tear out this page. Write the English words on the lines. Fold the paper along the dotted line to see the correct answers so you can check your work.

ahorrar _____

el banquero,
la banquera _____

capaz _____

casado, casada _____

el científico,
la científica _____

el cocinero,
la cocinera _____

el contador,
la contadora _____

cuidadoso,
cuidadosa _____

dedicarse a _____

desempeñar un cargo _____

el diseñador,
la diseñadora _____

diseñar _____

emprendedor,
emprendedora _____

la empresa _____

las finanzas _____

Fold In

Tear out this page. Write the Spanish words on the lines. Fold the paper along the dotted line to see the correct answers so you can check your work.

to save   _____

banker   _____

                         _____

able   _____

married   _____

scientist   _____

                         _____

cook   _____

                         _____

accountant   _____

                         _____

careful   _____

                         _____

to dedicate oneself to   _____

to hold a position   _____

designer   _____

                         _____

to design   _____

enterprising   _____

                         _____

business   _____

finance   _____

Fold In ←

Realidades 3

Nombre _____

Hora _____

Capítulo 6

Fecha _____

Vocabulary Check, Sheet 3

Tear out this page. Write the English words on the lines. Fold the paper along the dotted line to see the correct answers so you can check your work.

graduarse (u➔ú) _____

hacerse _____

el hombre de negocios,
la mujer de negocios _____

el ingeniero,
la ingeniera _____

el jefe, la jefa _____

el juez, la jueza _____

lograr _____

maduro, madura _____

mudarse _____

el peluquero,
la peluquera _____

el programador,
la programadora _____

el redactor, la redactora _____

seguir una carrera _____

soltero, soltera _____

el traductor,
la traductora _____

traducir (zc) _____

Fold In

Realidades 3

Capítulo 6

Nombre _____

Hora _____

Fecha _____

Vocabulary Check, Sheet 4

Tear out this page. Write the Spanish words on the lines. Fold the paper along the dotted line to see the correct answers so you can check your work.

to graduate _____

to become _____

businessman, _____
businesswoman _____

engineer _____
_____

boss _____

judge _____

to achieve, to manage to _____

mature _____

to move to _____

hairstylist _____
_____

programmer _____
_____

editor _____

to pursue a career _____

single _____

translator _____
_____

to translate _____

Fold In ←

realidades.com
• Web Code: jed-0602

Realidades **3**

Capítulo 6

Nombre _____

Fecha _____

Hora _____

Guided Practice Activities, Sheet 1

El futuro (p. 260)

- You already know at least two ways to express the future in Spanish: by using the present tense or by using **ir** + **a** + *infinitive*:

  Mañana *tengo* **una entrevista.**   *I have an interview tomorrow.*

  Vamos a **traducir el documento.**   *We are going to translate the document.*

- The future can also be expressed in Spanish by using the *future tense*. The endings for the future tense are the same for regular **-ar**, **-er**, and **-ir** verbs. For regular verbs, the endings are attached to the infinitive. See two examples below:

estudiar		repetir	
estudiar**é**	estudiar**emos**	repetir**é**	repetir**emos**
estudiar**ás**	estudiar**éis**	repetir**ás**	repetir**éis**
estudiar**á**	estudiar**án**	repetir**á**	repetir**án**

A. Read each of the following statements and decide if it describes something that took place in the past, or something that will take place in the future. Mark your answer. Follow the model.

Modelo   Montaba en triciclo.   ___✓___ en el pasado   _____ en el futuro

1. Manejaremos coches eléctricos.   _____ en el pasado   _____ en el futuro

2. Nadábamos en la piscina.   _____ en el pasado   _____ en el futuro

3. Todos viajarán a otros planetas.   _____ en el pasado   _____ en el futuro

4. Los teléfonos no existían.   _____ en el pasado   _____ en el futuro

5. Las enfermedades serán eliminadas.   _____ en el pasado   _____ en el futuro

B. Choose the correct verb form to complete each prediction about what will happen in the year 2025. Follow the model.

Modelo   Los estudiantes ((usarán)/ usará) computadoras todos los días.

1. Yo (**será / seré**) banquero.

2. Mi mejor amigo y yo (**vivirá / viviremos**) en la Luna.

3. Mi profesor/a de español (**conseguirá / conseguirás**) un puesto como director/a.

4. Mis padres (**estarás / estarán**) jubilados.

5. Tú (**hablarás / hablarán**) con los extraterrestres.

6. Nosotros (**disfrutaremos / disfrutarán**) mucho.

Realidades 3

Capítulo 6

Nombre _____

Hora _____

Fecha _____

Guided Practice Activities, Sheet 2

C. Complete each sentence with the correct form of the future tense of the verb given. Follow the model. **¡Recuerda!** All forms except **nosotros** have an accent mark.

Modelo   Nosotros ___*trabajaremos*___ en una oficina. (**trabajar**)

1. Lidia _____ una madre estupenda. (**ser**)

2. Mi familia _____ _____ a una ciudad más grande. (**mudarse**)

3. Yo _____ un cargo de contadora. (**desempeñar**)

4. Nosotros _____ mucho dinero en el banco. (**ahorrar**)

5. Tú _____ _____ una carrera muy interesante. (**seguir**)

- Some verbs have irregular stems in the future tense. You will use these stems instead of the full infinitive. Note that the irregular verbs have the same future endings as regular verbs. Look at the list of irregular stems below.

tener: **tendr-**	decir: **dir-**
salir: **saldr-**	poder: **podr-**
venir: **vendr-**	haber: **habr-**
poner: **pondr-**	hacer: **har-**
saber: **sabr-**	querer: **querr-**

  -é, -ás, -á, -émos, -éis, -án

D. Write the irregular future tense verbs for each subject and infinitive.

Modelo   nosotros (**salir**) ___*saldremos*___

1. yo (**poder**) _____

2. ellas (**querer**) _____

3. él (**hacer**) _____

4. tú (**tener**) _____

5. Uds. (**decir**) _____

6. yo (**saber**) _____

7. nosotras (**poner**) _____

8. ella (**venir**) _____

E. Complete each sentence about your hopes for the future using the future tense of the irregular verbs in parentheses.

Modelo   Mis padres _____*podrán*_____ mandarme a una universidad famosa. (**poder**)

1. Mis amigos _____ mucho sobre tecnología. (**saber**)

2. Mi esposo y yo _____ una casa grande. (**tener**)

3. _____ un robot que limpie toda la casa. (**haber**)

4. Mis colegas y yo _____ de la oficina temprano los viernes. (**salir**)

5. Mi jefa _____ que yo soy más capaz que los otros. (**decir**)

Realidades 3

Capítulo 6

Nombre _____

Fecha _____

Hora _____

Guided Practice Activities, Sheet 3

El futuro (*continued*)

F. Write sentences based upon the pictures. Use the information in parentheses in your sentences, including the future tense of the infinitives.

Modelo (Rafael / ser / _____ / algún día)

Rafael será diseñador algún día.

1. (Eugenio / estudiar para ser / _____)

_____

2. (en nuestra comunidad / haber muchos / _____)

_____

3. (yo / trabajar como / _____)

_____

4. (nosotros / conocer a / _____ / muy capaz)

_____

5. (el autor / querer trabajar con / _____ / bueno)

_____

6. (tú / hacerse / _____)

_____

Realidades 3

Capítulo 6

Nombre _____

Hora _____

Fecha _____

Guided Practice Activities, Sheet 4

El futuro de probabilidad (p. 263)

- You can use the future tense in Spanish to express uncertainty or probability about the present.

  Some equivalent expressions in English are *I wonder, it's probably,* and *it must be.*

  ¿Hará frío hoy?   *I wonder if it's cold today.*

  Mis guantes y mi chaqueta *estarán* en el armario.
  My gloves and jacket must be in the closet.

A. A person is very disoriented. Underline the phrases in their sentences that use the future of probability. Then find the best way of expressing this phrase in English in the word bank. Write the letter of the English phrase.

  A. I wonder what time it is. / What time must it be?
  B. I wonder where my parents are. / Where might my parents be?
  C. I wonder why there are so many people here.
  D. I wonder what today's date is. / What must today's date be?
  E. I wonder who he is. / Who could he be?
  F. I wonder what my brothers are doing.

1. ¿Qué harán mis hermanos? _____

2. ¿Qué hora será? _____

3. ¿Dónde estarán mis padres? _____

4. ¿Cuál será la fecha de hoy? _____

5. ¿Por qué habrá tantas personas aquí? _____

6. ¿Quién será él? _____

B. You are daydreaming during your Spanish class. Use the elements given and the future of probability to tell what you imagine your friends and family must be doing. Follow the model.

Modelo   Mi madre / estar / en su oficina   *Mi madre estará en su oficina.*

1. Mis amigos / jugar fútbol / en la clase de educación física

_____

2. Mi perro / dormir / en el sofá _____

3. Mis abuelos / dar una caminata / por el parque

_____

4. ¿Qué / hacer / mi padre? _____

5. Mi mejor amiga / dar / un examen difícil / en la clase de matemáticas

_____

realidades.com
- Web Code: jed-0604

Realidades ❸

Capítulo 6

Nombre _____

Hora _____

Fecha _____

Vocabulary Flash Cards, Sheet 6

Write the Spanish vocabulary word below each picture. If there is a word or phrase, copy it in the space provided. Be sure to include the article for each noun.

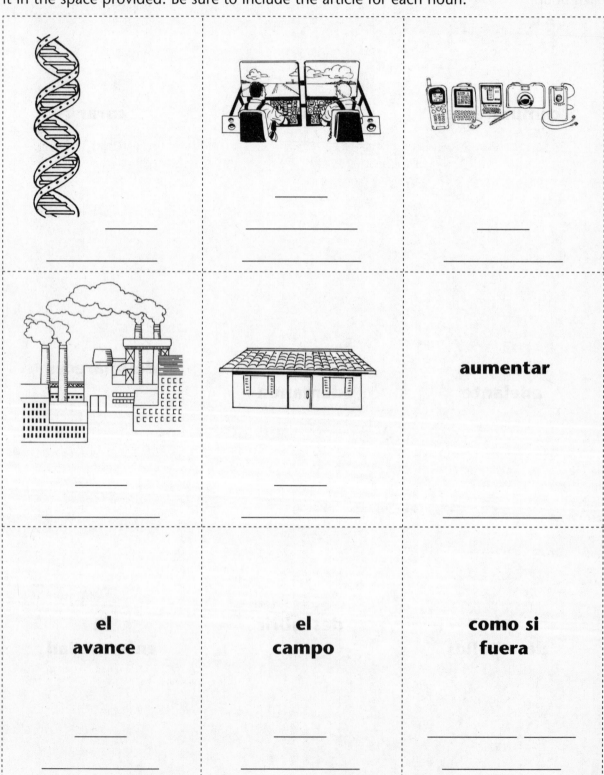

aumentar

el
avance

el
campo

como si
fuera

Realidades **3**

Nombre _____

Hora _____

Capítulo 6

Fecha _____

Vocabulary Flash Cards, Sheet 7

Copy the word or phrase in the space provided. Be sure to include the article for each noun.

comunicarse	**contaminar**	**curar**
_____	_____	_____
de hoy en adelante	**la demanda**	**desaparecer**
_____	_____	_____
el desarrollo	**descubrir**	**la enfermedad**
_____	_____	_____

Realidades ③

Capítulo 6

Nombre _____

Fecha _____

Hora _____

Vocabulary Flash Cards, Sheet 8

Copy the word or phrase in the space provided. Be sure to include the article for each noun.

enterarse	**la estrategia**	**la fuente de energía**
_____	_____	_____
la genética	**la hospitalidad**	**la industria**
_____	_____	_____
la informática	**inventar**	**el invento**
_____	_____	_____

Copy the word or phrase in the space provided. Be sure to include the article for each noun.

la máquina	**la mayoría**	**los medios de comunicación**
___	___	___
_____	_____	_____
el mercado	**el ocio**	**predecir**
___	___	
_____	_____	_____
el producto	**prolongar**	**reducir**
___		
_____	_____	_____

Tear out this page. Write the English words on the lines. Fold the paper along the dotted line to see the correct answers so you can check your work.

el aparato _____

aumentar _____

el avance _____

averiguar _____

el campo _____

comunicarse _____

curar _____

desaparecer _____

el desarrollo _____

descubrir _____

enterarse _____

la estrategia _____

la fábrica _____

la fuente de energía _____

el gen (*pl.* los genes) _____

la genética _____

la hospitalidad _____

la industria _____

Fold In →

Tear out this page. Write the Spanish words on the lines. Fold the paper along the dotted line to see the correct answers so you can check your work.

gadget _____

to increase _____

advance _____

to find out (inquire) _____

field _____

to communicate _____

to cure _____

to disappear _____

development _____

to discover _____

to find out _____

strategy _____

factory _____

energy source _____

gene (genes) _____

genetics _____

hospitality _____

industry _____

Fold In ←

Tear out this page. Write the English words on the lines. Fold the paper along the dotted line to see the correct answers so you can check your work.

la informática _____

_____

el invento _____

la máquina _____

la mayoría _____

los medios de _____
comunicación

el mercadeo _____

el ocio _____

predecir _____

prolongar _____

la realidad virtual _____

reducir (zc) _____

reemplazar _____

el servicio _____

tener en cuenta _____

vía satélite _____

la vivienda _____

Fold In

Realidades **3**

Capítulo 6

Nombre _____

Fecha _____

Hora _____

Vocabulary Check, Sheet 8

Tear out this page. Write the Spanish words on the lines. Fold the paper along the dotted line to see the correct answers so you can check your work.

information technology _____

invention _____

machine _____

the majority _____

media _____

_____

marketing _____

free time _____

to predict _____

to prolong, to extend _____

virtual reality _____

to reduce _____

to replace _____

service _____

to take into account _____

via satellite _____

housing _____

Fold In ←

Realidades 3

Capítulo 6

Nombre _____

Fecha _____

Hora _____

Guided Practice Activities, Sheet 5

El futuro perfecto (p. 273)

- The future perfect tense is used to talk about what *will have happened* by a certain time. You form the future perfect by using the future of the verb **haber** with the past participle of another verb. Below is the future perfect of the verb **ayudar**.

ayudar	
habré ayudado	habremos ayudado
habrás ayudado	habréis ayudado
habrá ayudado	habrán ayudado

- The future perfect is often used with the word **para** to say "by (a certain time)" and with the expression **dentro de** to say "within (a certain time)".

   Para el año 2050 *habremos reducido* la contaminación del aire.
   By the year 2050, we will have reduced air pollution.

   Los médicos *habrán eliminado* muchas enfermedades *dentro de* 20 años.
   Doctors will have eliminated many illnesses within 20 years.

A. Read each statement and decide if it will happen in the future (future tense), or if it will have happened by a certain point of time in the future (future perfect). Check the appropriate column.

Modelo Cada estudiante habrá comprado
un teléfono celular para el año 2016.   ____ futuro   _✓_ futuro perfecto

1. Los estadounidenses trabajarán menos horas.   ____ futuro   ____ futuro perfecto

2. Todas las escuelas habrán comprado una
computadora para cada estudiante.   ____ futuro   ____ futuro perfecto

3. Los coches volarán.   ____ futuro   ____ futuro perfecto

4. Alguien habrá inventado un robot que
maneje el carro.   ____ futuro   ____ futuro perfecto

B. Circle the correct form of the verb **haber** to complete each sentence.

Modelo Los médicos (habrá /(habrán)) descubierto muchas medicinas nuevas antes del fin del siglo.

1. Nosotros (**habrán** / **habremos**) conseguido un trabajo fantástico dentro de diez años.

2. Los científicos (**habrás** / **habrán**) inventado muchas máquinas nuevas dentro de cinco años.

3. Tú (**habrá** / **habrás**) aprendido a usar la energía solar antes del fin del siglo.

4. Yo (**habré** / **habrá**) traducido unos documentos antes de graduarme.

Realidades 3

Nombre _____

Hora _____

Capítulo 6

Fecha _____

Guided Practice Activities, Sheet 6

C. Complete each sentence with the future perfect of the verb in parentheses.
¡Cuidado! Some verbs have irregular past participles. Refer to page 79 in your textbook for the list of irregular forms.

| Modelo | (decir) La presidente ___ *habrá* ___ *dicho* ___ que es necesario usar otras fuentes de energía. |

1. **(poner)** Yo _____ _____ agua en mi coche en vez de gasolina.

2. **(reemplazar)** Los robots _____ _____ a muchos trabajadores humanos dentro de 100 años.

3. **(empezar)** Nosotros _____ _____ a usar muchas fuentes de energía dentro de poco tiempo.

4. **(curar)** Los médicos _____ _____ muchas enfermedades graves para el año 2025.

5. **(volver)** Tú _____ _____ de un viaje a Marte con una novia extraterrestre.

6. **(descubrir)** Alguien _____ _____ una cura para el resfriado.

- The future perfect tense is also used to speculate about something that may have happened in the past.

   Mis amigos no están aquí. ¿Adónde habrán ido?
   My friends are not here. I wonder where they might have gone.

D. Your Spanish teacher is not at school today. You and other students are discussing what may have happened to her. Write complete sentences below with the future perfect tense. Follow the model.

| Modelo | ir a una conferencia ___ *Habrá ido a una conferencia.* ___ |

1. visitar a un amigo en otra ciudad _____

2. enfermarse _____

3. salir para una reunión importante _____

4. hacer un viaje a España _____

realidades.com ✔
• Web Code: jed-0607

Realidades 3

Capítulo 6

Nombre _____

Fecha _____

Hora _____

Guided Practice Activities, Sheet 7

Uso de los complementos directos e indirectos (p. 275)

- Review the list of direct and indirect object pronouns. You may remember them from Chapter 3 in your textbook.

Direct Object Pronouns	
me	nos
te	os
lo / la	los / las

Indirect Object Pronouns	
me	nos
te	os
le	les

- You can use a direct and an indirect object pronoun together in the same sentence. When you do so, place the indirect object pronoun before the direct object pronoun.

  La profesora me dio un examen. *Me lo* dio el martes pasado.
  The teacher gave me an exam. She gave <u>it to me</u> last Tuesday.

A. Marcos was very busy yesterday. Complete each sentence with the correct direct object pronoun: **lo, la, los, las.** Follow the model.

Modelo   Marcos compró un libro de cocina española ayer. __*Lo*__ compró en la Librería Central.

1. Preparó una paella deliciosa. _____ preparó en la cocina de su abuela.

2. Encontró unas flores en el jardín y _____ trajo para poner en el centro de la mesa.

3. Decidió comprar unos tomates. _____ compró para preparar una ensalada.

4. Encontró una botella de vino y _____ abrió.

5. Marcos terminó de cocinar el pan y _____ sirvió.

B. Read the sentences again in exercise A and look at the direct object pronouns you wrote. Then, based on the cue in parentheses, add the indirect object pronoun **me, te,** or **nos** to create new sentences telling whom Marcos did these things for. Write both pronouns in the sentence. Follow the model.

Modelo   (para ti)   __*Te*__ __*lo*__ compró en la Librería Central.

1. (para nosotros) _____ _____ preparó en la cocina de su abuela.

2. (para mí) _____ _____ trajo para poner en el centro de la mesa.

3. (para ti) _____ _____ compró para preparar una ensalada.

4. (para mí) _____ _____ abrió.

5. (para nosotros) _____ _____ sirvió.

Realidades 3

Capítulo 6

Nombre _____

Hora _____

Fecha _____

Guided Practice Activities, Sheet 8

- In sentences with two object pronouns, sometimes the pronouns **le** and **les** have to be changed. If the **le** or **les** comes before the direct object pronoun **lo, la, los,** or **las,** the **le** or **les** must change to **se.**

   Le compré unas flores a mi madre. Se las di esta mañana.
   I bought flowers for my mother. I gave <u>them to her</u> this morning.

- You often add the personal **a** + a pronoun, noun, or person's name to make it more clear who the **se** refers to.

   Mi tía Gloria le trajo regalos a Lupita. Se los dio *a ella* después de la fiesta.
   My aunt Gloria brought gifts for Lupita. She gave them <u>to her</u> after the party.

C. Read the first sentence in each pair and underline the direct object. Then, circle the correct combination of indirect and direct object pronouns to complete the second sentence. Follow the model.

Modelo   Patricia le comprará <u>un anillo</u> a su hermana. (**Se lo** / Se la) comprará
en Madrid.

1. El Sr. Gómez les escribirá unas cartas de recomendación a sus estudiantes.
(**Se lo / Se las**) escribirá el próximo fin de semana.

2. Nosotros le enviaremos regalos a nuestra prima. (**Se los / Se las**) enviaremos
muy pronto.

3. Yo les daré unas tareas a mis maestros. (**Se la / Se las**) daré en la próxima clase.

4. ¿Tú le prepararás un pastel a tu papá? ¿(**Se la / Se lo**) prepararás para su
cumpleaños?

5. Le pagaremos dinero a la contadora. (**Se la / Se lo**) pagaremos por su dedicación
en el trabajo.

D. Complete each rewritten sentence using both indirect and direct object pronouns.
Follow the model.

Modelo   La profesora les leyó un cuento muy cómico a los estudiantes. La profesora
___*se*___ ___*lo*___ leyó.

1. Mis padres le dieron unos regalos a mi profesora. Mis padres _____ _____ dieron.

2. Yo te compré unas camisetas nuevas. Yo _____ _____ compré.

3. Nuestra directora nos explicó las reglas de la escuela. _____ _____ explicó.

4. El científico les enseño una técnica a sus asistentes. Él _____ _____ enseñó.

5. Mi profesora me escribió unos comentarios. Ella _____ _____ escribió.

Realidades 3

Capítulo 6

Nombre _____

Fecha _____

Hora _____

Reading Activities, Sheet 1

Puente a la cultura (pp. 278–279)

A. This reading is about the buildings of the future. Write three characteristics that you would expect the buildings of the future to have. Look at the photos in the reading to help you think of ideas. One example has been done for you.

buildings will use more technology _____

_____ _____

B. Look at the excerpt from the reading in your textbook. Try to figure out what the highlighted phrase means by using the context of the reading. Answer the questions below.

« *Cada vez habrá más **edificios "inteligentes"**, en otras palabras, edificios en los que una computadora central controla todos los aparatos y servicios para aprovechar (utilize) mejor la energía eléctrica...* »

1. What does the phrase **edificios "inteligentes"** mean in English?

_____ _____

2. What does this phrase mean in the context of this reading?

a. usarán más ladrillo   **b.** serán más altos   **c.** usarán mejor tecnología

C. Use the following table to help you keep track of the architects and one important characteristic of each of the buildings mentioned in the reading. The first one has been done for you.

Edificio	Arquitecto	Característica importante
1. las Torres Petronas	*César Pelli*	*los edificios más altos del mundo*
2. el Faro de Comercio		
3. el Hotel Camino Real		
4. el Milwaukee Art Museum		

Realidades 3

Capítulo 6

Nombre _____

Fecha _____

Hora _____

Reading Activities, Sheet 2

Lectura (pp. 284–286)

A. You will encounter many words in this reading that you do not know. Sometimes these words are cognates, which you can get after reading them alone. Look at the following cognates from the reading and write the corresponding English word.

1. superiores _____

2. la indignación _____

3. contemplado _____

4. ambiciones _____

5. una trayectoria _____

6. entusiasmo _____

B. This story contains a great deal of dialogue, but quotation marks are not used. Instead, Spanish uses another type of mark, **la raya** (—), to indicate direct dialogue. In the following paragraph, underline the section of text that is dialogue. Look for verbs such as **dijo** and **expresó** to help you determine where dialogue appears.

1. —¡Hoy es el día! —el tono de Rosa expresó cierta zozobra, la sensación de una derrota ineludible.

   —¿Por qué habrán decidido eso?

2. —A cualquiera le gustaría estar allí —dijo Rosa sin énfasis—. Pero creo que ya soy demasiado vieja.

C. Look at the following excerpts from page 285 of your reading. Circle the best translation for each by deciding whether it expresses a definite future action or a probability. Also use context clues to help you with meaning.

1. ‖ —Por eso **querrán** trasladarte. **Necesitarán** tus servicios en otra parte. Quizá te lleven al Centro Nacional de Comunicaciones. ‖

   a. That is why they will want to move you. They will need your services somewhere else. Perhaps they will bring you to the National Center for Communications.

   b. That must be why they want to move you. They probably need your services somewhere else. They might bring you to the National Center for Communications.

2. ‖ —Siempre serás un ejemplo para nosotras, Rosa. —Nadie será capaz de reemplazarte. Estamos seguras. ‖

   a. You will always be an example for us, Rosa. No one will be able to replace you. We are sure.

   b. You most likely will always be an example for us, Rosa. No one may be able to replace you. We are sure.

Realidades 3

Capítulo 6

Nombre _____

Fecha _____

Hora _____

Reading Activities, Sheet 3

D. Decide whether the following statements are true or false about what happens in the story. Write **C** for **cierto** or **F** for **falso**. Then, correct the false statements to make them true.

1. _____ Rosa está nerviosa porque tiene que ir a un lugar desconocido.

_____

2. _____ Las amigas de Rosa se llaman Marta y Pancha.

_____

3. _____ Rosa ha trabajado en su compañía por treinta años.

_____

4. _____ Rosa ha sido una buena trabajadora.

_____

5. _____ Las amigas piensan que Rosa recibirá un mejor trabajo.

_____

6. _____ Cinco robots vienen a sacar a Rosa de su trabajo.

_____

7. _____ Rosa recibe un buen trabajo nuevo al final del cuento.

_____

E. This story has a surprise ending. Finish the following sentence by circling the correct answers to explain what the "twist" ending reveals.

*Rosa no es un ser humano. Ella es (**una computadora / un animal**) y los hombres del cuento van a (**darle un premio / destruirla**) porque en el futuro (**los seres humanos / las máquinas**) controlarán el mundo.*

Realidades 3

Capítulo 7

Nombre _____

Hora _____

Fecha _____

AVSR, Sheet 1

Las construcciones negativas (p. 293)

- Look at the following lists of affirmative and negative words.

Affirmative		Negative	
algo	*something*	nada	*nothing*
alguien	*someone*	nadie	*no one*
alguno/a (*pron.*)	*some*	ninguno/a	*none, not any*
algún/alguna (*adj.*)	*some*	ningún/ninguna	*none, not any*
algunos/as (*pron/adj*)	*some*	ningunos/as (*pron/adj*)	*none, not any*
siempre	*always*	nunca	*never*
también	*also*	tampoco	*either, neither*

A. Learning words as opposites is a good strategy. Match each of the following affirmative words with the negative word that means the opposite.

_____ **1.** alguien

_____ **2.** algo

_____ **3.** algunos

_____ **4.** siempre

_____ **5.** también

A. nada

B. tampoco

C. nadie

D. ningunos

E. nunca

B. Circle the correct affirmative or negative word to complete each sentence. Follow the model.

Modelo   No hay (**algo** /(**nada**)) interesante en esa plaza. Salgamos ahora.

1. (**Siempre / Nunca**) voy al desierto porque no me gusta el calor.

2. El Sr. Toledo encontró (**algún / ningún**) artefacto de oro por estas partes.

3. —Me encanta acampar en las montañas.

—A mí (**también / tampoco**).

4. Mis vecinos se mudaron y ahora no vive (**nadie / alguien**) en esa casa.

5. (**Ningún / Algún**) día voy a ser un cantante famoso porque practico todos los días.

realidades.com

• Web Code: jcd-0701

Realidades ③

Capítulo 7

Nombre _____

Fecha _____

Hora _____

AVSR, Sheet 2

- It is important to remember that the adjectives **algún, alguna, algunos, algunas** and **ningún, ninguna, ningunos, ningunas** agree in number and gender with the noun they modify.

  *Hay **algunas** esculturas en el templo.*

  *No hay **ningún** bosque en esa parte del país.*

C. Complete the sentences with the correct affirmative word (**algún, alguna, algunos, algunas**) or negative word (**ningún, ninguna, ningunos, ningunas**). Follow the model.

Modelo Vimos _____*algunos*_____ ríos muy impresionantes.

1. No había _____ palacio antiguo en la ciudad.

2. Visitamos _____ montañas muy altas y bonitas.

3. ¿Hay _____ edificio de piedra por aquí?

4. No conocíamos a _____ persona en el pueblito.

5. Los arquitectos no han encontrado _____ objeto interesante en ese sitio.

6. Descubrimos _____ monumentos hermosos en el centro.

- Remember that to make a sentence negative in Spanish, you must put **no** in front of the conjugated verb.

  ***No** olvidé nada para mi viaje.*

- However, if a sentence starts with a negative word, like **nunca** or **nadie**, do not use the word **no** in front of the verb.

  ***Nadie** puede explicar ese fenómeno increíble.*

D. Change each of the following statements so they mean exactly the opposite.

Modelo Conocimos a alguien interesante en la plaza.

No conocimos a nadie interesante en la plaza.

1. Siempre llevo aretes de plata. _____

2. Hay algún río por aquí. _____

3. Nadie sube la escalera. _____

4. No hay nada en ese castillo. _____

5. Quiero hacer algo. _____

Los adjetivos usados como sustantivos (p. 295)

- When speaking about two similar things in Spanish you can avoid repetition by using the adjective as a noun. Look at the examples below.

   ¿Te gustan más los perros grandes o *los pequeños?*
   Do you like big dogs more or little ones?

   Tengo un pájaro blanco y *uno rojo.*
   I have a white bird and a red one.

- Note that you use the definite article (**el, la, los, las**) or indefinite article (**un, una, unos, unas**) and an adjective that agrees in gender and number with the noun it replaces.

- Note also that **un** becomes **uno** when it is not followed by a noun.

A. Read each sentence. The underlined adjective is being used as a noun to avoid repeating the original noun in the sentence. Circle the original noun. Follow the model.

Modelo Me gustan (las camisas) azules pero no me gustan nada <u>las amarillas</u>.

1. Tengo miedo de los animales grandes pero no me molestan <u>los pequeños</u>.

2. Anoche hubo una tormenta fuerte y esta noche va a haber <u>una pequeña</u>.

3. En el parque zoológico hay un elefante viejo y <u>uno joven</u>.

4. Las hormigas negras no pican pero <u>las rojas</u> sí.

5. La cebra flaca no come mucho porque <u>la gorda</u> se come toda la comida.

6. En ese acuario hay unos peces anaranjados y <u>unos azules</u>.

B. Choose the correct form of each adjective being used as a noun. Follow the model.

Modelo Los osos de color café son más grandes que ((los blancos) / las blancas).

1. No quiero un cuaderno rojo. Quiero (**uno gris** / **una gris**).

2. Las moscas grandes me molestan más que (**los pequeños** / **las pequeñas**).

3. El mono gris es más agresivo que (**la negra** / **el negro**).

4. Hubo un incendio pequeño en la ciudad y (**una grande** / **uno grande**) en el campo.

5. Va a haber muchas flores de color rosa y (**unas amarillas** / **unos amarillos**) en mi jardín esta primavera.

Realidades **3**

Capítulo 7

Nombre _____

Fecha _____

Hora _____

AVSR, Sheet 4

- You can also use the definite or indefinite article with a prepositional phrase beginning with **a**, **de**, or **para** to avoid repetition.

  *¿Son más grandes los pájaros de Guatemala o **los de Costa Rica**?*

  *Esta comida es para un perro joven, no **para uno viejo**.*

C. Cross out the noun that is repeated in each sentence. Then, write the remaining phrase including **a**, **de**, or **para** that replaces the repeated noun. Follow the model.

> **Modelo** La entrenadora de fútbol y la ~~entrenadora~~ de béisbol son buenas amigas.
>
> *la de béisbol*_____

1. Las entradas del cine cuestan menos que las entradas de la obra de teatro.

   _____

2. Unos estudiantes de primer año y unos estudiantes de tercer año están de excursión hoy.

   _____

3. La clase de literatura y la clase de ciencias sociales tienen lugar en el teatro de la escuela.

   _____

4. El profesor de inglés es más exigente que el profesor de anatomía.

   _____

5. Nos quedamos para este mes y no para el mes que viene.

   _____

- You can also place **lo** in front of a masculine singular adjective to make it into a noun. This creates the equivalent of "the (adjective) thing . . ." in English.

  Lo bueno del verano es que no hay clases.

  The good thing about summer is that there are no classes.

D. Use the adjectives in parentheses as nouns at the beginning of each of the following sentences. Follow the model.

> **Modelo** __Lo__ __cómico__ de la situación es que Lidia no es profesora. (**cómico**)

1. _____ _____ de la clase es que hay mucha tarea. (**malo**)

2. _____ _____ del libro es que no tiene narrador. (**interesante**)

3. _____ _____ del invierno es que podemos esquiar. (**divertido**)

4. _____ _____ de esta tarea es que no comprendo el vocabulario. (**difícil**)

5. _____ _____ de esos pájaros es que pueden volar por varias millas sin descansar. (**impresionante**)

Realidades 3

Nombre _____

Hora _____

Capítulo 7

Fecha _____

Vocabulary Flash Cards, Sheet 1

Write the Spanish vocabulary word or phrase below each picture. Be sure to include the article for each noun.

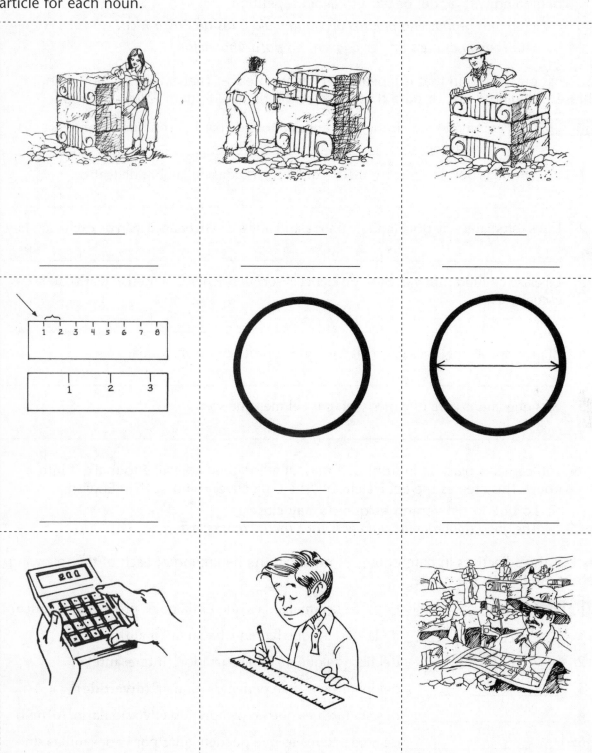

Realidades **3**

Nombre _____

Hora _____

Capítulo 7

Fecha _____

Vocabulary Flash Cards, Sheet 2

Write the Spanish vocabulary word or phrase below each picture. Be sure to include the article for each noun.

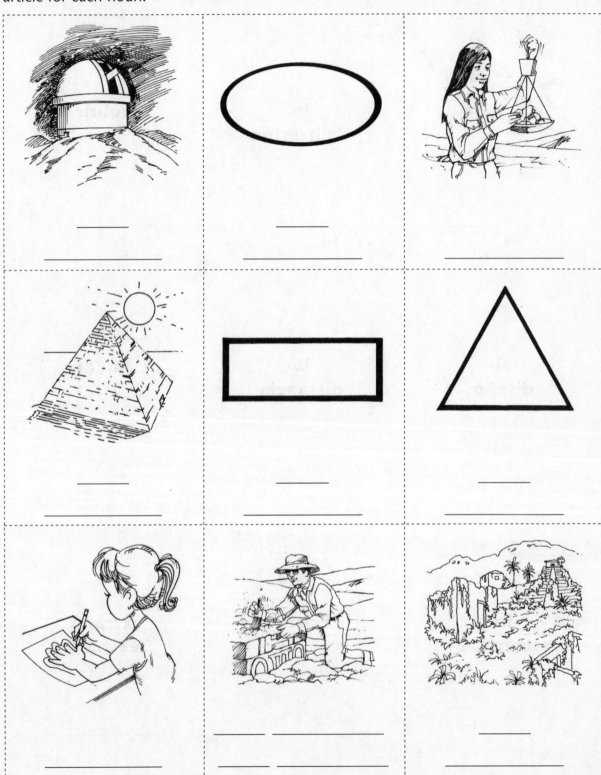

Realidades 3

Capítulo 7

Nombre

Hora

Fecha

Vocabulary Flash Cards, Sheet 3

Write the Spanish vocabulary word below each picture. If there is a word or phrase, copy it in the space provided. Be sure to include the article for each noun.

	la civilización	cubrir
el diseño	la distancia	dudar
la estructura	existir	extraño, extraña

Realidades 3

Capítulo 7

Nombre _____

Hora _____

Fecha _____

Vocabulary Flash Cards, Sheet 4

Copy the word or phrase in the space provided. Be sure to include the article for each noun.

el fenómeno	**la función**	**improbable**
_____ _____	_____ _____	_____
inexplicable	**probable**	**el pueblo**
_____	_____	_____ _____
redondo, redonda	**resolver**	**la tonelada**
_____ _____	_____	_____ _____

These blank cards can be used to write and practice other Spanish vocabulary for the chapter.

_____   _____   _____

_____   _____   _____

_____   _____   _____

Realidades 3

Capítulo 7

Nombre _____

Hora _____

Fecha _____

Vocabulary Check, Sheet 1

Tear out this page. Write the English words on the lines. Fold the paper along the dotted line to see the correct answers so you can check your work.

el alto _____

el ancho _____

el arqueólogo,
la arqueóloga _____

calcular _____

_____

el círculo _____

la civilización _____

cubrir _____

el diámetro _____

el diseño _____

la distancia _____

excavar _____

dudar _____

extraño, extraña _____

el fenómeno _____

la función _____

geométrico,
geométrica _____

improbable _____

Fold In →

Realidades 3

Capítulo 7

Nombre _____

Hora _____

Fecha _____

Vocabulary Check, Sheet 2

Tear out this page. Write the Spanish words on the lines. Fold the paper along the dotted line to see the correct answers so you can check your work.

height _____

width _____

archaeologist _____

_____

to calculate,
to compute _____

circle _____

civilization _____

to cover _____

diameter _____

design _____

distance _____

to dig _____

to doubt _____

strange _____

phenomenon _____

function _____

geometric(al) _____

_____

unlikely _____

Fold In ←

Realidades 3

Capítulo 7

Nombre _____

Fecha _____

Hora _____

Vocabulary Check, Sheet 3

Tear out this page. Write the English words on the lines. Fold the paper along the dotted line to see the correct answers so you can check your work.

inexplicable _____

el largo _____

medir (e➜i) _____

la nave espacial _____

el observatorio _____

el óvalo _____

pesar _____

la pirámide _____

probable _____

el pueblo _____

el rectángulo _____

redondo, redonda _____

resolver (o➜ue) _____

las ruinas _____

la tonelada _____

el triángulo _____

trazar _____

Fold In ⟵

Realidades 3

Capítulo 7

Nombre _____

Hora _____

Fecha _____

Vocabulary Check, Sheet 4

Tear out this page. Write the Spanish words on the lines. Fold the paper along the dotted line to see the correct answers so you can check your work.

inexplicable _____

length _____

to measure _____

spaceship _____

observatory _____

oval _____

to weigh _____

pyramid _____

likely _____

people _____

rectangle _____

round _____

to solve _____

ruins _____

ton _____

triangle _____

to trace, to draw _____

Fold In ←

realidades.com

• Web Code: jed-0702

Realidades **3**

Capítulo 7

Nombre _____

Fecha _____

Hora _____

Guided Practice Activities, Sheet 1

El presente y el presente perfecto del subjuntivo con expresiones de duda (p. 306)

- When you want to express doubt, uncertainty, or disbelief about actions in the present, you use the present subjunctive.

  Dudo que los arqueólogos tengan todos sus instrumentos.
  I doubt the archaeologists have all their instruments.

  Other verbs and expressions that indicate doubt, uncertainty, and disbelief include:

No creer	**Es improbable**	**Es dudoso**
Es probable	**Es imposible**	

- In contrast, expressions of belief, knowledge, or certainty are usually followed by the indicative.

  Es verdad que los arqueólogos trabajan mucho.
  It's true that the archaeologists work a lot.

  Other verbs and expressions of belief, knowledge, or certainty include:

Creer	**No dudar**	**Es cierto**
Estar seguro/a de	**Saber**	**Es evidente**

A. Circle the verb in each of the following sentence endings. Then, choose the appropriate sentence starter. If the verb you circled is in the subjunctive or present perfect subjunctive, check the column that says "**Dudamos.**" If the verb is in the indicative, check the column that says "**Estamos seguros de.**"

Modelo   ... que los marcianos (vivan) en nuestro planeta.

☑ Dudamos ...   ☐ Estamos seguros de ...

1. ... que Chichén Itza es el sitio arqueológico más famoso del mundo.

   ☐ Dudamos ...   ☐ Estamos seguros de ...

2. ... que muchas ruinas mayas están en el Yucatán.

   ☐ Dudamos ...   ☐ Estamos seguros de ...

3. ... que existan evidencias de una nave espacial.

   ☐ Dudamos ...   ☐ Estamos seguros de ...

4. ... que los arqueólogos resuelvan todos los misterios de la civilización maya.

   ☐ Dudamos ...   ☐ Estamos seguros de ...

5. ... que el observatorio está en el centro de la ciudad.

   ☐ Dudamos ...   ☐ Estamos seguros de ...

Realidades 3

Nombre _____

Hora _____

Capítulo 7

Fecha _____

Guided Practice Activities, Sheet 2

B. Find the expression that indicates doubt (subjunctive) or certainty (indicative) in each sentence below. Write **S** for subjunctive and **I** for indicative. Then, complete the sentences with the correct form of the verb in parentheses. Follow the model.

Modelo   __I__   Es cierto que nadie _____puede_____ explicar todo lo misterioso de nuestro universo. (**poder**)

1. _____ Es dudoso que los arqueólogos _____ hoy porque llueve. (**excavar**)

2. _____ Creo que los diseños geométricos _____ un diámetro de cinco metros. (**tener**)

3. _____ Los arqueólogos saben que nosotros _____ investigar ese sitio. (**querer**)

4. _____ Es cierto que la arqueóloga _____ una línea entre los dos edificios. (**trazar**)

5. _____ Es posible que los estudiantes _____ unos fenómenos extraños durante su viaje a Perú. (**ver**)

- When you express doubt or uncertainty about actions that took place in the past, use the present perfect subjunctive.

  Es dudoso que los arqueólogos *hayan medido* todas las pirámides.
  It's doubtful that the archaeologists measured (have measured) all the pyramids.

- Use the present perfect indicative after expressions of belief, knowledge, or certainty.

  Es verdad que los arqueólogos *han encontrado* unos objetos de cerámica.
  It is true that the archaeologists found (have found) some ceramic objects.

C. First, underline the expression that indicates doubt or certainty in each sentence. Then, complete the sentences with the present perfect indicative or present perfect subjunctive. Follow the models.

Modelos   (**ver**)   <u>No creo</u> que ellos ___*hayan*___ ____*visto*____ una nave espacial.

(**pesar**)   <u>Es evidente</u> que los científicos ___*han*___ ___*pesado*___ las piedras.

1. (**estudiar**)   Es evidente que los mayas _____ _____ mucho la astronomía.

2. (**ver**)   Dudamos que tú _____ _____ un extraterrestre.

3. (**hacer**)   No es probable que ellos _____ _____ todos los viajes que planearon.

4. (**ir**)   Estamos seguros que tú _____ _____ a un sitio muy famoso.

5. (**comunicar**)   Los científicos no creen que los incas se _____ _____ con los extraterrestres.

realidades.com

- Web Code: jed-0703

Realidades 3

Capítulo 7

Nombre _____

Fecha _____

Hora _____

Vocabulary Flash Cards, Sheet 6

Write the Spanish vocabulary word below each picture. If there is a word or phrase, copy it in the space provided. Be sure to include the article for each noun.

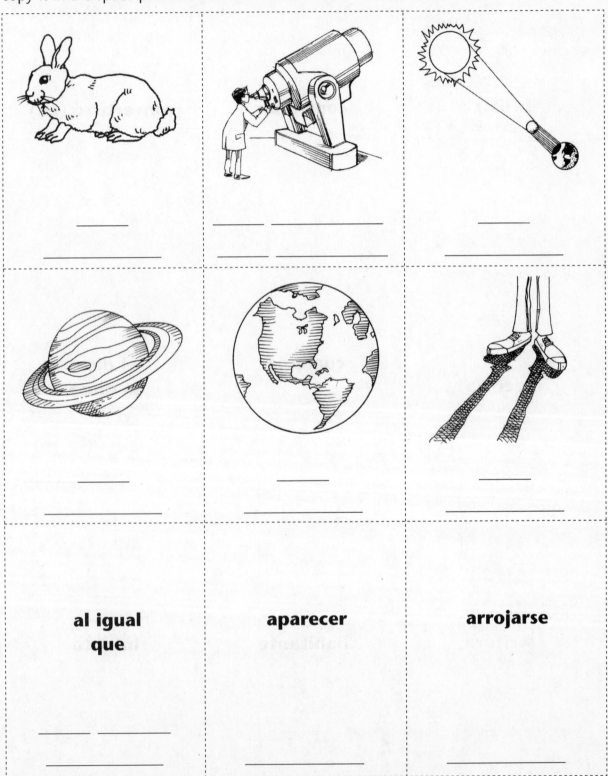

al igual que

_____

aparecer

_____

arrojarse

_____

Realidades 3

Capítulo 7

Nombre _____

Fecha _____

Hora _____

Vocabulary Flash Cards, Sheet 7

Copy the word or phrase in the space provided. Be sure to include the article for each noun.

brillar	**contribuir**	**convertirse (en)**
_____	_____	_____
la creencia	**cualquier**	**el dios, la diosa**
_____	_____	_____ _____
la escritura	**el/la habitante**	**el intento**
_____	_____	_____

Realidades 3

Capítulo 7

Nombre _____

Fecha _____

Hora _____

Vocabulary Flash Cards, Sheet 8

Copy the word or phrase in the space provided. Be sure to include the article for each noun.

la leyenda	**la Luna**	**el mito**
o sea que	**el origen**	**ponerse (el sol)**
sagrado, sagrada	**el símbolo**	**sino (que)**

Realidades 3

Capítulo 7

Nombre _____

Hora _____

Fecha _____

Vocabulary Flash Cards, Sheet 9

Copy the word or phrase in the space provided. Be sure to include the article for each noun. The blank cards can be used to write and practice other Spanish vocabulary for the chapter.

la teoría _____ _____	**el universo** _____ _____	**ya que** _____ _____
    _____	 _____	 _____
    _____	 _____	 _____

Tear out this page. Write the English words on the lines. Fold the paper along the dotted line to see the correct answers so you can check your work.

al igual que _____

aparecer (zc) _____

arrojar(se) _____

el astrónomo,
la astrónoma _____

brillar _____

convertirse (en) _____

_____

contribuir (u→y) _____

la creencia _____

cualquier,
cualquiera _____

el dios, la diosa _____

la escritura _____

el eclipse _____

el/la habitante _____

el intento _____

Fold In

Tear out this page. Write the Spanish words on the lines. Fold the paper along the dotted line to see the correct answers so you can check your work.

as, like   _____

to appear   _____

to throw (oneself)   _____

astronomer   _____

_____

to shine   _____

to turn (into);
to become   _____

to contribute   _____

belief   _____

any   _____

_____

god, goddess   _____

writing   _____

eclipse   _____

inhabitant   _____

attempt   _____

Fold In

Realidades ③

Capítulo 7

Nombre _____

Fecha _____

Hora _____

Vocabulary Check, Sheet 7

Tear out this page. Write the English words on the lines. Fold the paper along the dotted line to see the correct answers so you can check your work.

la leyenda _____

la Luna _____

el mito _____

el origen _____

o sea que _____

el planeta _____

ponerse (el sol) _____

sagrado, sagrada _____

el símbolo _____

sino (que) _____

la sombra _____

la teoría _____

la Tierra _____

el universo _____

Fold In

Tear out this page. Write the Spanish words on the lines. Fold the paper along the dotted line to see the correct answers so you can check your work.

legend _____

moon _____

myth _____

origin _____

in other words _____

planet _____

to set (sun) _____

sacred _____

symbol _____

but; but instead _____

shadow _____

theory _____

Earth _____

universe _____

Fold In

• Web Code: jed-0706

Realidades **3**

Capítulo 7

Nombre _____

Fecha _____

Hora _____

Guided Practice Activities, Sheet 3

Pero y sino (p. 319)

- To say the word "but" in Spanish, you usually use the word **pero**.

    *Hoy hace mal tiempo, **pero** vamos a visitar las pirámides.*

    However, there is another word in Spanish, **sino**, that also means "but." **Sino** is used after a negative, in order to offer the idea of an alternative: "not this, but rather that."

    Los aztecas no tenían un sólo dios *sino* muchos dioses diferentes.
    The Aztecs did not have only one god, but (rather) many different gods.

A. Underline the verb in the first part of each sentence. If the verb is affirmative, circle **pero** as the correct completion. If the verb is negative, circle **sino** as the correct completion. Note: if the verb is negative, you will also need to underline "**no**" if it is present. Follow the models.

Modelos Mi tío <u>no es</u> arquitecto ((sino)/ **pero**) arqueólogo.

Mi hermano <u>lee</u> libros sobre las civilizaciones antiguas (**sino** /(pero)) nunca ha visitado ninguna.

1. Esta escritura azteca me parece muy interesante (**sino** / **pero**) no la puedo leer.

2. Los mayas no estudiaban la arqueología (**sino** / **pero**) la astronomía.

3. Esta historia no es una autobiografía (**sino** / **pero**) una leyenda.

4. Los conejos son animales muy simpáticos (**sino** / **pero**) mi mamá no me permite tener uno en casa.

5. Va a haber un eclipse lunar este viernes (**sino** / **pero**) no podré verlo porque estaré dormido.

B. Choose either **pero** or **sino** to complete each of the following sentences.

Modelo Ese mito es divertido ((pero)/ **sino**) no creo que sea cierto.

1. Los mayas no eran bárbaros (**pero** / **sino**) muy intelectuales y poseían una cultura rica.

2. El alfabeto azteca no usaba letras (**pero** / **sino**) símbolos y dibujos.

3. Los mayas y los aztecas no vivían en España (**pero** / **sino**) en México.

4. Tengo que preparar un proyecto sobre los aztecas (**pero** / **sino**) no lo he terminado todavía.

5. Según los aztecas, uno de sus dioses se convirtió en el Sol (**pero** / **sino**) al principio no podía moverse.

- Web Code: jed-0707

Pero y sino (continued)

- **Sino** is also used in the expression **no sólo... sino también...** , which means *not only... but also.*

   *Los mayas **no sólo** estudiaban las matemáticas **sino también** la astronomía.*

C. Finish each sentence with the "**no sólo... sino también**" pattern using the elements given. Follow the model.

Modelo   Al niño *no sólo le gusta el helado sino también las galletas* .
             (le gusta el helado / galletas)

1. Hoy _____. (**hace sol / calor**)

2. Esta profesora _____.
   (**es cómica / inteligente**)

3. Las leyendas _____.
   (**son interesantes / informativas**)

4. Mis amigos _____.
   (**son comprensivos / divertidos**)

5. La comida mexicana _____.
   (**es nutritiva / deliciosa**)

- When there is a conjugated verb in the second part of the sentence, you should use **sino que**.

   Ella no perdió sus libros *sino que* se los prestó a una amiga.

   She didn't lose her books but (rather) she lent them to a friend.

D. Choose either **sino** or **sino que** to complete each of the following sentences.

Modelo   Los aztecas no tenían miedo de los fenómenos naturales (**sino** /(sino que))
             trataban de explicarlos.

1. Los españoles no aceptaron a los aztecas (**sino** / **sino que**) destruyeron su imperio.

2. Según los aztecas, no se ve la cara de un hombre en la luna (**sino** / **sino que**) un conejo.

3. Los arqueólogos no vendieron los artefactos (**sino** / **sino que**) los preservaron en un museo.

4. Esta leyenda no trata de la creación de los hombres (**sino** / **sino que**) del origen del día y de la noche.

El subjuntivo en cláusulas adjetivas (p. 320)

- Sometimes you use an entire clause to describe a noun. This is called an adjective clause, because, like an adjective, it *describes.* When you are talking about a specific person or thing that definitely exists, you use the indicative.

    Tengo unas fotos *que muestran* los templos mayas.
    I have some photos that show the Mayan temples.

- If you are not talking about a specific person or thing, or if you are not sure whether the person or thing exists, you must use the subjunctive.

    Busco un libro *que tenga* información sobre el calendario maya.
    I am looking for a book that has information about the Mayan calendar.

    Sometimes **cualquier(a)** is used in these expressions.

    Podemos visitar *cualquier* templo *que nos interese.*
    We can visit whatever temple interests us.

A. Circle the adjective clause in each of the following sentences. Follow the model.

Modelo   Queremos leer un cuento (que sea más alegre)

1. Busco una leyenda que explique el origen del mundo.

2. Los arqueólogos tienen unos artefactos que son de cerámica.

3. Queremos tomar una clase que trate de las culturas indígenas mexicanas.

4. Conocemos a un profesor que pasa los veranos en México excavando en los sitios arqueológicos.

5. Los estudiantes necesitan unos artículos que les ayuden a entender la escritura azteca.

B. First, find the adjective clause in each statement and decide whether it describes something that exists or possibly does not exist. Place an **X** in the appropriate column. Then, circle the correct verb to complete the sentence. Follow the model.

	Existe	Posiblemente no existe
Modelo Busco un artículo que (**tiene** / **tenga**) información sobre los mayas.	_____	**X**
1. Necesito el artículo que (**está** / **esté**) en esa carpeta.	_____	_____
2. Visitamos un museo que (**tiene** / **tenga**) una exhibición nueva.	_____	_____
3. Voy a llevar cualquier vestido que (**encuentro** / **encuentre**) en el armario.	_____	_____
4. En mi clase hay un chico que (**puede** / **pueda**) dibujar bien.	_____	_____
5. Queremos ver unas pirámides que (**son** / **sean**) más altas que éstas.	_____	_____

Realidades 3

Nombre _____

Hora _____

Capítulo 7

Fecha _____

Guided Practice Activities, Sheet 6

C. Complete each sentence using the present indicative or the present subjunctive mood of the verb in parentheses. Follow the model.

Modelo   (tener) Necesitamos usar una computadora que ___*tenga*___ más memoria.

1. (ser) Tengo una clase de arqueología que _____ muy divertida.

2. (poder) Buscamos una profesora que _____ ayudarnos con nuestro proyecto sobre los aztecas.

3. (medir) En el museo de arte hay una estatua maya que _____más de dos metros.

4. (conocer) Quiero un amigo que _____ todos los mitos indígenas.

5. (querer) La sociedad arqueológica busca dos estudiantes que _____ir a México este verano.

- The subjunctive is also used in adjective clauses when they describe something that doesn't exist, using a negative word such as **nadie, nada,** or **ninguno(a).**

   No hay *nadie* aquí *que pueda* interpretar el calendario maya.
   There is no one here who can interpret the Mayan calendar.

- When an adjective clause refers to something or someone unknown in the past, or something that does not exist or has not happened in the past, you can use the present perfect subjunctive.

   Quiero un profesor *que haya estudiado* el calendario maya.
   I want a professor who studied (has studied) the Mayan calendar.

D. First, read each sentence and determine if the adjective clause describes something that exists (affirmative) or something that may not exist (negative). Place a checkmark in either the "+" or "–" column to indicate your choice. Then, circle the correct verb for the sentence. Follow the model.

	+	–
Modelo Aquí tengo un libro que (**da** / **dé**) información interesante sobre los mayas.	✓	____
1. No hay nada en este museo que (**es** / **sea**) de los mayas.	____	____
2. En México, D.F. hay unos murales que (**ilustran** / **ilustren**) la vida de los indígenas.	____	____
3. Yo encontré un artefacto que (**tiene** / **tenga**) un significado religioso.	____	____
4. En mi familia no hay nadie que (**sabe** / **sepa**) más que yo sobre las civilizaciones mesoamericanas.	____	____
5. Buscamos a alguien en la escuela que (**ha visitado** / **haya visitado**) Chichén Itzá.	____	____

realidades.com
• Web Code: jed-0708

Realidades 3

Capítulo 7

Nombre _____

Fecha _____

Hora _____

Reading Activities, Sheet 1

Puente a la cultura (pp. 324–325)

A. Look at the photos of the Moai statues on page 324 and the Olmec head on page 325 in your textbook. Below are some ideas for what each photo might represent. Choose which you think is the best explanation for each artifact and explain why you chose it.

Polynesian people	Kings	Spanish conquistadors	
extraterrestrials	Gods	athletic champions	political figureheads

1. estatua moai _____

2. cabeza olmeca _____

B. Read the following excerpt and check off the sentence that best represents the main point.

> … *Allí se encuentran los moai, unas estatuas enormes de piedra que representan enormes cabezas con orejas largas y torsos pequeños. Se encuentran en toda la isla y miran hacia el cielo como esperando a algo o alguien. Pero la pregunta es ¿cómo las construyeron y las movieron los habitantes indígenas a la isla? Se sabe que no conocían ni el metal ni la rueda.*

a. ____ Las estatuas tienen orejas largas y torsos pequeños.

b. ____ Nadie sabe cómo las estatuas llegaron allí.

c. ____ Las estatuas miran hacia el cielo.

d. ____ Los indígenas no conocían ni el metal ni la rueda.

C. After reading about the Olmecs and the Nazca lines, complete the following by writing an **O** next to the statement if it corresponds to the creations of the **olmecas** and an **N** if it refers to the **líneas de Nazca**.

1. ____ Vivieron en México.

2. ____ Sólo es posible verlas completamente desde un avión.

3. ____ Construyeron cabezas gigantescas.

4. ____ La primera gran civilización de Mesoamérica.

5. ____ Representan figuras y animales.

Realidades 3

Capítulo 7

Nombre _____

Hora _____

Fecha _____

Reading Activities, Sheet 2

Lectura (pp. 330–332)

A. The excerpt you are about to read is from a well-known piece of literature about a man who *thinks* he is a knight. Think about what other depictions of knights you have seen in literature and/or movies.

1. What are knights usually like?

_____

2. Are the portrayals you have seen usually serious, comical, or both?

_____

B. Look at the excerpt below from page 331 of your textbook and answer the questions that follow.

> —Así es —dijo Sancho.
>
> —Pues —dijo su amo [master]—, aquí puedo hacer mi tarea: deshacer fuerzas y ayudar a los miserables.

1. To whom is Sancho speaking?

_____

2. What does Sancho's master say is his duty?

_____

3. Does this duty sound like something a knight would do?

_____

4. What kind of person or profession would do this duty in today's society?

_____

C. Read the following sentences about the reading in your textbook. Write **C** (for **cierto**) if they are true and **F** (for **falso**) if they are false.

_____ **1.** Cuando Don Quijote ve a los hombres, él sabe que son prisioneros.

_____ **2.** El primer prisionero con quien habla Don Quijote le dice que va a la prisión por amor.

_____ **3.** El segundo prisionero con quien habla Don Quijote le dice que va a la prisión por robar una casa.

_____ **4.** El tercer prisionero lleva más cadenas porque tiene más crímenes que todos.

_____ **5.** A Don Quijote le parece injusto el tratamiento de los prisioneros.

_____ **6.** Don Quijote y Sancho liberan a los prisioneros.

_____ **7.** Don Quijote quiere que los prisioneros le den dinero.

_____ **8.** Los prisioneros le tiran piedras a Don Quijote.

D. Read the following excerpt from the reading in your textbook and answer the questions that follow.

> *Don Quijote llamó entonces a los prisioneros y así les dijo:*
>
> *—De gente bien educada es agradecer (to thank) los beneficios que reciben. Les pido que vayan a la ciudad del Toboso, y allí os presentéis ante la señora Dulcinea del Toboso y le digáis que su caballero, el de la Triste Figura, ha tenido esta famosa aventura.*

1. First, find the following cognates in the passage above and circle them. Then write their meanings on the spaces below.

a. aventura _____   **c.** educada _____

b. beneficios _____   **d.** prisioneros _____

2. In this excerpt, Don Quijote uses the **vosotros** command form when addressing the prisoners. First, underline the following two commands in the passage above. Then choose the correct meaning for each.

os presentéis   **le digáis**

□ present yourselves   □ give her

□ provide yourselves   □ tell her

Realidades ③

Capítulo 8

Nombre _____

Fecha _____

Hora _____

AVSR, Sheet 1

Las palabras interrogativas (p. 339)

- Interrogative words are words used to ask questions. In Spanish, all interrogative words have a written accent mark. Look at the list of important interrogative words below.

¿cuándo? = *when?*	**¿para qué?** = *for what reason/purpose?*
¿dónde? = *where?*	**¿qué?** = *what?*
¿adónde? = *to where?*	**¿por qué?** = *why?*
¿cómo? = *how?*	

A. Circle the correct interrogative word in each short dialogue below. Follow the model.

Modelo —¿(**Por qué** /**Cuándo**) es el partido?
　　　　—Mañana a las cuatro.

1. —¿(**Dónde** / **Cuál**) está José?
　　—En el museo.

2. —¿(**Cómo** / **Cuándo**) se llama ese hombre viejo?
　　—Sr. Beltrán.

3. —¿(**Qué** / **Por qué**) vas al teatro?
　　—Necesito hablar con el director.

4. —¿(**Cuánto** / **Qué**) haces mañana?
　　—Voy a la plaza a ver unos monumentos.

- Some interrogative words must agree with the nouns they modify.

　　¿cuál?/¿cuáles?　　　　**¿quién?/¿quiénes?**
　　¿cuánto?/¿cuánta?　　　**¿cuántos?/¿cuántas?**

- Note that **¿quién(es)?** and **¿cuál(es)?** must agree in number with the nouns they modify.

　　¿Quiénes son los actores?　　*¿Cuál es el teatro nuevo?*

- Note that **¿cuánto(s)?** and **¿cuánta(s)?** must agree in number *and* gender with the nouns they modify.

　　¿Cuánto tiempo?　　　　*¿Cúantas sinagogas hay?*

B. In each question below, underline the noun that is modified by the interrogative word. Then, circle the interrogative word that agrees with the noun you underlined.

Modelo　¿(**Cuál** /**Cuáles**) son los <u>monumentos</u> más antiguos?

1. ¿(**Cuánto** / **Cuánta**) gente hay en la sinagoga?

2. ¿(**Cuál** / **Cuáles**) es la fecha de hoy?

3. ¿(**Quién** / **Quiénes**) es el presidente de México?

4. ¿(**Cuánto** / **Cuánta**) tarea tienes esta noche?

5. ¿(**Cuál** / **Cuáles**) son las calles que llevan al puente?

- Web Code: jed-0801

Realidades 3

Nombre _____

Hora _____

Capítulo 8

Fecha _____

AVSR, Sheet 2

- When you need to use a preposition with an interrogative word, you must always place it ahead of the interrogative word.

    ¿Con quién vas a la mezquita?   *With whom are you going to the mosque?*

    ¿De dónde es Marta?   *Where is Marta from?*

- Note that with the word **Adónde**, the preposition, **a**, is attached to the interrogative word. In all other cases, however, the preposition is a separate word.

C. Circle the correct interrogative phrase to complete each dialogue below. Look at the responses given to each question to help you make your choice. Follow the model.

Modelo   —¿(De dónde / Adónde) es tu profesora de español?
                —Ella es de Madrid.

1.   —¿(**De quién / Con quién**) es la mochila?

     —Es de mi amiga Josefina.

2.   —¿(**Para quién / De quién**) es ese regalo?

     —Es para mi hermano Roberto. Hoy es su cumpleaños.

3.   —¿(**Adónde / De dónde**) vas?

     —Voy al edificio histórico para estudiar la arquitectura.

4.   —¿(**Por qué / Para qué**) se usa un puente?

     —Se usa para cruzar un río.

- When interrogative words are used in indirect questions, or statements that imply a question, they also have a written accent.

    *No sé **dónde** está el palacio.*

D. Choose the interrogative word from the word bank that best completes each sentence and write it in the space provided. Follow the model.

cuál	cuántas	dónde	quién	por qué

Modelo   Necesito saber ____*cuál*____ de estos estudiantes es Juan.

1.   Quiero saber _____ está la iglesia.

2.   Tenemos que saber _____ causó ese accidente horrible.

3.   Mi profesor me preguntó _____ no había asistido a clase.

4.   Voy a averiguar _____ bebidas necesitamos comprar.

Realidades 3

Capítulo 8

Nombre _____

Hora _____

Fecha _____

AVSR, Sheet 3

Verbos con cambios en el pretérito (p. 341)

- Remember that some verbs have a spelling change in the preterite. The verb **oír** and verbs that end in **-uir, -eer, -aer** have a "y" in the **Ud./él/ella** and **Uds./ellos/ellas** forms. The verb **leer** is conjugated below as an example.

leer	
leí	leímos
leíste	leísteis
leyó	**leyeron**

A. Complete each sentence with the correct preterite form of the verb in parentheses.

Modelo (oír) Los cajeros ___*oyeron*___ una explosión en el mercado.

1. (**incluir**)   Yo _____ unas piedras preciosas en el collar que hice en la clase de arte.

2. (**destruir**) El dueño se puso enojado cuando un criminal _____ su tienda.

3. (**creer**)   Los policías no _____ las mentiras del ladrón.

4. (**caerse**)   Nosotros _____ _____ cuando corríamos porque teníamos mucho miedo del oso.

5. (**leer**)   Jorge _____ un artículo sobre cómo regatear en los mercados mexicanos.

- Remember that **-ar** and **-er** verbs have no stem changes in the preterite. Stem-changing **-ir** verbs have changes in the **Ud./él/ella** and **Uds./ellos/ellas** forms of the preterite.
- In verbs like **dormir** and **morir** (o→ue), the stem changes from **o** to **u** in these forms. In verbs like **sentir** and **preferir** (e→ie), or **pedir** and **seguir** (e→i), the stem changes from **e** to **i** in these forms.

B. Give the correct form of each of the following verbs in the preterite. Be careful not to make any stem changes where you don't need them!

Modelo (él) **morir** ___*murió*___

1. (nosotros) **almorzar** _____
2. (los profesores) **servir** _____
3. (yo) **repetir** _____
4. (nosotros) **perder** _____

5. (tú) **contar** _____
6. (Uds.) **dormir** _____
7. (él) **mentir** _____
8. (tú) **pedir** _____

realidades.com

• Web Code: jed-0801

- There are several irregular verbs in the preterite. Remember that some verbs such as **decir**, **traer**, and **traducir** have irregular stems in the preterite, but they share the same endings.

  decir: **dij-**

  traer: **traj-** ⎫ **Endings:** -e, -iste, -o, -imos, -isteis, -eron

  traducir: **traduj-** ⎭

C. Complete each sentence with the appropriate form of the verb in the preterite tense.

Modelo (decir) (Yo) Le _____*dije*_____ a mi mamá: «Estoy asustado».

1. (**traducir**) El traductor _____ las instrucciones para el producto nuevo del español al inglés.

2. (**traer**) Nosotros _____ algunos aretes de oro al mercado para venderlos.

3. (**decir**) Tú _____ cosas terribles durante la pelea con tu novia.

4. (**traer**) Los dos estudiantes _____ su parte del proyecto y colaboraron para terminarlo.

5. (**traducir**) Mis profesores de español _____ unos documentos y la compañía les pagó muy bien.

- Another set of irregular verb stems share a slightly different set of endings.

andar	estar	tener	poder	poner	saber	venir
anduv-	**estuv-**	**tuv-**	**pud-**	**pus-**	**sup-**	**vin-**

Endings: -e, -iste, -o, -imos, -isteis, -ieron.

- The verb **hacer** is also irregular in the preterite:

  hice, hiciste, hizo, hicimos, hicisteis, hicieron

Notice that these verbs do not have written accent marks in the preterite.

D. Complete each sentence with the correct preterite form of the verb in parentheses.

Modelo (venir) Cuando estudiaba en España, mis padres _____*vinieron*_____ a visitarme.

1. (**estar**) La policía capturó al ladrón y éste _____ en la cárcel 20 años.

2. (**poder**) Nosotros no _____ refugiarnos en la cueva porque había un oso allí.

3. (**hacer**) Ellos _____ todo lo posible por resolver el conflicto.

4. (**andar**) ¿Tú _____ solo por el bosque? ¿No tenías miedo?

5. (**tener**) Ayer yo _____ que salvar a mi hermanito porque se cayó en un río.

Realidades 3

Capítulo 8

Nombre _____

Hora _____

Fecha _____

Vocabulary Flash Cards, Sheet 1

Write the Spanish vocabulary word below each picture. If there is a word or phrase, copy it in the space provided. Be sure to include the article for each noun.

_____

_____

_____

_____

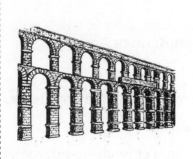

_____

_____

_____

_____

_____

_____

_____

_____

anteriormente

_____

_____

el/la árabe

_____

_____

la arquitectura

_____

_____

Realidades 3

Capítulo 8

Nombre _____

Fecha _____

Hora _____

Vocabulary Flash Cards, Sheet 2

Copy the word or phrase in the space provided. Be sure to include the article for each noun.

asimilar(se) _____	**la conquista** _____ _____	**conquistar** _____
la construcción _____ _____	**cristiano, cristiana** _____, _____	**dejar huellas** _____ _____
dominar _____	**la época** _____ _____	**grupo étnico** _____ _____

Realidades 3

Capítulo 8

Nombre _____

Hora _____

Fecha _____

Vocabulary Flash Cards, Sheet 3

Copy the word or phrase in the space provided. Be sure to include the article for each noun.

expulsar	**fundar(se)**	**gobernar**
_____	_____	_____
el idioma	**el imperio**	**la influencia**
___	___	___
_____	_____	_____
integrarse	**invadir**	**el judío, la judía**
		____ ____
_____	_____	____ ____

Realidades **3**

Nombre _____

Hora _____

Capítulo 8

Fecha _____

Vocabulary Flash Cards, Sheet 4

Copy the word or phrase in the space provided. Be sure to include the article for each noun.

la maravilla	**maravilloso, maravillosa**	**el musulmán, la musulmana**
_____	_____	____ ____
	_____	____ ____
ocupar	**la población**	**reconquistar**
	_____	
_____	_____	_____
el romano, la romana	**la unidad**	**único, única**
____ ____	_____	_____
_____	_____	_____

These blank cards can be used to write and practice other Spanish vocabulary for the chapter.

_____   _____   _____

_____   _____   _____

_____   _____   _____

Tear out this page. Write the English words on the lines. Fold the paper along the dotted line to see the correct answers so you can check your work.

el acueducto _____

anteriormente _____

el/la árabe _____

el arco _____

la arquitectura _____

asimilar(se) _____

el azulejo _____

el balcón,
(*pl. los balcones*) _____

la conquista _____

conquistar _____

la construcción _____

cristiano, cristiana _____

dejar huellas _____

dominar _____

la época _____

expulsar _____

fundarse _____

gobernar (ie) _____

Fold In →

Tear out this page. Write the Spanish words on the lines. Fold the paper along the dotted line to see the correct answers so you can check your work.

aqueduct _____

before _____

Arab _____

arch _____

architecture _____

to assimilate _____

tile _____

balcony _____

_____

conquest _____

to conquer _____

construction _____

Christian _____

to leave marks, traces _____

to dominate _____

time, era _____

to expel _____

to found _____

to rule, to govern _____

Fold In

Realidades 3

Capítulo 8

Nombre _____

Fecha _____

Hora _____

Vocabulary Check, Sheet 3

Tear out this page. Write the English words on the lines. Fold the paper along the dotted line to see the correct answers so you can check your work.

el grupo étnico _____

el idioma _____

el imperio _____

integrarse _____

invadir _____

el judío, la judía _____

la maravilla _____

maravilloso, maravillosa _____

el musulmán, la musulmana _____

ocupar _____

la población _____

la reja _____

el romano, la romana _____

la torre _____

la unidad _____

único, única _____

Fold In →

Realidades ③

Capítulo 8

Nombre _____

Hora _____

Fecha _____

Vocabulary Check, Sheet 4

Tear out this page. Write the Spanish words on the lines. Fold the paper along the dotted line to see the correct answers so you can check your work.

ethnic group _____

language _____

empire _____

to integrate _____

to invade _____

Jewish _____

marvel, wonder _____

wonderful _____

_____

Muslim _____

_____

to occupy _____

population _____

railing, grille _____

Roman _____

tower _____

unity _____

only _____

Fold In ←

• Web Code: jed-0802

Realidades 3

Capítulo 8

Nombre _____

Fecha _____

Hora _____

Guided Practice Activities, Sheet 1

El condicional (p. 352)

- To talk about what you *would* do in a hypothetical situation or what things *would* be like, you use the conditional tense in Spanish. To form the conditional of regular verbs, you add the endings to the infinitive of the verb. Look at the examples below.

fundar		invadir	
fundar**ía**	fundar**íamos**	invadir**ía**	invadir**íamos**
fundar**ías**	fundar**íais**	invadir**ías**	invadir**íais**
fundar**ía**	fundar**ían**	invadir**ía**	invadir**ían**

- Note that the endings are the same for **-ar**, **-er**, and **-ir** verbs.

A. Alejandro is thinking about what his life would be like if he lived in Spain. Choose the correct form of the conditional tense to complete each sentence.

Modelo   (Yo) (comería / comerías) tortilla española todos los días.

1. Mis amigos y yo (hablarían / **hablaríamos**) español perfectamente.

2. Mi familia (**viviría** / vivirías) en una casa bonita con un jardín y muchas flores.

3. Mis hermanos (**estudiarían** / estudiaríamos) en la universidad de Madrid.

4. Mis profesores me (**enseñarían** / enseñaría) sobre los Reyes Católicos.

5. Mis compañeros de clase y yo (prepararían / **prepararíamos**) un proyecto sobre la conquista de España por los árabes.

B. Some students were interviewed about what they would do if they were studying abroad in a Spanish-speaking country. Complete each sentence with correct form of the verb in the conditional tense.

Modelo   (escribir) Yo les ___escribiría___ cartas a mis abuelos todos los días.

1. (visitar)   Mi mejor amigo _____ todos los museos para aprender sobre las épocas pasadas.

2. (conocer)   Nosotros _____ a personas de varios grupos étnicos.

3. (conversar) Todos los estudiantes _____ en español todo el día.

4. (estudiar)   ¿Tú _____ la influencia de las diferentes culturas en el país?

5. (sacar)   Un estudiante _____ fotos de todos los lugares turísticos.

6. (ir)   Nosotros _____ a ver todos los sitios históricos del país.

- Web Code: jed-0803

- Some verbs have irregular stems in the conditional. These are the same irregular stems used to form the future tense. Look at the list below to review them.

hacer: **har-**	decir: **dir-**
poder: **podr-**	saber: **sabr-**
poner: **pondr-**	componer: **compondr-**
salir: **saldr-**	querer: **querr-**
tener: **tendr-**	contener: **contendr-**
venir: **vendr-**	haber: **habr-**

C. Fill in the correct stems of the irregular conditional verbs to complete the sentences about what people would do on a family trip to Spain. Follow the model.

Modelo   (querer) Mis padres y yo _____*querr*_ íamos ver los azulejos.

1. (**salir**)   Yo _____ía a las discotecas a bailar.

2. (**poder**) Mis hermanos _____ían ver los acueductos.

3. (**tener**)   Tú _____ías que acostumbrarte al acento español.

4. (**decir**) Nosotros _____íamos muchas cosas buenas sobre el Alcázar Real.

5. (**hacer**) Yo _____ía un viaje a Barcelona.

6. (**saber**) Toda la familia _____ía mucho más sobre la cultura española.

D. Conjugate the verb given in the conditional to write complete sentences about what would happen if people won the lottery.

Modelo   Mis padres / no / tener / que trabajar más
     Mis padres no tendrían que trabajar más. _____

1. Yo / poder / comprar / un carro nuevo

     _____

2. Mis amigos / venir / a cenar / a mi casa / todas las noches

     _____

3. Nosotros / querer / donar / dinero / a las personas pobres

     _____

4. Haber / una fuente / en el pasillo / de mi casa

     _____

5. Mi mamá / poner / pinturas de artistas famosos / en las paredes

     _____

realidades.com ✔
- Web Code: jed-0803

Write the Spanish vocabulary word below each picture. If there is a word or phrase, copy it in the space provided. Be sure to include the article for each noun.

_____

_____

_____

_____

_____

_____

_____

_____

_____

_____

_____

_____

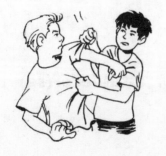

_____

_____

adoptar

_____

africano, africana

_____

_____

Realidades **3**

Nombre _____

Hora _____

Capítulo 8

Fecha _____

Vocabulary Flash Cards, Sheet 7

Copy the word or phrase in the space provided. Be sure to include the article for each noun.

al llegar _____ _____	**los antepasados** _____ _____	**la colonia** _____ _____
componerse de _____ _____	**la descendencia** _____ _____	**desconocido, desconocida** _____ _____
el encuentro _____ _____	**enfrentar(se)** _____ _____	**establecer(se)** _____ _____

Realidades 3

Capítulo 8

Nombre _____

Hora _____

Fecha _____

Vocabulary Flash Cards, Sheet 8

Copy the word or phrase in the space provided. Be sure to include the article for each noun.

europeo, europea	**la guerra**	**la herencia**
_____ _____	_____	_____ _____
el/la indígena	**el intercambio**	**la lengua**
_____	_____	_____
la mezcla	**el poder**	**poderoso, poderosa**
_____	_____	_____ _____

Realidades 3

Nombre _____

Hora _____

Capítulo 8

Fecha _____

Vocabulary Flash Cards, Sheet 9

Copy the word or phrase in the space provided. Be sure to include the article for each noun. The blank card can be used to write and practice another Spanish vocabulary word or phrase for the chapter.

la raza ___ _____	**rebelarse** ___ _____	**el resultado** ___ _____
el reto ___ _____	**la riqueza** ___ _____	**la semejanza** ___ _____
la tierra ___ _____	**la variedad** ___ _____	___ _____

Realidades ③

Capítulo 8

Nombre _____

Hora _____

Fecha _____

Vocabulary Check, Sheet 5

Tear out this page. Write the English words on the lines. Fold the paper along the dotted line to see the correct answers so you can check your work.

adoptar _____

africano, africana _____

el antepasado _____

el arma (*pl.* las armas) _____

la batalla _____

la colonia _____

componerse de _____

desconocido, desconocida _____

enfrentarse _____

el encuentro _____

establecer (zc) _____

europeo, europea _____

la guerra _____

la herencia _____

el/la indígena _____

el intercambio _____

Fold In

Realidades **3**

Capítulo 8

Nombre _____

Hora _____

Fecha _____

Vocabulary Check, Sheet 6

Tear out this page. Write the Spanish words on the lines. Fold the paper along the dotted line to see the correct answers so you can check your work.

to adopt _____

African _____

ancestor _____

weapon _____

battle _____

colony _____

to be formed by _____

unknown _____

_____

to face, to confront _____

meeting _____

to establish _____

European _____

war _____

heritage _____

native _____

exchange _____

Fold In →

Tear out this page. Write the English words on the lines. Fold the paper along the dotted line to see the correct answers so you can check your work.

la lengua _____

luchar _____

la mercancía _____

la mezcla _____

la misión _____

el misionero,
la misionera _____

el poder _____

poderoso,
poderosa _____

la raza _____

rebelarse _____

el resultado _____

el reto _____

la riqueza _____

la semejanza _____

el/la soldado _____

la tierra _____

la variedad _____

Fold In ←

Realidades 3

Nombre _____

Hora _____

Capítulo 8

Fecha _____

Vocabulary Check, Sheet 8

Tear out this page. Write the Spanish words on the lines. Fold the paper along the dotted line to see the correct answers so you can check your work.

language, tongue   _____

to fight   _____

merchandise   _____

mix   _____

mission   _____

missionary   _____

_____

power   _____

powerful   _____

_____

race   _____

to rebel, to revolt   _____

result, outcome   _____

challenge   _____

wealth   _____

similarity   _____

soldier   _____

land   _____

variety   _____

Fold In

realidades.com

• Web Code: jed-0806

El imperfecto del subjuntivo (p. 364)

- You have already learned how to use the subjunctive to persuade someone else to do something, to express emotions about situations, and to express doubt and uncertainty. If the main verb is in the present tense, you use the present subjunctive.

  Nos alegramos de que la fiesta sea divertida.   *We are happy the party is fun.*

- If the main verb is in the preterite or imperfect, you must use the *imperfect subjunctive* in the second part of the sentence.

  Él se alegró de que *comieran* **buena comida.**   *He was happy they ate authentic food.*

- To form the imperfect subjunctive, first put a verb in the **ellos/ellas/Uds.** form of the preterite tense and remove the **-ron**. Then, add the imperfect subjunctive endings. Look at the two examples below.

luchar (ellos) = luch**aron** (pretérito)		**establecer** (ellas) = establec**ieron**	
luch~~aron~~		establec~~ieron~~	
luch**ara**	luch**áramos**	establec**iera**	establec**iéramos**
luch**aras**	luch**arais**	establec**ieras**	establec**ierais**
luch**ara**	luch**aran**	establec**iera**	establec**ieran**

- Note: The **nosotros** form of each verb has an accent at the end of the stem.

A. Circle the correct form of the imperfect subjunctive to complete the following sentences.

Modelo   La profesora recomendó que los estudiantes (**estudiara** / **estudiaran**) los aztecas.

1. A los conquistadores no les gustaba que los aztecas (**practicara** / **practicaran**) una religión diferente.

2. El rey español quería que Hernán Cortés (**enseñara** / **enseñaras**) su religión a los aztecas.

3. Fue excelente que nosotros (**miraran** / **miráramos**) una película sobre el imperio azteca.

4. Los españoles dudaban que el rey azteca (**se rebelaran** / **se rebelara**), pero eso fue lo que ocurrió.

- Any verbs that have stem changes, spelling changes, or irregular conjugation in the **ellos/ellas/Uds.** form of the preterite will also have these changes in the imperfect subjunctive. Look at a few examples of stems below.

leer-	leyeron-	**leye-**	ir-	fueron-	**fue-**
hacer-	hicieron-	**hicie-**	dormir-	durmieron-	**durmie-**

B. In the first space, write the **ellos/ellas/Uds.** preterite form of the verb. Then, conjugate the verb in the **él/ella/Ud.** form of the imperfect subjunctive. Follow the model.

Modelo   (construir) ___*construyeron*___ : el trabajador ___*construyera*___

1. (**dar**) _____ : el rey _____

2. (**ir**) _____ : la reina _____

3. (**poder**) _____ : Papá _____

4. (**morir**) _____ : Ud. _____

5. (**sentir**) _____ : Juanita _____

6. (**andar**) _____ : Carlitos _____

C. In the following sentences, conjugate the first verb in the imperfect indicative and the second verb in the imperfect subjunctive to create complete sentences. Follow the model.

Modelo   Yo / querer / que / mi profesor / mostrar / un video / sobre los aztecas
    Yo quería que mi profesor mostrara un video sobre los aztecas.

1. Ser / necesario / que / los aztecas / defender / su imperio

    _____

2. Los aztecas / dudar / que / Hernán Cortés / tener razón

    _____

3. Yo / alegrarse / de que / los estudiantes / estar / interesados / en la cultura azteca

    _____

4. Nosotros / no estar seguros / de que / los aztecas / poder / preservar todas sus tradiciones

    _____

5. Ser / malo / que / muchos aztecas / morirse / de enfermedades

    _____

realidades.com ✓
- Web Code: jed-0807

El imperfecto del subjuntivo con *si* (p. 367)

- The two tenses you have learned in this chapter, the conditional and the imperfect subjunctive, are often combined in sentences where you talk about hypothetical, unlikely, or untrue events. These sentences include the word **si** ("if") followed by the imperfect subjunctive and a main clause with a verb in the conditional tense. Look at the following examples.

  > **Si viviera en España, podría ver la influencia árabe en la arquitectura.**
  > *If I lived in Spain, I would be able to see the arabic influence in the architecture.*

  > **Haríamos un viaje a México para ver las pirámides si tuviéramos tiempo.**
  > *We would take a trip to Mexico to see the pyramids if we had time.*

- Notice that the order of the phrase can vary, but the imperfect subjunctive must **always** be paired with the **si**.

A. Complete the sentences with the conditional of the verb in parentheses. Follow the model.

> **Modelo** (comprar) Si tuviera un millón de dólares, yo _**compraría**_ un carro.

1. **(ir)** Si tuviera un avión, yo _____ a una isla privada.

2. **(ser)** Si pudiera tener cualquier trabajo, yo _____ embajador a España.

3. **(ver)** Si pudiera ver cualquier película esta noche, yo _____ una romántica.

4. **(sentirse)** Si tuviera que tomar cinco exámenes hoy, yo ____ _____ enfermo.

B. What would happen if you participated in an exchange program in Mexico? Read the following statements and decide which part of the sentence would use the imperfect subjunctive form of the verb and which part would use the conditional. Circle your choice in each part of the sentence. Follow the model.

> **Modelo** Si ((comiera) / comería) en un restaurante mexicano, (pidiera / (pediría)) platos auténticos.

1. Si nuestros profesores (**fueran** / **serían**) más exigentes, nos (**dieran** / **darían**) exámenes todos los días.

2. Yo (**fuera** / **iría**) a las montañas si (**tuviera** / **tendría**) un caballo.

3. Si nosotros (**trabajáramos** / **trabajaríamos**) para el gobierno (**fuéramos** / **seríamos**) muy poderosos.

4. Si tú (**vendieras** / **venderías**) unas mercancías, (**ganaras** / **ganarías**) mucho dinero.

El imperfecto del subjuntivo con *si* (*continued*)

C. Conjugate the boldface verbs in the imperfect subjunctive and the underlined verbs in the conditional tense to form complete sentences. Follow the model.

Modelo Si / yo / **tener** / dinero / <u>comprar</u> / unas joyas preciosas

Si yo tuviera dinero, compraría unas joyas preciosas. _____

1. Si / nosotros / **hablar** / con nuestros antepasados / <u>aprender</u> / cosas interesantes

_____

2. Si / tú / **ir** / a México / el 1 de noviembre / <u>celebrar</u> / el Día de los Muertos

_____

3. Si / yo / **tener** / un examen sobre los aztecas / <u>sacar</u> / una buena nota

_____

4. Si / mis amigos / **tocar** / instrumentos / <u>tener</u> / una banda

_____

5. Si / yo / **hacer** / un viaje a la Costa del Sol / <u>nadar</u> en el mar

_____

_____

• After **como si** ("as if") you must **always** use the imperfect subjunctive. The other verb can be in either the present or the past tense.

> **Martín habla como si *fuera* un hombre poderoso.**
> *Martin speaks as if he were a powerful man.*

> **La comida del restaurante era tan buena que él se sentía como si *estuviera* en España.**
> *The food at the restaurant was so good that he felt as if he were in Spain.*

D. Complete each of the following sentences with the imperfect subjunctive form of the verb given. Follow the model.

Modelo (tener) Juan Pablo Fernández tiene 80 años, pero baila como si ___*tuviera*___ 20.

1. (hacer) Hace calor hoy, pero Pepita está vestida como si _____ frío.

2. (querer) Marta hablaba de México como si _____ vivir allí.

3. (ser) Rafael cocinaba como si _____ un chef profesional.

4. (estar) ¡Mi mamá habla como si _____ enojada conmigo!

5. (tener) Conchita gasta dinero como si _____ un millón de dólares.

• Web Code: jed-0808

Realidades ③

Capítulo 8

Nombre _____

Fecha _____

Hora _____

Reading Activities, Sheet 1

Puente a la cultura (pp. 370–371)

A. You are about to read an article about missions established in California in the 18th century. Check off all of the items in the following list that you think would be found in these missions. You can use the pictures in your textbook to give you ideas.

soldier barracks _____   dance halls _____   a pool _____

eating areas _____   a church _____   rooms for priests _____

B. Look at the following excerpts from your reading and decide which is the best definition for each highlighted word. Circle your answer.

1. «...tenían la función de recibir y **alimentar** a las personas que viajaban a través del territorio desconocido»

   a. educar   **b.** aconsejar   **c.** dar comida

2. «Las misiones incluían una iglesia, cuartos para los sacerdotes, depósitos, casas para mujeres **solteras**...»

   a. tristes   **b.** no son casadas   **c.** con sombra

3. «Muchas personas **recorren** hoy el Camino Real...»

   a. viajar por   **b.** correr rápidamente   **c.** nadar

C. Read the following excerpt from the reading. List the three functions of the missions mentioned.

> Las misiones fueron creadas no sólo para enseñar la religión cristiana a los indígenas sino también para enseñarles tareas que pudieran realizar en la nueva sociedad española. Asimismo (Likewise) tenían la función de recibir y alimentar a las personas que viajaban a través del territorio desconocido de California.

1. _____

2. _____

3. _____

D. Look at the paragraph on page 371 of the reading and fill in the key pieces of information below.

1. El nombre del hombre que fundó las misiones: _____

2. El número de misiones que fundó: _____

3. El nombre de la ruta en la que se encuentran las misiones: _____

Realidades 3

Capítulo 8

Nombre

Hora

Fecha

Reading Activities, Sheet 2

Lectura (pp. 376–378)

A. In this story, a modern-day teenager is transported into the world of the Aztecs just prior to the arrival of Hernán Cortés. What background information do you remember about the Aztecs from what you have learned in this chapter? List two elements in each category below.

1. religion: _____ ,

   _____

2. architecture: _____ ,

   _____

B. The first part of this story finds the protagonist, Daniel, in a very confusing situation. How does he figure out where he is? Check off all of the clues below that he uses to try to determine where, and when he is.

☐ está durmiendo en un *petate* y no en su cama

☐ lleva jeans y una camiseta

☐ el emperador Moctezuma está en su casa

☐ habla un idioma extraño

☐ su novia lo llama "Tozani" y "esposo"

C. Daniel determines the date by using his knowledge of the Aztec calendar and the Aztec dates his "wife" gives him. Read the excerpt and fill in the dates below in the Aztec and then the modern form.

—*Acatl. El año 1-Caña, el día de 2-Casas.*
Trato de recordar el calendario azteca. Un escalofrío (chill) me invade el cuerpo cuando por fin descifro el significado de aquella fecha. Acatl, equivalente al año 1519 del calendario cristiano. El día 2-Casas, o sea, el 29, probablemente del mes de junio. Un mes antes de la entrada de Hernán Cortés en Tenochtitlán.

Azteca   **Moderna**

El año _____1-Caña_____   El año _____

El día _____   El día _____

D. According to this account, does it seem the "beings" look more like humans or animals? Give examples below from the excerpt.

> *Los mensajeros de Moctezuma que han visto a estos seres, cuentan que son grandes de estatura, que tienen la cara cubierta de cabello. Y algunos de ellos tienen cuatro patas enormes y dos cabezas, una de animal y otra de hombre.*

1. According to this passage, who has seen these "beings"? _____

2. What does it seem the "beings" look more like, man or animal, according to this account? Give examples.

   _____

   _____

3. These beings are described as tall and some as "two-headed." Why might Moctezuma think they were gods?

   _____

   _____

E. As you read the story, you have gone on a path of discovery with Daniel to find out who he is, where he is, and what he is supposed to do. By the end of the story, he has his situation figured out, but does not like the task he is given. Number the following statements in the order in which Daniel experiences them. Then, answer the question that follows.

_____ Daniel se da cuenta de que su misión es llevar regalos a los «dioses blancos» y guiarlos a la ciudad de Tenochtitlán.

_____ Daniel se da cuenta de que su nombre es «Tozani» y que tiene una esposa llamada «Chalchi».

_____ Daniel se da cuenta de que tiene que ir a un lago y luego al Templo Mayor.

When Daniel has realized who he is and what he has been told to do, what is his reaction? Why does he react this way? (*Hint:* does he know something others do not?)

_____

_____

Realidades 3

Capítulo 9

Nombre _____

Hora _____

Fecha _____

AVSR, Sheet 1

Verbos como *gustar* (p. 385)

- Remember that you use the verb **gustar** to talk about likes and dislikes. When you use **gustar**, the subject of the sentence is the thing that is liked or disliked.
- If the thing liked or disliked is a singular object or a verb, use the singular form of **gustar**.

   *(A mí) me **gusta** el camión amarillo.   ¿Te **gusta** conducir?*

- If the thing liked or disliked is a plural object, use the plural form of **gustar**.

   *Nos **gustan** los cuadernos con papel reciclado.*

A. First, underline the subject of each sentence. Then, circle the correct form of **gustar** to complete the sentence. **¡Recuerda!** The subject is the thing that is liked or disliked.

| Modelo | A los padres de Juana les ((gusta)/ gustan) <u>el parque</u>.

1. A nadie le (gusta / gustan) la contaminación.

2. A mí me (gusta / gustan) los ríos claros.

3. A nosotros nos (gusta / gustan) el barrio Norte.

4. A mi hermano le (gusta / gustan) los coches rojos.

- **Gustar** is used with an indirect object pronoun to indicate to whom something is pleasing. The indirect object pronouns appear below.

me	nos
te	os
le	les

- To clarify the person to whom the indirect object pronoun refers, use the personal *a* plus a noun or a subject pronoun. This is often used with the pronouns **le** and **les**.

   ***A ella** le gustan los grupos que protegen el medio ambiente.*

   ***A los voluntarios** les gusta mejorar las condiciones para la gente.*

   You can also use the personal **a** plus a pronoun for emphasis.

   *A Marta le gusta pasear en barco pero **a mí** no me gusta porque no puedo nadar.*

B. Match the beginning of each of the following sentences with the correct ending. The first one has been done for you.

_D_ 1. A los estudiantes...

_____ 2. A la gente...

_____ 3. A mí...

_____ 4. ¿A ti...

_____ 5. A mis amigos y a mí...

A. ...nos gusta colaborar.

B. ...le gusta la naturaleza.

C. ...te gusta hacer trabajo voluntario?

~~**D.** ...no les gusta el tráfico.~~

E. ...me gusta pasar tiempo en el aire libre.

realidades.com ✓

• Web Code: jed-0901

Realidades 3

Capítulo 9

Nombre _____

Fecha _____

Hora _____

AVSR, Sheet 2

- There are several other Spanish verbs that often follow the same pattern as **gustar**. Look at the list below.

encantar	to love	**doler**	to ache, to be painful
molestar	to bother	**faltar**	to lack, to be missing
preocupar	to worry	**quedar (bien/mal)**	to fit (well / poorly)
importar	to matter	**parecer**	to seem
interesar	to interest		

C. Write the correct indirect object pronoun and circle the correct form of the verb to complete each sentence. Follow the model.

Modelo   A mis padres _____ ((encantaba)/ encantaban) montar en bicicleta.

1. A mí _____ (interesaba / interesaban) los insectos.

2. A mis amigos _____ (preocupaba / preocupaban) la contaminación del lago que estaba cerca de su casa.

3. A nosotros _____ (dolía / dolían) la espalda después de subir árboles.

4. A mi mejor amiga _____ (importaba / importaban) reciclar papel.

5. A ti _____ (quedaba / quedaban) mal los zapatos de tu papá.

D. Use the elements below to write complete sentences. You will need to add the appropriate indirect object pronoun and conjugate the verb in the present tense.

Modelo   a mis padres / molestar / zonas de construcción.

    A mis padres les molestan las zonas de construcción.

1. a mí / doler / los pies / después de correr

   _____

2. a ti / faltar / dinero / para comprar el carro

   _____

3. a nosotras / preocupar / las causas de la contaminación

   _____

4. a la profesora / importar / las buenas notas en los exámenes

   _____

5. a mí / encantar / manejar el camión de mi abuelo

   _____

Uses of the definite article (p. 387)

- In general, the definite article (**el, la, los, las**) is used in Spanish the same way it is in English, whenever you need the word "the." However, it is also sometimes used in Spanish when it is not needed in English, in the following ways:

- When you are referring to someone by a name and title, in front of the title (Note: This is not used when speaking directly to the person.)

    El doctor Fuentes no está aquí hoy.   *Hola, profesora Martínez.*

- With a street, avenue, park, or other proper name.

    La avenida Yacútoro es una calle muy larga.

- In front of a noun that represents an entire species, institution or generality.

    Los gatos duermen más que los perros.   *La felicidad es fundamental.*

A. Read the following sentences to determine the reason the underlined definite article is needed. Write **T** for title (such as profession), **P** for proper name, and **G** for generality.

Modelo   _G_ El chocolate es delicioso.

1. _____ La profesora Corzano llega a las nueve.

2. _____ Las universidades son instituciones importantes.

3. _____ La Torre Eiffel está en Francia.

4. _____ El Parque Nacional de Yellowstone es impresionante.

5. _____ Los policías de nuestro barrio son valientes.

6. _____ Caminamos por la calle Córdoba.

B. Complete each sentence with the appropriate definite article. Follow the model.

Modelo   Mi profesor de biología es __el__ Sr. Rivera.

1. _____ hormigas son insectos que me molestan mucho.

2. Hay un semáforo en la esquina de _____ avenidas Santiago y Castillo.

3. _____ señora Ramos fue a las montañas para acampar.

4. Voy a ir a Guatemala con _____ doctor Jiménez para estudiar la selva tropical.

5. _____ respeto es una parte importante de las relaciones.

6. _____ terremotos destruyen muchas casas cada año.

realidades.com
- Web Code: jed-0901

- The definite articles are also used with certain time expressions that refer to age, days of the week, hours (time of day) and seasons. Look at the examples below.

    *Aprendí a manejar a **los 16 años**.*   *Vamos a salir a **las 8** de la mañana.*

    *La cena para los honrados es **el viernes**.*   ***El verano** es mi estación favorita.*

C. Circle the correct definite article to complete each sentence. Follow the model.

Modelo   Voy a graduarme de la escuela secundaria a (las /(los) 18 años.

1. Me gusta muchísimo (**el / la**) otoño porque hace fresco.

2. La tormenta empezó a (**los / las**) diez de la noche.

3. El viaje al bosque es (**el / los**) miércoles que viene.

4. A (**los / la**) 5 años, mi papá vio un oso feroz en el bosque.

- The definite article is also included when it is an inseparable part of the name of a country or city, such as **El Salvador, La Paz,** and **La Habana**.

- Remember that the combination **a** + **el** produces the contraction *al* and the combination **de** + **el** produces the contraction *del*.

    *Salimos **del** parque zoológico y después caminamos **al** parque nacional.*

- However, when **el** is part of a proper name, it does not combine with **a** or **de**.

    *Viajamos **a El** Paso, Texas.*   *Somos **de El** Salvador.*

D. Combine the first part of the sentence with the phrase in parentheses, creating **al** or **del** when necessary. Remember, this only occurs with the article **el**, but not with proper names. Follow the model.

Modelo   Vamos a ir a (el campo). Vamos a ir ____*al campo*____.

1. Mis amigos salieron de (el desierto). Mis amigos salieron _____.

2. Dimos una caminata a (las montañas). Dimos una caminata _____.

3. Quiero viajar a (el desierto africano). Quiero viajar _____.

4. Nosotros venimos de (La Paz). Venimos _____.

5. Me gustaría viajar a (el fondo del mar). Me gustaría viajar _____.

6. Carlos viene de (El Cajón), California. Viene _____.

Write the Spanish vocabulary word below each picture. If there is a word or phrase, copy it in the space provided. Be sure to include the article for each noun.

_____

_____

_____

_____

_____

_____

agotar(se)

_____

amenazar

_____

castigar

_____

Realidades 3

Capítulo 9

Nombre _____

Fecha _____

Hora _____

Vocabulary Flash Cards, Sheet 2

Copy the word or phrase in the space provided. Be sure to include the article for each noun.

colocar	conservar	la contaminación
_____	_____	_____

crecer	dañar	debido a
_____	_____	_____ _____

depender de	deshacerse de	desperdiciar
_____ _____	_____	_____

Realidades 3

Capítulo 9

Nombre _____

Hora _____

Fecha _____

Vocabulary Flash Cards, Sheet 3

Copy the word or phrase in the space provided. Be sure to include the article for each noun.

económico, económica	la electricidad	en cuanto
la escasez	estar a cargo (de)	fomentar
el gobierno	grave	limitar

Copy the word or phrase in the space provided. Be sure to include the article for each noun.

el pesticida ___ _____	**promover** _____	**la protección** ___ _____
químico, química _____ _____	**el recipiente** ___ _____	**el recurso natural** ___ _____ _____
suficiente _____	**tan pronto como** ___ ___ _____ _____	**tomar medidas** _____ _____

Copy the word or phrase in the space provided. Be sure to include the article for each noun. The blank cards can be used to write and practice other Spanish vocabulary for the chapter.

ambiental _____	**la atmósfera** _____ _____	**la amenaza** _____ _____
la fábrica _____ _____	**en vez de** _____ _____ _____	 _____
    _____	 _____	 _____

Tear out this page. Write the English words on the lines. Fold the paper along the dotted line to see the correct answers so you can check your work.

agotar(se) _____

la amenaza _____

amenazar _____

ambiental _____

castigar _____

colocar _____

conservar _____

la contaminación _____

contaminado,
contaminada _____

crecer _____

dañar _____

debido a _____

depender de _____

deshacerse de _____

desperdiciar _____

el desperdicio _____

Fold In

Realidades 3

Nombre _____

Hora _____

Capítulo 9

Fecha _____

Vocabulary Check, Sheet 2

Tear out this page. Write the Spanish words on the lines. Fold the paper along the dotted line to see the correct answers so you can check your work.

to exhaust, to run out   _____

threat   _____

to threaten   _____

environmental   _____

to punish   _____

to put, to place   _____

to preserve   _____

pollution   _____

polluted   _____

    _____

to grow   _____

to damage   _____

due to   _____

to depend on   _____

to get rid of   _____

to waste   _____

waste   _____

Fold In

Tear out this page. Write the English words on the lines. Fold the paper along the dotted line to see the correct answers so you can check your work.

echar _____

la electricidad _____

la escasez _____

estar a cargo de _____

fomentar _____

el gobierno _____

grave _____

limitar _____

el pesticida _____

el petróleo _____

la pila _____

promover _____

químico, química _____

el recipiente _____

tomar medidas _____

el veneno _____

Fold In

Tear out this page. Write the Spanish words on the lines. Fold the paper along the dotted line to see the correct answers so you can check your work.

to throw (away)   _____

electricity   _____

shortage   _____

to be in charge of   _____

to encourage   _____

government   _____

serious   _____

to limit   _____

pesticide   _____

oil   _____

battery   _____

to promote   _____

chemical   _____

container   _____

to take steps (to)   _____

poison   _____

Fold In ←

realidades.com
• Web Code: jed-0902

Conjunciones que se usan con el subjuntivo y el indicativo (p. 398)

- Spanish has several conjunctions that refer to time.

  cuando: when   **en cuanto:** as soon as

  después (de) que: after   **mientras:** while, as long as

  tan pronto como: as soon as   **hasta que:** until

- These time conjunctions are followed by the subjunctive when they refer to actions that have not yet occurred.

  Vamos a usar coches eléctricos *tan pronto como* se agote el petróleo.
  We are going to use electric cars as soon as oil runs out.

A. Complete each sentence with the correct form of the present subjunctive.

Modelo   **(sembrar)** Habrá peligro de deforestación mientras nosotros no
<u> sembremos </u> suficientes árboles.

1. **(terminar)** Reciclaré el periódico cuando yo _____ de leerlo.

2. **(estar)** Vamos a colocar estos recipientes en el depósito de reciclaje tan pronto como _____ vacíos.

3. **(dejar)** La contaminación no se eliminará hasta que la fábrica _____ de echar sustancias químicas al lago.

4. **(beber)** En cuanto _____ este refresco, voy a reciclar la botella.

- These time conjunctions are followed by the preterite when the action that follows has already taken place.

  Jorge recicló las latas tan pronto como *tuvo* tiempo.
  Jorge recycled the cans as soon as he had time.

- If the action occurs regularly, the verb will be in the present indicative.

  Uso productos reciclados cuando *puedo*.   *I use recycled products when I can.*

B. Look at the underlined part of each sentence below and write **I** if it is in the indicative mood or **S** if it is in the subjunctive mood. Base your decision on whether the underlined part is something that has already happened or occurs regularly (indicative) or whether it has not yet happened (subjunctive). Follow the model.

Modelo   ___*I*___ Los peces mueren cuando <u>el agua del lago se contamina</u>.

1. _____ El agricultor usó pesticidas hasta que <u>encontró productos orgánicos</u>.

2. _____ El medio ambiente sufrirá mientras <u>no conservemos los recursos naturales</u>.

3. _____ Dejaré de molestarte en cuanto <u>tú aprendas a reciclar</u>.

4. _____ Usan pesticidas mientras <u>los insectos se comen las verduras</u>.

realidades.com
- Web Code: jed-0903

Realidades 3

Capítulo 9

Nombre _____

Hora _____

Fecha _____

Guided Practice Activities, Sheet 2

C. Look at the first verb in each sentence to determine how to conjugate the second verb. If the verb is an action that happened, use the preterite; if the action has not yet taken place, use the present subjunctive; and if the first verb describes something that occurs regularly, use the present indicative. Follow the model.

Modelo (beber) **a.** Yo reciclo las botellas cuando ___*bebo*___ jugo.

b. Yo reciclaré esta botella cuando ___*beba*___ el jugo.

c. Yo reciclé la botella cuando ___*bebí*___ jugo ayer.

1. (lavar) **a.** Yo cerraré la llave del agua tan pronto como _____ estos platos.

b. Yo cerré la llave del agua tan pronto como _____ los platos ayer.

c. Yo siempre cierro la llave del agua tan pronto como _____ los platos.

2. (leer) **a.** Los estudiantes trabajaron para resolver el problema después de que la profesora les _____ un artículo.

b. Los estudiantes trabajarán para resolver el problema después de que la profesora les _____ un artículo.

c. Los estudiantes generalmente trabajan para resolver problemas después de que la profesora les _____ artículos.

- You must always follow the conjunction **antes de que** with the subjunctive.
  *Voy a comprar un carro eléctrico antes de que este verano **termine**.*
- With the conjunctions **antes de, después de,** and **hasta,** conjugate the verbs only if there is a subject change. If there is no subject change, use the infinitive.
  Voy a comprar un carro eléctrico después de ahorrar mucho.

D. Circle the choice that correctly completes each sentence. If there is only one subject, choose the infinitive. If there are two subjects, choose the subjunctive.

Modelo Estaré a cargo del club estudiantil después de que la presidenta actual (graduarse /(se gradúe)).

1. Reciclaremos este papel después de (**escribir** / **escribamos**) el reportaje.

2. Los estudiantes empezarán a escribir antes de que la profesora (**llegar** / **llegue**).

3. Estudiarás hasta (**aprender** / **aprendas**) más sobre el medio ambiente.

4. Usaremos más energía solar después de que el petróleo (**agotarse** / **se agote**).

5. Limpiaremos el lago antes de que los peces (**morir** / **mueran**).

realidades.com

• Web Code: jed-0903

Los pronombres relativos *que, quien,* y *lo que* (p. 402)

- Relative pronouns are used to combine two sentences or to provide clarifying information. In Spanish, the most commonly used relative pronoun is **que**. It is used to refer either to people or to things, and can mean "that," "which," "who," or "whom."

    Se deshicieron del veneno *que* mató las hormigas.
    They got rid of the poison that killed the ants.

A. Your biology class is touring the community with an environmental expert. Match the beginnings of the tour guide's sentences with the most logical endings.

__*C*__ 1. Estos son los contaminantes...

_____ 2. Ésta es la fábrica...

_____ 3. Éstos son los recipientes...

_____ 4. La profesora Alcatrán es la persona...

_____ 5. Ésas son las estudiantes...

A. ... que produce los contaminantes.

B. ... que hacen trabajo voluntario para educar a las personas sobre la contaminación.

~~**C.** ... que dañan el medio ambiente.~~

D. ... que dirige la organización *Protege la tierra.*

E. ... que contienen los productos químicos.

- When you use a preposition, such as **a, con,** or **en,** with a relative pronoun, **que** refers to things and **quien(es)** refers to people.

    El producto *con que* lavé el piso contiene algunos químicos.
    The product with which I washed the floor contains some chemicals.

    La mujer *de quien* hablo es una científica importante.
    The woman about whom I am speaking is an important scientist.

    Los jefes *para quienes* trabajo insisten en que reciclemos.
    The bosses for whom I work insist that we recycle.

- Notice that you use **quien** if the subject is singular and **quienes** if it is plural.

B. Read each sentence and determine whether the subject refers to a person or a thing. Then, circle the correct relative pronoun to complete the sentence.

Modelo El profesor a (**que** / **quien**) le hicimos las preguntas es el Sr. Rodríguez.

1. La situación en (**que** / **quien**) me encuentro es divertida.

2. Los reporteros a (**quien** / **quienes**) pedí prestado el video ya salieron.

3. Los recursos con (**que** / **quienes**) trabajamos son escasos.

4. Los estudiantes con (**que** / **quienes**) hicimos los experimentos desaparecieron.

- Web Code: jed-0904

C. Fill in the sentences with **que**, **quien**, or **quienes**. Remember that **quien(es)** is only used after a preposition. When you refer to people without a preposition, use **que**.

Modelo   El muchacho con _____*quien*_____ trabajé limpiando una sección del río se llama Manuel.

1. Nosotros vivimos en una comunidad _____ se preocupa mucho por conservar los recursos naturales.

2. Hay un autobús _____ va directamente al centro comercial. No es necesario ir en carro.

3. Los estudiantes de _____ hablo trabajan en una fábrica durante el verano.

4. El senador a _____ le escribí una carta me respondió la semana pasada.

- The relative phrase **lo que** is used to refer to situations, concepts, actions, or objects that have not yet been identified.

   Todos escuchamos con atención *lo que* el profesor dijo sobre la protección del planeta.
   We all listened carefully to what the professor said about the protection of the planet.

   ***Lo que* necesitamos es más voluntarios.**
   What (The thing) we need is more volunteers.

- As seen in the example above, **lo que** often occurs at the beginning of a sentence.

D. Complete each of the following sentences with **que** or **lo que**. Remember that you will use **que** to clarify a specific thing and **lo que** to refer to something abstract or not yet mentioned. Follow the model.

Modelo   ____*Lo que*____ me molesta más es el uso de los contaminantes.

1. La organización _____ escribió esos artículos hace muchas cosas buenas.

2. No podemos hacer todo _____ queremos para mejorar las condiciones.

3. Ayer hubo un accidente _____ afectó el medio ambiente.

4. _____ queremos hacer es crear un grupo para limpiar una sección de la carretera.

5. Hay muchos contaminantes en el aire, _____ no es bueno para la respiración.

6. El petróleo _____ usamos se va a agotar algún día.

Realidades ③

Capítulo 9

Nombre _____

Hora _____

Fecha _____

Vocabulary Flash Cards, Sheet 6

Write the Spanish vocabulary word or phrase below each picture. Be sure to include the article for each noun.

_____

_____

_____

_____

_____

_____

_____

_____

_____

_____

_____

_____

_____

_____

_____

Realidades 3

Nombre _____

Hora _____

Capítulo 9

Fecha _____

Vocabulary Flash Cards, Sheet 7

Write the Spanish vocabulary word below each picture. If there is a word or phrase, copy it in the space provided. Be sure to include the article for each noun.

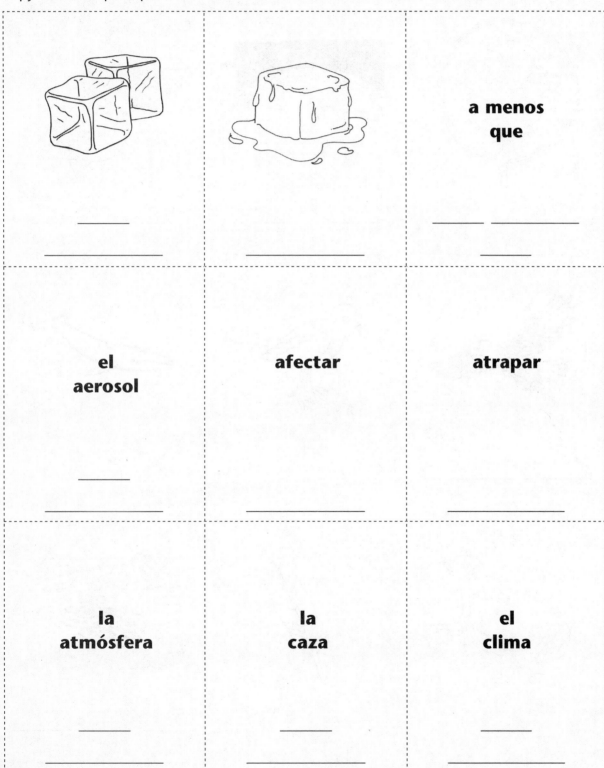

a menos
que

_____ _____

el
aerosol

afectar

atrapar

la
atmósfera

la
caza

el
clima

Copy the word or phrase in the space provided. Be sure to include the article for each noun.

con tal que	**detener**	**disminuir**
_____ _____	_____	_____
_____		
la especie	**excesivo, excesiva**	**explotar**
_____	_____	_____
_____		
la falta	**la limpieza**	**en peligro de extinción**
_____	_____	_____ _____
_____	_____	_____ _____

Copy the word or phrase in the space provided. Be sure to include the article for each noun.

la piel	**la preservación**	**producir**
el recalentamiento global	**el rescate**	**la reserva natural**
salvaje	**la selva tropical**	**tomar conciencia de**

Realidades **3**

Capítulo 9

Nombre _____

Fecha _____

Hora _____

Vocabulary Check, Sheet 5

Tear out this page. Write the English words on the lines. Fold the paper along the dotted line to see the correct answers so you can check your work.

el aerosol _____

afectar _____

el agujero _____

el águila calva _____
(*pl. las águilas calvas*)

atrapar _____

el ave _____

la ballena _____

la caza _____

la capa de ozono _____

el clima _____

el derrame _____
de petróleo

derretir _____

detener _____

disminuir _____

_____

el efecto _____
invernadero

Fold In

Tear out this page. Write the Spanish words on the lines. Fold the paper along the dotted line to see the correct answers so you can check your work.

aerosol   _____

to affect   _____

hole   _____

bald eagle   _____

        _____

to catch, to trap   _____

bird   _____

whale   _____

hunting   _____

ozone layer   _____

weather   _____

oil spill   _____

        _____

to melt   _____

to stop   _____

to decrease,   _____
to diminish

greenhouse effect   _____

        _____

Fold In

Tear out this page. Write the English words on the lines. Fold the paper along the dotted line to see the correct answers so you can check your work.

en peligro
de extinción   _____

_____

la especie   _____

excesivo, excesiva   _____

explotar   _____

_____

la falta   _____

la foca   _____

el hielo   _____

la limpieza   _____

la piel   _____

la pluma   _____

la preservación   _____

el recalentamiento
global   _____

el rescate   _____

la reserva natural   _____

salvaje   _____

la selva tropical   _____

tomar conciencia de   _____

Fold In

Tear out this page. Write the Spanish words on the lines. Fold the paper along the dotted line to see the correct answers so you can check your work.

(in) danger of
extinction, endangered   _____

species   _____

excessive   _____

to exploit,
to overwork   _____

lack   _____

seal   _____

ice   _____

cleaning   _____

skin   _____

feather   _____

conservation   _____

global warming   _____

rescue   _____

nature preserve   _____

wild   _____

tropical forest   _____

to become aware of   _____

Fold In

realidades.com
• Web Code: jed-0906

Más conjunciones que se usan con el subjuntivo y el indicativo (p. 412)

- Earlier in this chapter, you learned some conjunctions that can be followed by the subjunctive or the indicative. Below is another list of conjunctions. These conjunctions are usually followed by the subjunctive to express the purpose or intention of an action.

  con tal (de) que: provided that   **para que**: so that

  a menos que: unless   **sin que**: without

  aunque: even if, even though, although

  Las águilas calvas despaderán *a menos que* trabajemos para protegerlas.
  Bald eagles will disappear <u>unless</u> we work to protect them.

A. Circle the conjunction that most logically completes each sentence, according to the context. Follow the model.

Modelo   Van a la marcha ((para que) / a menos que) los animales estén protegidos.

1. No podemos usar aerosoles (**sin que / a menos que**) produzcan agujeros en la capa de ozono.

2. Las selvas tropicales serán bonitas (**a menos que / con tal de que**) no las explotemos.

3. El presidente va a crear una ley (**para que / sin que**) nadie pueda cazar las ballenas.

4. Tenemos que tomar conciencia de los problemas (**para que / aunque**) sea difícil hacerlo.

5. El grupo de voluntarios construirá una reserva natural (**sin que / a menos que**) no tenga suficiente dinero.

B. Complete the sentences with the correct present subjunctive form of the verbs in parentheses. Follow the model.

Modelo   (**usar**) Puedes protegerte de los rayos ultravioleta con tal de que
_____*uses*_____ anteojos de sol y loción protectora para sol.

1. (**proteger**)   Las especies en peligro de extinción no van a sobrevivir a menos que nosotros las _____.

2. (**hacer**)   La condición del planeta no puede mejorar sin que todas las personas _____ un esfuerzo.

3. (**tener**)   El gobierno va a crear varias reservas naturales para que los animales _____ un lugar protegido donde vivir.

4. (**poder**)   Es importante entender los peligros del efecto invernadero, aunque tú no _____ ver todos sus efectos personalmente.

- With the conjunctions **para** and **sin**, use the infinitive if the subject of the sentence does not change.

  Trabajo *para proteger* los animales.   *I work to protect animals.*

C. Complete each sentence below. If there is no subject change, choose **para** or **sin**. If there is a subject change, choose **para que** or **sin que**.

Modelo   No debes comprar estos productos ((sin) / sin que) pensar.

1. La policía investigará el problema (**sin / sin que**) la compañía lo sepa.

2. Distribuiremos los artículos (**para / para que**) los lea el dueño.

3. Ellos se pondrán camisetas y anteojos (**para / para que**) protegerse la piel.

4. Los turistas deben disfrutar del parque (**sin / sin que**) dañarlo.

D. Circle the conjunction in each sentence. Then, complete each sentence with the infinitive or the present subjunctive of the verb in parentheses.

Modelo   (rescatar) Nosotros hacemos un viaje (para)   *rescatar*   las ballenas.

1. (**conseguir**) No podemos visitar la selva tropical sin _____ una guía.

2. (**poder**)   Debo salir de la cocina para que mamá _____ cocinar.

3. (**dar**)   Esa foca no va a sobrevivir sin que nosotros le _____ comida.

4. (**explicar**)   Un científico vino a la clase para _____ el efecto invernadero.

- The conjunction **aunque** is followed by the subjunctive when it expresses uncertainty. It is followed by the indicative when there is no uncertainty.

  Aunque la ballena esté muy enferma, vamos a cuidarla.
  Even though the whale <u>may be</u> very sick, we are going to take care of it.

  Aunque la ballena está muy enferma, vamos a cuidarla.
  Even though the whale <u>is</u> very sick, we are going to take care of it.

E. Select the best English translation for the underlined portion of each sentence.

1. Aunque no <u>haya mucha gente</u>, debemos continuar con la marcha.

   ☐ there aren't a lot of people   ☐ there may not be a lot of people

2. Aunque <u>son nuevos</u>, los viajes de ecoturismo son muy populares.

   ☐ they are new   ☐ they may be new

3. Aunque <u>no te guste</u>, es más importante protegerte del sol que estar bronceado.

   ☐ you don't like it   ☐ you may not like it

4. Aunque <u>el hielo se derrite</u>, no habrá una inundación en este lugar.

   ☐ the ice is melting   ☐ the ice may be melting

- Web Code: jed-0907

Realidades 3

Nombre _____

Hora _____

Capítulo 9

Fecha _____

Reading Activities, Sheet 1

Puente a la cultura (pp. 416–417)

A. This reading contains several *cognates,* or words that look and sound like English words with the same meaning. See if you can determine what the following words mean:

1. volcánico: _____

2. piratas: _____

3. tortugas: _____

4. velocidad: _____

5. mamíferos: _____

6. flora y fauna: _____

B. Look at the statements below and match them with the century (**siglo**) in which they happened according to the reading. Use the topic sentences in the reading to help you.

a. el siglo XX (1900s)

b. el siglo XVIII (1700s)

c. el siglo XVII (1600s)

d. el siglo XIX (1800s)

1. _____ Los piratas ingleses llegaron a las islas.

2. _____ Los balleneros llegaron y cazaron muchas tortugas.

3. _____ Charles Darwin llegó a las islas e hizo un estudio para escribir su libro *El origen de las especies.*

4. _____ El gobierno ecuatoriano estableció una reserva natural.

C. The Galápagos Islands, once a perserved paradise, have suffered greatly in recent years. Look at the following list and cross out the one item that is *not* an issue that has affected the Galápagos Islands.

extinción de algunas especies	terremotos
exceso de población	faltas de recursos del gobierno ecuatoriano

D. In the Galápagos Islands, the government needed to get involved in order to save rare species of plants and animals. Can you think of other places where the government or environmental organizations have helped with preservation efforts? Think of the places you have studied or visited. Explain why outside involvement was needed to help save local wildlife.

_____

_____

_____

Realidades 3

Capítulo 9

Nombre

Hora

Fecha

Reading Activities, Sheet 2

Lectura (pp. 422–424)

A. You are about to read an article about the monarch butterfly. Based on your previous knowledge or what you can determine from the pictures accompanying the text, write three characteristics that describe a monarch butterfly.

1. _____

2. _____

3. _____

B. Try to use context to help you detemine the meaning of the terms from the reading in your textbook which you may not know. Read the following selections and write the letter of the definition that best corresponds with the highlighted phrase.

    a. en la última parte de   **b.** aproximadamente   **c.** setenta y cinco por ciento

1. «*Tres cuartas partes* de los animales que viven en la tierra son insectos.» _____

2. «*Las mariposas, en general, viven* **alrededor de** *24 días*» _____

3. « *Llegan* **a fines de** *octubre a la zona entre...*» _____

C. The introduction to the reading in your textbook includes several descriptions of the monarch butterfly. Read the first two paragraphs on page 422 and decide which of the following descriptions of the monarch butterfly are mentioned. Indicate with a check mark.

1. _____ hermosa

2. _____ más grande que la mayoría de las mariposas

3. _____ agente polinizador

4. _____ vive más tiempo que otras mariposas

5. _____ sólo vive en lugares tropicales

6. _____ resistente a las condiciones del clima

D. Look at each section title on pages 423 and 424 of the reading in your textbook. Based on the title given, decide which choice would most accurately represent what that section is about. Circle your choice.

1. **Llegada a México**

    a. los conquistadores españoles llegan a México
    b. el camino de la mariposa monarca

2. **Hibernación**

    a. cómo pasan el invierno   **b.** cómo pasan de un lugar al otro

3. **Migración**

    a. cómo sobreviven mudándose de un lugar al otro
    b. qué comen

4. **Refugios**

    a. dónde se reunen para pasar el invierno   **b.** sus colores

5. **Peligros**

    a. dónde viven   **b.** qué los amenaza

E. Now look more closely at each section. Use the following cues to help you look for a key piece of information in each section. Write in the most appropriate words to complete the statements from each section.

1. **Llegada a México**

    Las mariposas monarca vuelan de _____ a _____ antes de octubre, y regresan en abril.

2. **Hibernación**

    Las mariposas monarca pasan el invierno en _____, unas montañas que se encuentran entre Michoacán y el Estado de México.

3. **Migración**

    El número de mariposas monarca que llega a México para pasar el invierno todos los años está entre _____ y _____ millones.

4. **Refugios**

    Las mariposas monarca pasan el invierno en _____ al lado de las montañas.

5. **Peligros**

    Dos acontecimientos que causaron posibles peligros a las mariposas monarca fueron un _____ en 2001 y una _____ en 2003.

Realidades 3

Capítulo 10

Nombre _____

Fecha _____

Hora _____

AVSR, Sheet 1

Pretérito vs. imperfecto (p. 431)

- Remember that you must determine whether to use the preterite or the imperfect when speaking in Spanish about the past.

  Use the preterite:
  - to talk about past actions or a sequence of actions that are considered complete.

    *Mis padres **fueron** a la escuela y **hablaron** con mi profesor.*

  Use the imperfect:
  - to talk about repeated or habitual actions in the past

    *Yo siempre **hacía** mis tareas después de la escuela.*

  - to provide background information or physical and mental descriptions

    *Nacha, una chica que **tenía** diez años, **estaba** enojada.*

  - to convey two or more actions that were taking place simultaneously in the past.

    *Yo **leía** mientras mis padres **preparaban** la cena.*

A. Read the following sentences and decide if the action is a completed action (**C**), a habitual/repeated action (**H**), or background information (**B**). Follow the model.

Modelo Los científicos **trabajaban** todos los días para proteger el medio ambiente.	C	(H)	B

1. El martes pasado el presidente **habló** sobre la injusticia.　　C　H　B

2. Mi hermano mayor **tenía** 22 años.　　C　H　B

3. Nuestro vecino nos **trajo** unos panfletos sobre la economía.　　C　H　B

4. Los estudiantes siempre **luchaban** por leyes más justas.　　C　H　B

5. Los miembros de la comunidad **estaban** muy entusiasmados.　　C　H　B

B. Conjugate the verbs in parentheses in the preterite or imperfect to complete the sentences. Follow the model.

Modelo El verano pasado nosotros _____*fuimos*_____ (ir) a un concierto en beneficio de los niños diabéticos.

1. Cuando mis padres _____ (**ser**) niños, ellos siempre _____ (**obedecer**) las reglas de su escuela.

2. De niña, mi vecina _____ (**tener**) pelo muy largo.

3. Yo _____ (**cumplir**) con todas mis responsabilidades hoy.

4. En sus conciertos de escuela, mi prima _____ (**cantar**) mientras mi primo _____ (**tocar**) el piano.

5. Todos los estudiantes _____ (**disfrutar**) de la fiesta del sábado pasado.

realidades.com

- Web Code: jed-1001

Pretérito vs. imperfecto (p. 431)

- You may use the preterite and imperfect together in one sentence when one action (preterite) interrupts another action that was already taking place (imperfect).

    *Nosotros **hacíamos** las tareas cuando nuestro vecino **llamó**.*

C. Complete the following sentences with the preterite or imperfect of the verbs in parentheses. Remember to put the background action in the imperfect and the interrupting action in the preterite.

> **Modelo**   Los soldados __*luchaban*__ (**luchar**) cuando __*empezó*__ (**empezar**) a llover.

1. Mi hermana menor _____ (**estar**) en la clase de ciencias cuando _____ (**sonar**) la alarma contra incendios.

2. Nosotros _____ (**hablar**) de las obligaciones de la sociedad cuando mi amigo _____ (**salir**).

3. Constantino _____ (**caerse**) cuando _____ (**correr**) en el centro de la comunidad.

4. Yo _____ (**jugar**) al fútbol con mis amigos cuando José _____ (**meter**) un gol.

5. ¿Tú _____ (**ver**) el accidente cuando _____ (**caminar**) a la escuela?

D. Read the following paragraph about a surprising turn of events. Conjugate the verbs given in the preterite or imperfect, according to the context. The first one has been done for you.

Ayer después de clases, yo (1) _____*salí*_____ (**salir**) con mis padres. Yo (2)

_____ (**sentirse**) impaciente porque (3) _____ (**tener**) mucha

tarea y (4) _____ (**querer**) ver a mi novio. De repente, mi papá (5)

_____ (**parar**) el coche enfrente de mi restaurante favorito. Cuando nosotros

(6) _____ (**entrar**) al restaurante, (yo) (7) _____ (**ver**) que (8)

_____ (**estar**) todos mis amigos con un pastel grande en honor de mi

cumpleaños. ¡Qué sorpresa!

Realidades 3

Capítulo 10

Nombre _____

Hora _____

Fecha _____

AVSR, Sheet 3

Verbos con distinto sentido en el pretérito y en el imperfecto (p. 433)

- Remember that some verbs change meaning depending on whether they are used in the preterite or the imperfect tense. Look at the chart below for a reminder.

Verb	Preterite	Imperfect
conocer	met for the first time *Marta **conoció** a su mejor amiga en la escuela primaria.*	knew someone *El abogado y el juez **se conocían** muy bien.*
saber	found out, learned *El policía **supo** que el criminal se había escapado.*	knew a fact *Los ciudadanos **sabían** que tenían que obedecer la ley.*
poder	succeeded in doing *Después de mucho trabajo, la policía **pudo** arrestar al ladrón.*	was able to, could *El juez nos dijo que no **podíamos** hablar con nadie sobre el caso.*
querer	tried ***Quisimos** resolver el conflicto, pero fue imposible.*	wanted *El gobierno **quería** escuchar las opiniones de la gente.*
no querer	refused ***No quise** reunirme con el jefe. Salí temprano.*	didn't want *Nosotros **no queríamos** ir a la manifestación, pero fuimos.*

A. Match the conjugated forms of the following preterite and imperfect verbs with their English meanings. The first one has been done for you.

_D_ **1.** supe

_____ **2.** pude

_____ **3.** sabía

_____ **4.** quise

_____ **5.** conocí

_____ **6.** no quería

A. I met (somebody) for the first time

B. I didn't want to

C. I tried to

D. ~~I found out, learned~~

E. I knew

F. I managed to, succeeded in

B. Circle the preterite or the imperfect form of the verb, according to the context.

Modelo (**Conocí** / **Conocía**) a mucha gente nueva en la manifestación.

1. (**Conocí** / **Conocía**) al hombre que la organizó. Era un amigo de mis padres.

2. No (**supe** / **sabía**) que la policía trabajaba con la organización.

realidades.com

• Web Code: jed-1001

3. Durante la manifestación, (**supe / sabía**) que un juez también luchaba contra el problema.

4. No (**supe / sabía**) mucho del problema antes de ir a la manifestación.

C. Circle the correct preterite or the imperfect form of the verb given, according to the context. The first one has been done for you.

No **1.**(**quise /** (**quería**)) salir el viernes pasado porque tenía mucha tarea, pero fui al cine

con mi mejor amiga. Después ella me preguntó si nosotras **2.**(**pudimos / podíamos**) ir a

un restaurante. Yo le dije que sí y cuando llegamos, ella pidió los calamares. ¡Qué asco! Yo

3.(**no quise / no quería**) comerlos así que pedí una pizza. Cuando recibimos la cuenta,

nos dimos cuenta de que no teníamos dinero. No **4.**(**quisimos / queríamos**) llamar a

nuestros padres, pero no había otra opción. Mi padre nos trajo dinero y por fin

5.(**podíamos / pudimos**) pagar la cuenta.

D. Conjugate the verbs in the following sentences in the correct preterite or the imperfect form, depending on context. Follow the model.

Modelo (querer) Mi madre no ___*quiso*___ comer en ese restaurante. Se quedó en casa.

1. (**poder**) Después de hacer un gran esfuerzo, mis padres _____ resolver el problema.

2. (**saber**) Yo siempre _____ que era muy importante decir la verdad.

3. (**conocer**) La semana pasada nosotros _____ al boxeador que ganó la pelea reciente.

4. (**poder**) La policía le aseguró a la víctima que _____ garantizar su seguridad.

5. (**querer**) Paco no _____ respetar el límite de velocidad, pero la policía le dijo que tenía que hacerlo.

6. (**conocer**) El presidente y la senadora se _____ muy bien y se confiaban mucho.

Realidades 3

Nombre _____

Hora _____

Capítulo 10

Fecha _____

Vocabulary Flash Cards, Sheet 1

Write the Spanish vocabulary word below each picture. If there is a word or phrase, copy it in the space provided. Be sure to include the article for each noun.

		el abuso
_____	_____	_____
adecuado, adecuada	**el/la adolescente**	**ambos**
_____	_____	_____
aplicar (las leyes)	**el apoyo**	**el armario**
_____	_____	_____

Copy the word or phrase in the space provided. Be sure to include the article for each noun.

el asunto	**la autoridad**	**el código de vestimenta**
de ese modo	**el deber**	**discriminado, discriminada**
discriminar	**en cuanto a**	**la enseñanza**

Realidades 3

Capítulo 10

Nombre _____

Hora _____

Fecha _____

Vocabulary Flash Cards, Sheet 3

Copy the word or phrase in the space provided. Be sure to include the article for each noun.

el estado _____ _____	**estar sujeto, sujeta a** ____ ____ ____	**la felicidad** _____ _____
funcionar _____ _____	**gozar de** _____ _____	**gratuito, gratuita** _____ _____
la igualdad _____ _____	**la injusticia** _____ _____	**la justicia** _____ _____

Realidades 3

Capítulo 10

Nombre _____

Hora _____

Fecha _____

Vocabulary Flash Cards, Sheet 4

Copy the word or phrase in the space provided. Be sure to include the article for each noun.

la libertad	libre	maltratar
el maltrato	el motivo	la niñez
obligar	el pensamiento	la pobreza

Realidades ③

Capítulo 10

Nombre _____

Hora _____

Fecha _____

Vocabulary Flash Cards, Sheet 5

Copy the word or phrase in the space provided. Be sure to include the article for each noun. The blank cards can be used to write and practice other Spanish vocabulary for the chapter.

la razón	**el respeto**	**satisfactorio, satisfactoria**
_____	_____	_____
_____	_____	_____
sufrir	**la tolerancia**	
	_____	
_____	_____	_____
_____	_____	_____

Tear out this page. Write the English words on the lines. Fold the paper along the dotted line to see the correct answers so you can check your work.

el abuso

adecuado, adecuada

ambos

aplicar (las leyes)

el apoyo

el armario

el asunto

la autoridad

el código de
vestimenta

el deber

discriminado,
discriminada

discriminar

la enseñanza

el estado

estar sujeto, sujeta a

la felicidad

funcionar

Fold In

Realidades 3

Capítulo 10

Nombre _____

Hora _____

Fecha _____

Vocabulary Check, Sheet 2

Tear out this page. Write the Spanish words on the lines. Fold the paper along the dotted line to see the correct answers so you can check your work.

abuse _____

adequate _____

both _____

to apply (the law) _____

support _____

locker _____

subject _____

authority _____

dress code _____

_____

duty _____

discriminated _____

_____

to discriminate _____

teaching _____

the state _____

to be subject to _____

happiness _____

to function _____

Fold In ←

Tear out this page. Write the English words on the lines. Fold the paper along the dotted line to see the correct answers so you can check your work.

gozar (de) _____

la injusticia _____

la libertad _____

maltratar _____

el maltrato _____

el motivo _____

la niñez _____

obligar _____

la paz _____

el pensamiento _____

la pobreza _____

la razón _____

el respeto _____

satisfactorio, _____
satisfactoria

sufrir _____

la tolerancia _____

votar _____

Fold In

Realidades **3**

Nombre _____

Hora _____

Capítulo 10

Fecha _____

Vocabulary Check, Sheet 4

Tear out this page. Write the Spanish words on the lines. Fold the paper along the dotted line to see the correct answers so you can check your work.

to enjoy _____

injustice _____

liberty _____

to mistreat _____

mistreatment _____

cause _____

childhood _____

to force _____

peace _____

thought _____

poverty _____

reason _____

respect _____

satisfactory _____

_____

to suffer _____

tolerance _____

to vote _____

Fold In ←

realidades.com ✓

• Web Code: jed-1002

Realidades **3**

Nombre _____

Hora _____

Capítulo 10

Fecha _____

Guided Practice Activities, Sheet 1

La voz pasiva: *ser* + participio pasado (p. 444)

- In a sentence written in the *active voice*, the subject performs the action.

  El gobierno estudiantil *organizó* el evento.
  The student government organized the event.

- In a sentence written in the *passive voice*, the subject does not *perform* the action, but rather has the action "done to it" or receives the action.

  El evento *fue organizado por* el gobierno estudiantil.
  The event was organized by the student government.

- The passive voice is formed by using the verb **ser** + the past participle of another verb. Note how the past participle functions as an adjective, modifying the subject of the verb **ser**. As an adjective, it must agree in number and gender with the subject.

  Las clases son planeadas por la maestra.
  The classes are planned by the teacher.

  El texto fue leído por todos los estudiantes.
  The article was read by all the students.

A. Read each of the following statements and decide if it is active voice or passive voice. Write an **A** in the space for **voz** *activa* or a **P** for **voz** *pasiva*. Follow the model.

| Modelo | _P_ | El pastel fue decorado por el cocinero. |

1. _____ El director registró los armarios.

2. _____ Los derechos fueron respetados por todos los estudiantes.

3. _____ Las leyes fueron aplicadas de una manera justa.

4. _____ La estudiante pidió permiso para usar el carro.

5. _____ La lista de derechos fue creada por los adolescentes.

B. Circle the correct form of **ser** (**fue** or **fueron**) in the sentences below. Then, write the correct ending of the past participle (**o, a, os,** or **as**) in the blank. Make sure the subject and participle of each sentence agree in number and gender. Follow the model.

| Modelo | La celebración ((**fue**) / fueron) organizad*a*___ por el club de español. |

1. Las leyes (**fue / fueron**) establecid____ por los líderes del país.

2. El presidente estudiantil (**fue / fueron**) elegid____ por los estudiantes.

3. Los abusos (**fue / fueron**) criticad____ por toda la gente justa.

4. La injusticia (**fue / fueron**) sufrid____ por los padres de la adolescente.

5. La lista (**fue / fueron**) hech____ por mamá.

La voz pasiva: *ser* + participio pasado (*continued*)

C. Underline the subject of each sentence. Then, write the correct preterite form of **ser** and the correct form of the past participle of the verb in parentheses. Follow the model. Remember to check number and gender agreement.

Modelo (aceptar) <u>Las reglas</u> <u>*fueron*</u> <u>*aceptadas*</u> por todas las personas en la reunión.

1. **(resolver)** Los conflictos _____ _____ por todos los miembros de la familia.

2. **(establecer)** El horario _____ _____ por los padres.

3. **(eliminar)** La discriminación _____ _____ en la escuela.

4. **(tomar)** Las decisiones _____ _____ por los miembros de la administración.

5. **(escribir)** Los documentos _____ _____ por los consejeros.

6. **(cancelar)** La reunión _____ _____ por el director porque nevaba.

- The passive voice can also be expressed by using the *impersonal se.* You often use the *impersonal se* when the person or thing who does the action is unknown. In these types of sentences, the verb usually comes before the subject. When the subject is an infinitive, the singular verb form is used.

  Se prohíbe la discriminación.   *Discrimination is prohibited*

  Se respetan los derechos.   *Rights are respected.*

D. Underline the subject of each sentence. Use the verb in parentheses to complete the sentence using the passive voice. Include the pronoun **se** with the correct third person form of the verb.

Modelo (necesitar) <u>*Se*</u> <u>*necesita*</u> <u>una discusión</u> para resolver los conflictos.

1. **(registrar)** _____ _____ los armarios una vez por mes.

2. **(querer)** _____ _____ igualdad entre todos los estudiantes.

3. **(poder)** _____ _____ votar en las elecciones.

4. **(respetar)** _____ _____ la autoridad de los maestros.

5. **(deber)** _____ _____ seguir el código de vestimenta.

6. **(aplicar)** _____ _____ las leyes en esta situación.

realidades.com ✔

• Web Code: jed-1003

El presente y el imperfecto del subjuntivo (p. 445)

- Use the *present subjunctive* or the *present perfect subjunctive* after "**que**" when the first verb is in the:

Present	***Espero** que tú **hayas recibido** una educación gratuita.*
Command form	***Díigales** que no **discriminen**.*
Present perfect	***Hemos exigido** que ellos **sean** justos.*
Future	***Será** excelente que nosotros **resolvamos** el conflicto.*

A. Circle the first verb of each sentence. On the line next to the sentence, write a **P** if that verb is in the present, **C** if it is a command, **PP** if it is in the present perfect and **F** if it is in the future. Then, underline the subjunctive verb.

Modelo   _P_ (Me alegro) de que todos <u>participen</u> en la vida de la escuela.

1. _____ Recomiéndenle que vaya a la reunión este viernes.

2. _____ Mis padres estarán felices con tal de que les diga adónde voy.

3. _____ Busco un horario que sea flexible.

4. _____ Hemos dudado que esa ley sea justa.

B. Circle the first verb in each sentence. Then, conjugate the verbs in the correct form of the present subjunctive to complete the sentences. Follow the model.

Modelo   (venir) (Será) necesario que todos los estudiantes _____*vengan*_____ a la reunión.

1. (**participar**) He esperado que Uds. _____ en la lucha por la igualdad.

2. (**compartir**) Dile al profesor que _____ esta información con sus estudiantes.

3. (**apoyar**) No hay nadie aquí que _____ los abusos del poder.

4. (**haber**) Este programa no funcionará bien a menos que _____ fondos adecuados.

Realidades 3

Capítulo 10

Nombre _____

Hora _____

Fecha _____

Guided Practice Activities, Sheet 4

El presente y el imperfecto del subjuntivo (*continued*)

- Use the *imperfect subjunctive* after **que** when the first verb is in the:

Verb Tense	Main Clause
Preterite	***Recomendé*** que ellos ***siguieran*** las reglas del club.
Imperfect	***Dudábamos*** que él ***gozara*** de libertad de expresión.
Pluperfect	El profesor ***había querido*** que los estudiantes ***se respetaran***.
Conditional	***Sería*** fantástico que ***se eliminara*** por completo la discriminación.

C. Underline the first verb in each sentence and determine whether the following verb will be present subjunctive or imperfect subjunctive. Circle your choice to complete each sentence. Follow the model.

Modelo <u>Era</u> importante que los profesores siempre (**respeten** /(**respetaran**)) a los estudiantes.

1. No creo que (**sea / fuera**) justo discriminar por razones de raza, nacionalidad o sexo.

2. Buscaremos un trabajo que (**tenga / tuviera**) un ambiente de paz y tolerancia.

3. El profesor recomendó que nosotros (**pensemos / pensáramos**) libremente.

4. Yo dudaba que (**haya / hubiera**) una solución fácil al problema de la pobreza.

5. Fue terrible que tantas personas (**sufran / sufrieran**) maltratos y abusos por razones de su nacionalidad.

D. Conjugate the verbs in the appropriate form of the imperfect subjunctive.

Modelo (**vivir**) Era triste que tantas personas _____*vivieran*_____ en un estado de pobreza.

1. (**establecer**) Nosotros habíamos sugerido que el comité _____ unas reglas nuevas.

2. (**ser**) Me gustaría que la educación universitaria _____ gratuita.

3. (**respetar**) El policía dudaba que el criminal _____ su autoridad.

4. (**ir**) Me gustaría que nosotras _____ a la manifestación.

5. (**discriminar**) Queríamos unas leyes que no _____.

realidades.com

• Web Code: jed-1004

Realidades 3

Capítulo 10

Nombre _____

Hora _____

Fecha _____

Vocabulary Flash Cards, Sheet 6

Write the Spanish vocabulary word below each picture. If there is a word or phrase, copy it in the space provided. Be sure to include the article for each noun.

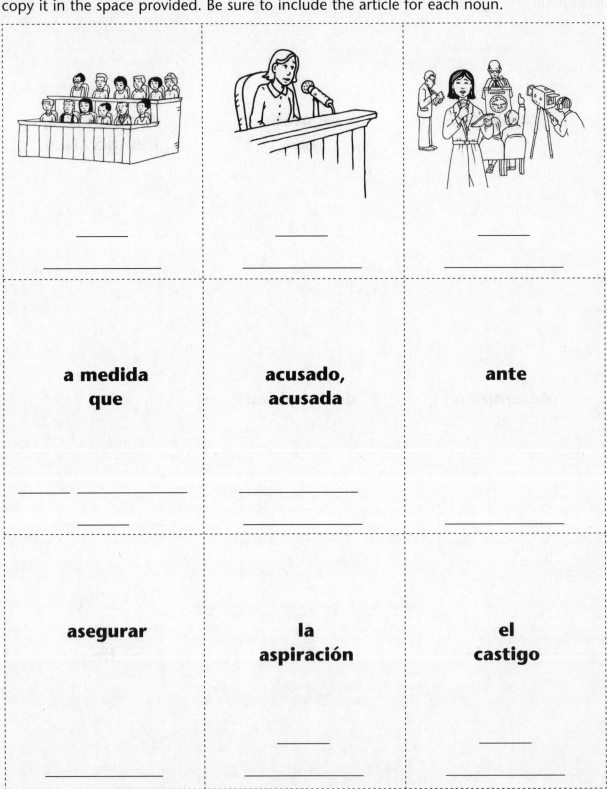

_____	_____	_____
a medida que	**acusado, acusada**	**ante**
_____	_____	_____
asegurar	**la aspiración**	**el castigo**
_____	_____	_____

Realidades 3

Capítulo 10

Nombre _____

Hora _____

Fecha _____

Vocabulary Flash Cards, Sheet 7

Copy the word or phrase in the space provided. Be sure to include the article for each noun.

culpable	de modo que	democrático, democrática
_____	_____ _____	_____
		_____

el desempleo	la desigualdad	detener
_____	_____	_____
_____	_____	

en lugar de	la falta de	el fin
_____	_____	_____
_____	_____	_____

Realidades 3

Capítulo 10

Nombre _____

Fecha _____

Hora _____

Vocabulary Flash Cards, Sheet 8

Copy the word or phrase in the space provided. Be sure to include the article for each noun.

fundamental _____	**la garantía** _____	**la igualdad** _____
inocente _____	**intercambiar** _____	**el juicio** _____
juzgar _____	**llegar a** ___ ___	**el modo** _____

Realidades 3

Capítulo 10

Nombre _____

Hora _____

Fecha _____

Vocabulary Flash Cards, Sheet 9

Copy the word or phrase in the space provided. Be sure to include the article for each noun.

opinar	**pacífico, pacífica**	**proponer**
_____	_____	_____
la propuesta	**el punto de vista**	**sospechoso, sospechosa**
_____	_____	_____
tratar	**el valor**	**violar**
_____	_____	_____

Tear out this page. Write the English words on the lines. Fold the paper along the dotted line to see the correct answers so you can check your work.

el acusado,
la acusada   _____

ante   _____

asegurar   _____

el castigo   _____

culpable   _____

la desigualdad   _____

el desempleo   _____

detener   _____

en lugar de   _____

la falta de   _____

el fin   _____

fundamental   _____

la garantía   _____

la igualdad   _____

inocente   _____

intercambiar   _____

el juicio   _____

Fold In

Realidades 3

Capítulo 10

Nombre _____

Hora _____

Fecha _____

Vocabulary Check, Sheet 6

Tear out this page. Write the Spanish words on the lines. Fold the paper along the dotted line to see the correct answers so you can check your work.

accused, defendant _____

_____

before _____

to assure _____

punishment _____

guilty _____

inequality _____

unemployment _____

to detain _____

instead of _____

lack of _____

purpose _____

fundamental, vital _____

guarantee _____

equality _____

innocent _____

to exchange _____

judgement _____

Fold In

Realidades 3

Capítulo 10

Nombre _____

Hora _____

Fecha _____

Vocabulary Check, Sheet 7

Tear out this page. Write the English words on the lines. Fold the paper along the dotted line to see the correct answers so you can check your work.

el jurado _____

la justicia _____

juzgar _____

llegar a _____

el modo _____

mundial _____

opinar _____

pacífico, _____
pacífica

la prensa _____

proponer _____

la propuesta _____

el punto de vista _____

sospechoso, _____
sospechosa

el/la testigo _____

tratar _____

el valor _____

violar _____

Fold In

Realidades 3

Capítulo 10

Nombre _____

Hora _____

Fecha _____

Vocabulary Check, Sheet 8

Tear out this page. Write the Spanish words on the lines. Fold the paper along the dotted line to see the correct answers so you can check your work.

jury _____

justice _____

to judge _____

to reach, to get to _____

the way _____

worldwide _____

to think _____

peaceful _____

_____

the press _____

to propose, to suggest _____

proposal _____

point of view _____

suspicious _____

_____

witness _____

to treat _____

value _____

to violate _____

Fold In ←

realidades.com

• Web Code: jed-1006

Realidades 3

Capítulo 10

Nombre _____

Hora _____

Fecha _____

Guided Practice Activities, Sheet 5

El pluscuamperfecto del subjuntivo (p. 456)

- The *pluperfect subjunctive* is used when describing actions in the past, when one action takes place before the other. In the following sentences, note that the first verb is in the preterite or imperfect and the verb after **que** is in the pluperfect subjunctive.

    Yo me alegré de que el juicio *hubiera terminado*.
    I was happy the trial had ended.

    Nosotros esperábamos que los estudiantes *hubieran hecho* la propuesta.
    We hoped the students had made *the proposal*.

    To form the pluperfect subjunctive, use the imperfect subjunctive of **haber** plus the past participle of another verb. Here are the imperfect subjunctive forms of the verb **haber**:

    hubiera, hubieras, hubiera, hubiéramos, hubierais, hubieran

A. Underline the first verb in each sentence. Then, circle the correct form of the pluperfect subjunctive to complete the sentence.

Modelo <u>Fue</u> una lástima que el ladrón (**hubieras cometido** / **hubiera cometido**) el crimen.

1. El abogado dudaba que los testigos (**hubiera dicho** / **hubieran dicho**) la verdad.

2. Nosotros habíamos dudado que el acusado (**hubiera sido** / **hubieran sido**) un niño pacífico.

3. No había ningún testigo que (**hubiera participado** / **hubieras participado**) en un juicio antes.

4. ¿El juez no creía que tú (**hubiera conocido** / **hubieras conocido**) al acusado antes?

B. Complete each of the following sentences with the pluperfect subjunctive by using the correct form of **haber** with the past participle of the verb in parentheses.

Modelo (estudiar) La profesora dudaba que sus estudiantes ___*hubieran*___ ___*estudiado*___ durante el verano.

1. (**hablar**) El presidente se alegró de que los líderes mundiales _____ _____ de los problemas internacionales.

2. (**ver**) No había nadie que no _____ _____ la contaminación ambiental en la ciudad.

3. (**subir**) Era una lástima que el nivel de desempleo _____ _____.

4. (**lograr**) A tus padres no les sorprendió que tú _____ _____ tus aspiraciones.

realidades.com

• Web Code: jed-1007

- The *pluperfect subjunctive* can also be used when the first verb is in the conditional tense.

    *Yo **me alegraría** de que ellos hubieran intercambiado sus ideas.*

C. In each of the following sentences, underline the verb in the conditional tense and then complete the sentence with the pluperfect subjunctive of the verb in parentheses. Follow the model.

Modelo (experimentar) Sería una lástima que los jóvenes _hubieran_ _experimentado_ desigualdad social.

1. **(tener)** Me gustaría mucho que mis padres _____ _____ las mismas aspiraciones que yo.

2. **(desaparecer)** Sería terrible que las oportunidades _____ _____.

3. **(violar)** No creería que tú _____ _____ la ley.

4. **(poder)** Sería excelente que nosotros _____ _____ ver un juicio verdadero.

5. **(ver)** No habría nadie que no _____ _____ algo sospechoso.

- The expression **como si** (*as if*) always refers to something that is contrary to the truth, or unreal. In Chapter 8, you saw that **como si** can be followed by the imperfect subjunctive. It can also be followed by the *pluperfect subjunctive*.

    El ladrón hablaba del crimen como si no *hubiera hecho* nada serio.

    The robber talked about the crime as if he hadn't done anything serious.

D. Complete the following sentences using **como si** with the appropriate form of the pluperfect subjunctive. Follow the model.

Modelo (ocurrir) El juez recordaba el juicio como si _hubiera_ _ocurrido_ ayer.

1. **(entender)** La testigo habló como si no _____ _____ la pregunta del abogado.

2. **(participar)** El juicio fue tan duro que el juez sintió como si todos _____ _____ en una guerra.

3. **(visitar)** Jorge habló de México como si _____ _____ el país varias veces.

4. **(ver)** El hombre culpable corrió como si _____ _____ un fantasma.

5. **(correr)** Después de tanto trabajo, nosotros sentíamos como si _____ _____ en un maratón.

realidades.com

- Web Code: jed-1007

El condicional perfecto (p. 459)

• The conditional perfect is used to talk about what *would have happened* (but didn't) in the past.

En esa situación, yo *habría dicho* la verdad.
In that situation, I would have told the truth.

Nosotros no *nos habríamos portado* así.   *We wouldn't have acted like that.*

To form the conditional perfect, use the conditional form of the verb **haber** plus the past participle of another verb. Here are the conditional forms of the verb **haber**:

habría, habrías, habría, habríamos, habríais, habrían

A. Pepe is making some statements about things he has done (present perfect) and some statements about things he would have done (conditional perfect), if he had studied abroad in Mexico. Mark the column labeled **Sí** if it is something he actually did, and **No** if it is something he didn't *actually* do, but would have done.

		Sí	No
Modelos	He comido enchiladas en la cena.	X	___
	Habría ido a la playa mucho.	___	___
1.	Habría visitado el Zócalo.	___	___
2.	He visto un partido del equipo de fútbol mexicano.	___	___
3.	Mis amigos y yo hemos ido al mercado.	___	___
4.	Habría ido a ver las pirámides aztecas.	___	___
5.	Habría conocido al presidente de México.	___	___

B. Complete each of the following sentences about what you and others would have done if school had been canceled today with the correct forms of the conditional perfect.

Modelo   (nadar) Mis amigas Lola y Rafaela ___*habrían*___ ___*nadado*___ en la piscina de la comunidad.

1. (terminar)   Yo _____ _____ mi proyecto de filosofía.

2. (dormir)   Nosotros _____ _____ hasta las diez.

3. (leer)   La profesora _____ _____ un libro de Gabriel García Márquez.

4. (jugar)   Mis hermanos menores _____ _____ al fútbol.

5. (ver)   Yo _____ _____ un juicio en la tele.

Realidades ③

Capítulo 10

Nombre _____

Hora _____

Fecha _____

Guided Practice Activities, Sheet 8

- To talk about what might have been if cirumstances had been different, you can use a **si** clause. In these sentences, you use the pluperfect subjunctive and the conditional perfect together.

  Si yo *hubiera visto* el crimen, *habría llamado* a la policía.
  If I had seen the crime, I would have called the police.

  Si nosotros no *hubiéramos hablado* del conflicto, no *habríamos encontrado* una solución.
  If we had not talked about the conflict, we would not have found a solution.

C. In each sentence below, underline the verb in the pluperfect subjunctive and complete the sentence with the conditional perfect of the verb in parentheses. Follow the model.

Modelo (**decir**) Si ellos no <u>hubieran estudiado</u> política, no ___*habrían*___ ___*entendido*___ lo que dijo el presidente.

1. (**agradecer**) Si yo hubiera conocido a Martin Luther King, Jr., le _____ _____ su trabajo para eliminar la discriminación.

2. (**tener**) Si tú hubieras hecho un esfuerzo, _____ _____ más oportunidades.

3. (**poder**) Si no hubiera nevado, los testigos _____ _____ llegar a la corte a tiempo.

4. (**recibir**) Si el acusado hubiera dicho la verdad _____ _____ una sentencia menos fuerte.

D. Form complete sentences by conjugating the infinitives in the pluperfect subjunctive and conditional perfect. Follow the model.

Modelo Si / yo / tomar / esa clase / aprender / mucho más
  Si yo hubiera tomado esa clase, habría aprendido mucho más.

1. Si / tú / venir / a la reunion / entender / el conflicto

   _____

2. Si / yo / experimentar discriminación / quejarse / al director

   _____

3. Si / ellas / tener más derechos / ser / más pacíficos

   _____

4. Si / tú / votar / en las últimas elecciones / cambiar / el resultado

   _____

- Web Code: jed-1008

Realidades 3

Capítulo 10

Nombre _____

Fecha _____

Hora _____

Reading Activities, Sheet 1

Puente a la cultura (pp. 462–463)

A. The reading in your textbook is about heroes. Think about what being a hero means to you. Write three characteristics of a hero in spaces below.

1. _____

2. _____

3. _____

B. When you encounter unfamiliar words in a reading, a good strategy is to look at the context for clues. The word **o** ("or") is often used to introduce a definition to a new or difficult word.

Look at the following excerpts from the reading and circle the definitions for the highlighted words.

1. «*Este territorio tenía aproximadamente 17 millones de habitantes y estaba dividido en cuatro* **virreinatos**, *o unidades políticas.*»

2. « *Al sentir que la monarquía estaba débil, los* **criollos**, *o hijos de españoles nacidos en América, se rebelaron contra la Corona, iniciando así un movimiento de independencia...*»

C. In the reading, you learn about 3 different heroes. Write a **B** next to the following characteristics if they apply to Simón Bolivar, an **M** if they apply to José Martí, or an **H** if they apply to Miguel Hidalgo.

1. _____ Llamó al pueblo mexicano a luchar durante un sermón.

2. _____ Fue presidente de la República de la Gran Colombia.

3. _____ Era un gran poeta.

4. _____ Fue a prisión por lo que escribió contra las autoridades españolas.

5. _____ Quería crear una gran patria de países latinos.

6. _____ Motivó a la gente indígena a participar en la lucha por la independencia.

D. Which of the three countries mentioned in the reading actually gained independence from Spain first?

    a. México   **b.** Bolivia   **c.** Cuba

Lectura (pp. 468–470)

A. In this article, you will read about some of the responsibilities the narrator has outside of school. Take a minute to think about your responsibilities and obligations outside of school (to family, sports teams, etc.). Write two of your responsibilities on the lines below.

1. _____

2. _____

B. Look at the excerpt from the reading in your textbook. What word or words are synonyms for each of the highlighted words?

> «...nosotros teníamos una vivienda que consistía en **una pieza** pequeñita donde no teníamos patio y no teníamos dónde ni con quiénes dejar a **las wawas**. Entonces, consultamos al director de la escuela y él dio permiso para llevar a mis hermanitas conmigo.»

C. Read the following excerpt carefully and put an **X** next to the tasks for which the narrator was responsible.

> Salía de la escuela, tenía que cargarme la niñita, nos íbamos a la casa y tenía yo que cocinar, lavar, planchar, atender a las wawas. Me parecía muy difícil todo eso. ¡Yo deseaba tanto jugar! Y tantas otras cosas deseaba, como cualquier niña.

1. _____ trabajar en la mina

2. _____ llevar a sus hermanas a la escuela con ella

3. _____ dar de comer a los animales

4. _____ limpiar la casa

5. _____ preparar la comida

Realidades ③

Capítulo 10

Nombre

Hora

Fecha

Reading Activities, Sheet 3

D. Use the following sentences to help you locate key information in the reading. The sentences are in order. Circle the choice that completes them with correct information about the story.

1. La narradora empezó a ir a la escuela sola porque (**sus hermanas tenían que trabajar / su profesora dijo que sus hermanas metían bulla**).

2. El papá de la hija quería que (**ella se graduara de la universidad / ella dejara de asistir a la escuela**).

3. Los problemas y la pobreza de la familia obligaron a los padres de la narradora a tener una actitud muy (**antipática / generosa**) hacia otras personas.

4. La narradora sufría castigos en la escuela porque (**no traía sus materiales a la escuela / no hacía su tarea**).

5. Cuando el profesor de la narradora le pidió que le contara lo que pasaba, ella (**le dijo la verdad / le mintió**).

6. La narradora tenía tantas responsabilidades porque (**su mamá había muerto / a su mamá no le gustaba trabajar**).

7. El padre de la narradora estaba (**muy enojado porque no tenía un hijo varón / muy orgulloso de sus hijas**).

E. Now look back at the opening line from the reading. Based on what you read after this, and using the excerpt below as a reference, answer the following questions.

«Bueno, en el 54 me fue difícil regresar a la escuela después de las vacaciones…»

1. Who is the narrator? Is this a fictional tale? Explain.

_____

_____

2. What is the tone of the reading? Is the author formal or informal? Explain.

_____

_____

3. How would you describe the main character of the book? Use adjectives and specific instances in the reading to support your answer.

_____

_____

Realidades 3

Nombre _____ Hora _____

Fecha _____ **Vocabulary Flash Cards**